Kicking Center

Critical Issues in Sport and Society

Michael Messner and Douglas Hartmann, Series Editors

Critical Issues in Sport and Society features scholarly books that help expand our understanding of the new and myriad ways in which sport is intertwined with social life in the contemporary world. Using the tools of various scholarly disciplines, including sociology, anthropology, history, media studies and others, books in this series investigate the growing impact of sport and sports-related activities on various aspects of social life as well as key developments and changes in the sporting world and emerging sporting practices. Series authors produce groundbreaking research that brings empirical and applied work together with cultural critique and historical perspectives written in an engaging, accessible format.

Rachel Allison, *Kicking Center: Gender and the Selling of Women's Professional Soccer*

Jules Boykoff, *Activism and the Olympics: Dissent at the Games in Vancouver and London*

Diana Tracy Cohen, *Iron Dads: Managing Family, Work, and Endurance Sport Identities*

Cheryl Cooky and Michael A. Messner, *No Slam Dunk: Gender, Sport, and the Unevenness of Social Change*

Jennifer Guiliano, *Indian Spectacle: College Mascots and the Anxiety of Modern America*

Kathryn E. Henne, *Testing for Athlete Citizenship: Regulating Doping and Sex in Sport*

Jeffrey L. Kidder, *Parkour and the City: Risk, Masculinity, and Meaning in a Postmodern Sport*

Michael A. Messner and Michela Musto, eds., *Child's Play: Sport in Kids' Worlds*

Jeffrey Montez de Oca, *Discipline and Indulgence: College Football, Media, and the American Way of Life during the Cold War*

Stephen C. Poulson, *Why Would Anyone Do That? Lifestyle Sport in the Twenty-First Century*

Nicole Willms, *When Women Rule the Court: Gender, Race, and Japanese American Basketball*

Kicking Center

Gender and the Selling of Women's Professional Soccer

RACHEL ALLISON

Rutgers University Press

New Brunswick, Camden, and Newark, New Jersey, and London

Library of Congress Cataloging-in-Publication Data

Names: Allison, Rachel, author.
Title: Kicking center : gender and the selling of women's professional soccer / Rachel Allison.
Description: New Brunswick, New Jersey : Rutgers University Press, [2018] | Series: Critical
issues in sport and society | Includes bibliographical references and index.
Identifiers: LCCN 2017033843 | ISBN 9780813586786 (cloth : alk. paper) |
ISBN 9780813586779 (pbk. : alk. paper)
Subjects: LCSH: Soccer for women—United States. | Women soccer players—United States. |
Soccer for women—Social aspects—United States. | Soccer—Social aspects—United States.
Classification: LCC GV944.5 .A44 2018 | DDC 796.334—dc23
LC record available at https://lccn.loc.gov/2017033843

A British Cataloging-in-Publication record for this book is available from the British Library.

∞ The paper used in this publication meets the requirements of the American National
Standard for Information Sciences—Permanence of Paper for Printed Library Materials,
ANSI Z39.48-1992.

www.rutgersuniversitypress.org

Manufactured in the United States of America

For Grant and Lynne Allison

Contents

Abbreviations

AYSO American Youth Soccer Organization

ESPN Entertainment and Sports Programming Network

FIFA Fédération Internationale de Football Association

FSC Fox Soccer Channel

MLB Major League Baseball

MLS Major League Soccer

NASL North American Soccer League

NBA National Basketball Association

NFL National Football League

NWSL National Women's Soccer League

WNBA Women's National Basketball Association

WPS Women's Professional Soccer

WUSA Women's United Soccer Association

Kicking Center

Introduction

────────────────────●

Kicking Center

July 10, 1999, found me huddled eagerly around the television with my parents and two younger sisters to watch the championship game of the Women's World Cup. I turned fourteen that summer and had played soccer for exactly half of my life. After beginning with what my dad jokingly calls "herd ball" in the local youth recreational program, my interest and skill in the sport had grown enough by the age of ten that I joined a competitive club team. By the time of the Women's World Cup, many of my weeknights and weekends revolved around soccer, with practices, games, and tournaments eating up much of my time outside of school. I proudly displayed a collection of gold-plated trophies in my bedroom and begged my mom to buy me a T-shirt reading, "Soccer is life. The rest is just details."

While not as excited about soccer as I was, my sisters also played sports. My middle sister was an accomplished gymnast, her prized possession a Wheaties box depicting the "Magnificent Seven" of the 1996 U.S. Olympic gymnastics team. My youngest sister preferred martial arts. In truth, almost every girl I knew at school played sports. Family members, teachers, church leaders, and coaches encouraged me, my sisters, and my schoolmates to compete, believing, as many do, that sports impart valuable lessons in hard work, camaraderie, and fair play.[1] And it was easy for my family to translate these beliefs into experiences, not only because we had the financial resources to support involvement in sports, but also because opportunities to play abounded. My middle school offered track and field, basketball, and volleyball, and the high school I would enter just after the Women's World Cup offered cross country, soccer, swimming and diving, and tennis, among other sports. Outside of school, citywide leagues, private organizations, and summer camps presented additional options. It simply never occurred to me as a child that I shouldn't play sports or that I couldn't if I wanted to. Organized sport was a routine part of white middle-class girlhood in 1990s Iowa.

Youth sports participation today is commonplace, a near ubiquitous experience along the road to adulthood for girls, and for white, class-privileged girls in particular.[2] Yet the seeming ordinariness of girls' involvement in sports is new within my lifetime. This has become clear to me in considering the experiences of my mom. Born in 1957, she was fifteen when Title IX was passed and opportunities to play sports began to open to girls. It wasn't until her junior year in high school that she joined an organized league in volleyball. In taking to the court, my mom was at the vanguard of the post–Title IX spike in youth sports participation, a trend driven largely by the increased participation of girls.[3] For instance, the National Federation of State High School Associations reported that more than 3 million high school girls played sports in 2013–2014, compared to just fewer than 300,000 in 1971–1972.[4] During this time, the number of high school boys participating in sports rose from 3.7 to 4.5 million.

In comparison to my mom, girls like me coming into our teenage years in the 1990s were a generation of "Title IX babies," the first cohort for whom opportunities to play sports had been present since birth.[5] Much like me, girls of this "Third Wave of female athleticism" often take sports for granted, ignorant to the history of cultural and legal struggle that predated our participation opportunities.[6]

This ignorance became untenable, however, during the 1999 Women's World Cup, where the positive consequences of these challenges to the landscape of women's athletics were made explicit. Prior to the final game of the tournament, commentator and former U.S. Women's National Team member Wendy Gebauer primed the television audience to understand the matchup within a legacy of change in the status of women's sports: "This is more than a game. This is a defining moment in women's sports history." And so despite the normality of sports participation in my life, I knew throughout this tournament that I was witness to something wonderfully atypical.

Apart from the Olympic Games, the broadcasts of which I devoured, I had almost never seen a women's sporting event on television. Even after a celebrated victory in the 1996 Atlanta Olympics, the first-ever games for women's soccer, I knew the names of only one or two players on the U.S. Women's National Team. I had no idea then that the 1999 tournament, taking place in the United States, was not the inaugural World Cup for women or that the United States had taken first place in 1991 and third place in 1995. While my ignorance was certainly attributable to youth, it was also an issue of access. Due to the lack of consistent media coverage of women's sports in this early era of the internet, I was not able to translate my passion for playing soccer into knowledgeable fandom of the women's game. The 1999 tournament, however, was different.

The Americans' final game, against China, was televised live to an estimated audience of forty million.[7] The Pasadena, California, Rose Bowl crowd of more than ninety thousand fans remains the single largest audience for a women's sporting event to date. And the game did not disappoint. A close contest between the teams remained scoreless after regulation and overtime play, sending the game to a tense round of penalty kicks. After her successful shot won the game for the United States, defender Brandi Chastain yanked off her jersey in celebration. While this is a staple of postgoal revelries in men's soccer games around the world, a woman had never done so in front of so large an audience. An image of the sports-bra-clad Chastain kneeling in exaltation was captured instantly by photographers and circulated widely in the ensuing weeks, gracing the covers of magazines like *Sports Illustrated* and *Newsweek*. Today, this image has become an iconic visual representation of the Women's World Cup and of U.S. women's achievements in sports more broadly. For many observers, the U.S. victory in 1999 was the culmination of decades of growth in women's sports participation and the proliferation of mass media images of women athletes as "cultural icons."[8] This image of Chastain was lauded as evidence of the positive transformation of cultural attitudes toward women's strength and athleticism in the United States.[9] As Chastain herself remarked in the 2006 HBO documentary *Dare to Dream*, "People constantly remind me of how special that tournament was and how it changed a lot of people's perceptions—not only about soccer in this country and women's soccer but I think about sports in general."

However, there was also a less congratulatory and more critical side to discussions of the popularity of Chastain's image. Scholars who have studied the 1999 tournament argue that the team gained a massive fan and media following as much for their white, middle-class "girls-next-door" image as for their accomplishments on the field. Gender and sexual normativity were key components of this image, as media coverage of the team focused persistently on the heterosexuality and stereotypically feminine "niceness" of the players.[10] Those white women whose self-presentations easily fit into this narrative received media and pop-culture attention over similarly skilled teammates like African American goalkeeper Briana Scurry and midfielder Michelle Akers.[11] Defining the (white) "girls of summer" as humble, approachable, and unfailingly feminine and heterosexual was a strategy to downplay the challenge that women's physical power posed to male superiority and to appeal to a white and heterosexual middle-class audience.[12] Sociologists Neal Christopherson, Michelle Janning, and Eileen Diaz McConnell argue that the team reached an apex of popularity because its players were offered as role models: "The players'

FIGURE 1 Brandi Chastain celebrates winning the Women's World Cup, July 10, 1999. PA
Images/Alamy Stock Photo.

popularity and public success stems from the fact that they are physically tough and competitive yet congenial and caring. These women are role models, yet they are real people because they seem as if they could be anybody's friend (if by 'anybody' we mean white middle-class Americans). Thus, people were watching not just because the team was successful, but also because the team was made up of women who represented what the media heralded as a new kind of woman."[13]

Given this basis for the team's appeal, critics deemed the circulation of Chastain's image problematic for its tendency to translate power into sexualized "striptease."[14] In many iterations of the image, it was less Chastain's skill than her physique on display, presented for the titillation of a presumably male audience. To some, the way that Chastain's image was used in popular culture was believed to compromise the National Team's draw as a "pure" variant of sport appropriate for the consumption of youth, and particularly for girls.[15] The image was also perceived to be an example of the sexual objectification of women athletes in mass media, a representation that compromised and undermined, rather than furthered, women's advancement in sports by emphasizing appearance over athleticism.[16] This interpretation of the photo was bolstered by coverage of the 1999 team within the immediate posttournament media frenzy. On David Letterman's late night show, for instance, the team was described as residing in "Babe City."[17]

Beyond the issue of sexualization, others pointed to the Nike swoosh that adorned Brandi Chastain's sports bra as a damning sign of corporate influence over women's soccer.[18] For some, corporate power thwarted the potential of the Women's World Cup victory to promote women's sports by linking it to the bottom line. Sociologist C. L. Cole has argued convincingly that while corporate buy-in to women's sports appears progressive in rewarding the meaningful connections that many women have with sports, most corporate-sponsored, mediated representations of sportswomen embrace a politically neutered platform of "empowerment" designed to "cultivate a particular fantasy of political efficacy through consumption."[19] Through Nike's involvement, women's soccer was less a movement than a product, a motivation to shop more than a call to action.

Within these debates over the meaning of Chastain's image lurked the supposition of a darker underbelly to the increased presence of women in sports than was commonly acknowledged at the time. Yes, athletic women had come to be accepted and even at times glorified in American culture. And to some extent, this trend marked real progress. Women who played or supported sports were overjoyed at seeing their experiences reflected back to them and reveled in the images of strong, talented sportswomen that became increasingly prevalent during the 1990s.[20] Yet much of the time, visibility and acceptance were predicated on an explicitly white and heterosexual femininity believed to make women athletes more palatable as women's sports became increasingly wrapped into commercial, corporate interests.[21] It was inclusion, but for whom, and at what cost?

Tensions between celebration and scrutiny of the Women's World Cup and its aftermath were largely invisible to me as a teen watching the tournament on television. My strongest memories are of excitement and inspiration as I marveled at the talents of Mia Hamm, Kristine Lilly, and their teammates. In the short term, this more optimistic, if sanitized, view of the Women's World Cup won out as the dominant public narrative. The unanticipated but welcome successes of the tournament in ticket sales, corporate sponsorship dollars, media airtime, and viewership sparked hope for "a new era for women and women's empowerment" in sports, purportedly signaling willingness among sports fans, media organizations, and corporations to welcome women's soccer into the center of U.S. sports culture.[22] The tournament hastened formation of the first fully professional league for women in U.S. history, the Women's United Soccer Association (WUSA). WUSA investors believed that they could translate the momentum generated by the Women's World Cup into lasting attention for a top-flight professional league.

Ultimately, however, this vision of a new age for women's sports on the national stage was never fully realized. As American studies scholar Cheryl Cooky notes of the 1999 Women's World Cup, "The celebratory moment would quickly fade."[23] Beginning play in 2001, WUSA went almost as quickly as it had come. The league folded after three seasons amid talk of gross overspending and disappointing attendance figures.[24]

While it certainly may be the case that the WUSA was mismanaged, what is of interest to me is not the singularity of this league's story, but the commonality of its trajectory with that of other women's professional team sports leagues throughout the 1990s and 2000s. During these decades, women's professional leagues in basketball, softball, volleyball, and football also failed after only a few seasons. Each failure was interpreted in turn as a referendum on the (non)viability of women's professional sports writ large. The much-vaunted movement of U.S. girls and women into sports as participants had done little to alter the gendered balance of power, resources, and opportunity at the highest level. Instead, the "institutional core" of professional sports remained firmly and intractably male dominated.[25]

Faced with an uneven history of both triumph and disappointment in women's soccer, as in women's professional sports more generally, the optimism of the Women's World Cup moment deflated after 2003. In its place grew a sense of uncertainty that lingers to this day. Why hadn't the demographic transformation of youth sports been accompanied by a similar change at the elite level? Why hadn't increased media visibility for some women athletes translated into increased interest and investment in women's professional sports leagues? Why did there seem to be a persistent glass ceiling on women's advancement into professional team sport?

Women on the Margins

In *Taking the Field: Women, Men, and Sports*, sociologist Michael Messner identifies sport as "among the most masculine of institutions."[26] What he is pointing to is the role that sports play in defining what it means to be a man. For example, consider that those qualities that we reward most highly in elite sports, like strength, aggression, and competitiveness, are also characteristics of dominant definitions of masculinity. In fact, modern, organized sports as we know them today in the United States were built by and for men. Organized sports emerged out of a perceived "crisis of masculinity" for white men bred by changing economic conditions in the late nineteenth century.[27] When work moved from the fields to the factories, it no longer required the physical exertion that purportedly demonstrated men's physical superiority to women. During and after World War II, the twin shifts of women's increasing entrée into the public sphere and the decreasing availability of jobs relying on physical labor contributed to men's renewed perception that their dominant social position was in jeopardy. Sociologist Michael Kimmel argues that the destabilization of white, heterosexual masculinity that took place throughout the nineteenth and twentieth centuries bred a cultural doctrine of physicality that sought new discipline over the male body. As part of this doctrine, organized sport emerged to "create young men imbued with the attributes of physical, moral, and spiritual fitness."[28]

Sports thus grew popular as a way for men to assert themselves as men. And the importance of sports to the meanings attached to manhood has not only continued but intensified given the vast array of economic, political, and cultural changes of the past half century that have spurred women's entrance into many institutional spheres previously defined as the domain of men.[29] Today, sports give men a socially acceptable way to connect to other men and share in symbolic constructions of male physical dominance. Sociologist Sara Crawley argues that sports generate "vicarious masculinity," where "male-bodied people align themselves with that subset of men (especially elite athletes, actors, and working-class men who do hard labor) who actually possess the buff ideal of the strong man."[30] While most men are unable to achieve the physique and bodily capacities of elite athletes themselves, they are nevertheless able to draw on the power these bodies represent through sharing their sports fandom with other men.

For sports to solidify the dominance of manhood, however, evidence of women's participation must be suppressed and women themselves marginalized, if not outright excluded. As women's presence in sport has grown, it has simultaneously been "contained and ghettoized" to minimize its challenge to the status quo.[31] Historically, this has been accomplished through powerful ideologies of gender and sexual difference and the working of these ideologies into organizational practices and policies.

In sport, where the performance of the body is front and center, the social and cultural meanings attached to bodies matter. What scholars of gender and sport call "essentialism" is a dominant cultural ideology relating gender to bodily capacities. Essentialism refers to the idea that differences between men and women are the result of biology. Essentialism often exists in tandem with the categorical belief that all men are distinct from all women.[32] Essentialist, categorical interpretations of sport hold that men are uniformly physically superior to women and that biological sex differences account for the comparatively marginal position of women in sport. If men and women are simply born with different and unequal physical abilities, then the lower status of women and women's sports compared to men and men's sports is to be expected. Inequality, from this perspective, is both natural and unchanging.

To make this case, essentialist, categorical arguments rely on social constructions of sex and gender as binary and oppositional. American cultural constructions of sex hold that there are two naturally occurring, mutually exclusive sex categories (male and female) that we are all born into. And binary sex is believed to map onto binary gender, with biological males and females becoming men and women. While binary sex and gender, and correspondence between the two, appear to be commonsense and well-established facts to many, however, they are not facts at all. The truth about bodies and identities is far more complex than ideas about binary sex and gender allow.

Approximately one in two thousand individuals is born with an intersex trait, referring to "the state of being born with a combination of characteristics (e.g., genital, gonadal, and/or chromosomal) that are typically presumed to be exclusively male or female."[33] The prevalence of intersex reveals that bodies naturally vary in their genetic, chromosomal, gonadal, and hormonal makeup beyond what we have defined as simply "male" or "female." To date, however, doctors have treated intersex not as natural variation but as a "problem" to be fixed through medical or surgical intervention, even though most intersex traits do not cause health issues. The result is that many in the intersex community have been lied to and misled by doctors, their bodies altered irreparably to fit into one of two socially constructed sex categories.[34] As with sex, gender too is not binary but varies beyond merely man-woman designations. And one's gender identity is not determined solely by assigned sex category at birth. The growing visibility and activism of those whose identities do not reflect binary or concordant definitions of sex and gender, including intersex, transgender, and genderqueer people, poses challenges to essentialist assumptions both inside and outside of sport.

It is also the case that gender does not solely determine capacity for physical performance. Men's and women's abilities range along an overlapping continuum, with more sameness than difference.[35] Of course, the extent of this overlap varies per the performance outcome that is measured. While on some measures, like upper-body strength, men will score higher on average than women, some women will score higher than many men, and this potential increases with training. For other measures, such as flexibility, the average woman will excel compared to the average man. And these average differences are made muddier still if we consider that sex and gender binaries are somewhat arbitrary constructions, rather than bodily realities. While we can identify some patterns based on gender categories, athletic performance is simply not determined by gender as much as we think it is.

Essentialism and categoricalism, then, fail to present an accurate account of the world we live in, and their explanation of gender inequality in sport is incomplete. What Messner calls "hard essentialism," or the duo of essentialism and categoricalism, is not reality but ideology, a powerful belief that shapes how we perceive and organize the world around us.[36] Hard essentialism upholds perceptions of men's superiority to women by making difference and inequality seem natural, total, and inevitable. As political scientists Andrei Markovits and Emily Albertson conclude, the result of accepting essentialism in contemporary sport is that gender inequality "is openly accepted, indeed officially sanctioned and—shockingly—barely contested."[37] While the essentialist linking of sex and gender to ability has been challenged in many areas of social life, sport has remained an acutely gendered and unequal social institution in part because essentialist beliefs seem more legitimate here than in, say, schools or the workplace.

We are constantly confronted with evidence that hard essentialist beliefs don't quite hold up. Women's athletic performances routinely show us the overlap between women and men's capabilities and demonstrate women's excellence in sport. Women's participation in sport has always contested definitions of femininity as passivity and weakness and undermined the ideology of men's physical superiority over women.[38] Yet in the face of substantial evidence to counter dominant beliefs about sex, gender, and bodily performance, these beliefs are rarely revised or discarded. Instead they are upheld, whether through making women's accomplishments invisible, downplaying women's achievements through comparing them to men's, situating individual women as exceptions to the rule, or changing the rules of the game itself. In other words, we perform what sociologist Faye Linda Wachs terms "ideological repair work" that upholds men's dominance over women.[39]

Sport as an institution continues to be cognitively associated with men and masculinity, despite the increased participation of girls and women.[40] Yet individual sports are "gender typed," meaning that they accrue affiliations with masculinities and/or femininities given their historical development, the organization of play, and the demographics of players.[41] Certain sports, such as American football, are widely recognized as "masculine," while others have more feminized reputations. Of course, the "gender" of a sport can change. As I show in chapter 1, for instance, soccer once had uniquely masculine associations in the United States given its early adoption by men but developed a gender-neutral or even feminized reputation over time with the increasing participation of girls and women.

The gendered meanings attached to sports influence whether and how people play them. The highly masculine nature of certain sports in tandem with the gender makeup of those who participate shape whether youth perceive a sport as appropriate for them to play.[42] Sports' gendered affiliations also articulate with sexuality. The assumptions of heterosexuality that accompany normative gender mean that participation in so-called gender-typical sports (e.g., American football for boys and men or dance for girls and women) establishes participants as firmly and "appropriately" heterosexual. In contrast, engagement in so-called gender-atypical sports generates associations with lesbian or gay sexualities. The acceptance of lesbian, gay, and bisexual (LGB), or sexual minority, athletes has grown, as is evident in the number of publicly "out" athletes. However, there remains a social stigma attached to real or perceived LGB sexualities, and boys and men experience somewhat more stigma for participation in gender-inappropriate sports than do girls and women. Feminist activism, advocacy, and research efforts have made major headway in expanding gender boundaries for women in ways that incorporate what were previously believed to be "masculine" characteristics. In contrast, however, definitions of manhood have been less subject to challenge and remain more rigid.[43] When men participate in "feminine" sports such as gymnastics or ice skating, they typically compete by a different set of rules and standards that establish the men's variant as more "masculine."[44]

Nevertheless, the deployment of a persistent homophobia in women's sports is one way that women athletes are kept in check.[45] As sport studies scholar Ann Hall argues, "The real issue behind so much attention to an athlete's femininity is the fear that she may be a lesbian."[46] As sport is perceived to be a masculine endeavor, women athletes are positioned as more masculine than their nonathletic counterparts. Because of their supposed masculinization, women athletes' heterosexuality becomes suspect.[47] While the most vitriolic forms of homophobia are declining with the growing visibility and acceptance of sexual minorities in the United States, studies document a continuing lesbian stigma attached to U.S. women's sports. The "female apologetic" whereby women demonstrate heterosexuality outside of play via markers of traditional femininity remains a common tactic employed by athletes to distance themselves from this stigma.[48] It is no surprise, then, that girls and women sometimes choose so-called feminine sports that allow them to play without compromising their adherence to "appropriate heterosexual femininity."[49] Yet if sport itself is linked to masculinity, one consequence of this choice is that feminized sports played by women are easily relegated to the margins as second-class, less "serious" sports or perhaps not even "real" sports at all.[50] Recent research on cheerleading, for example, shows that while young women use the feminized reputation of cheer to establish themselves as both athletic and feminine, the feminization of cheer simultaneously locates participants outside the realm of so-called real (read: masculine) sport.[51]

Thus the dominant gender and sexual meanings attached to sport place women athletes in a contradictory position. Within a social institution defined around maleness and masculinity, they are outsiders. To assert belonging, women could conform to the highly masculine values that organize sport. To some extent, women must do this to compete successfully at the highest level of play. Yet women who are "too" masculine may be stigmatized, marked as inadequately feminine and, by extension, suspected as lesbian.

In contrast, women could assert the value of femininity in direct opposition to sports' masculinity. The persistent lesbian stigma attached to women's sports may make this strategy appealing to some, as femininity is cultural code for heterosexuality, and the availability of "feminine" sports options provides opportunity. Yet because sport remains a masculine institutional sphere, this strategy confirms gender difference and may solidify perceptions of the inferiority of women's sports. While these strategies are neither mutually exclusive nor exhaustive, they do point to the requirement for women athletes to carefully and continually balance sport with gender. As kinesiology professors Melanie Sartore and George Cunningham summarize, "Women must not behave as too feminine for fear of being sexualized and trivialized, nor must they act too masculine for fear of being demonized."[52]

Cultural ideologies of women's difference from and physical inferiority to men also inform organizational and legal policies to relegate women to the margins of sport as a social institution. In some historical moments, women have been formally excluded from playing sports altogether, these restrictions justified by a belief that vigorous physical activity harms women's bodies.[53] For instance, several competitors sank to the ground in exhaustion after the women's eight-hundred-meter race at the 1928 Olympic Games. This action, also common after men's running events, was interpreted as evidence that women lacked the requisite physical stamina for competition. As a result, the women's eight-hundred-meter event was removed from Olympic track and field until 1960.[54] Exclusion has been particularly true for white women; historically, women of color participated in physical activity without being subject to the same fears for their bodily, and often their reproductive, capacities. As sport studies scholar Mary McDonald notes, explicitly racialized historical anxieties tied white women's motherhood to the propagation of white racial superiority.[55]

More common than formal exclusion today, however, is the "feminization" of sports rules.[56] Women often play modified or adapted versions of men's sports. For instance, the first Women's World Cup in 1991 set games at eighty minutes, instead of the standard ninety, out of concern for women's supposedly lower physical stamina compared to men. And in high-profile tennis tournaments today, women play to the best of three sets, while men play to the best of five. When women play by a different set of rules, this difference is commonly interpreted as evidence of their weakness compared to men.[57]

Perhaps foremost among the policies that contribute to women's marginalization in sport, however, is the near total sex segregation of sports at all levels. Except for those played by young children or coed recreational leagues for adults, sports separate boys and girls, men and women under the essentialist rationale of sex difference in athletic ability. In categorically assuming all women are physically inferior to all men, sex segregation becomes a protectionist rationale where women are shielded from the social or physical harms purported to come from playing with men. Sex segregation is also explained via reference to "fair play" under the assumption that no woman could compete successfully in a gender-integrated setting. While separate women's teams and leagues may in some cases maintain opportunities for women, the justification for universal sex segregation in sport falls apart rather easily under scrutiny. If our sports system does not restrict the smallest and most physically weak boys and men from participation against their larger, stronger, peers, why exclude girls and women who may be equally or more capable as many men? Systemic sex segregation in sports, then, reinforces ideologies of categorical sexual difference and women's athletic inferiority to men.[58]

Related to sex segregation is the sex testing (or, in some parlance, gender verification) of women athletes. Sex testing policies are justified as ensuring fair play in women's sports. While historically such policies were designed to detect men competing as women, they have more recently been framed as a method for determining competitors with the "unfair advantage" of naturally elevated hormone levels. Social scientists argue that instead of leveling the playing field within women's sport, athlete sex testing is a method of "gender policing" that reflects and perpetuates social anxieties around muscular, athletic women's bodies.[59] Several facts support this argument. First, women are tested, but men are not. The perceived need for testing policies only for women stems from binary understandings of sex and gender and an assumption of all men's physical superiority over all women, social ideas about the body that neglect the continuum that is biology. Also, testing is often implemented only when women athletes come to the attention of sport authorities. In some cases, domineering displays of athleticism may generate suspicion. Thus women's athletic performances may be used to call their gender into question. If a woman performs well, perhaps *too* well, is she really a woman? Additionally, a woman's self-presentation may trigger testing if she is deemed inadequately feminine. The markers used to identify athletes for testing often have more to do with appropriate gender display for women rather than biology, assuming congruence between the body and social behavior that has long been debunked by science.[60]

Sports organizations have used a bevy of measures since the 1960s to assess sex, including gynecological examinations, chromosomal or DNA tests, and assessments of hormone levels. Changes in how organizations have measured sex demonstrate the impossibility of definitively doing so. There is no one bodily characteristic that all women share in the same way. For national and international sport organizing bodies to continue the testing of women in sport despite scientific objection is to subject women and women only to harmful and invasive scrutiny. Quite recent policies of gender verification test not for sex per se but for "hyperandrogenism," or higher than average hormonal testosterone. While this form of testing purports to be fairer and less subject to error than earlier methods, it incorrectly identifies hormonal testosterone as an ubiquitous source of athletic advantage for women. Additionally, this policy punishes women for bodies that produce high levels of naturally occurring testosterone, enabling discrimination against athletes whose bodies do not adhere to socially constructed binaries, including intersex athletes.[61] Testing of this sort continues to disproportionately impact women whose self-presentations defy expectations of heterosexual femininity and women from the Global South whose hyperandrogenism was not previously detected or treated. Rather than ensuring fairness, gender verification creates unfairness.

At the level of professional sport, the containment of women's leagues has also been accomplished through the policies and practices of major sport and media organizations. Within the U.S. Soccer Federation and the global Fédération Internationale de Football Association (FIFA), levels of financial and resource investment between men and women's teams are nowhere near equal. Within U.S. soccer, gender compensation disparities persist despite the women's team's greater history of success in international play and substantial revenue generation. Travel and playing conditions are also inequitable, with the U.S. women's team alone historically assigned to more dangerous turf fields for international friendlies and tournament games. Further, FIFA has been plagued by blatant sexism and mistreatment of women on the playing fields and in the office. For instance, despite former FIFA president Sepp

Blatter's assertion that "the future of football [soccer] is feminine," he suggested in 2004 that to draw more attention to their sport, women's soccer players "could, for example, have tighter shorts."[62]

In addition, mainstream mass media coverage of elite women's sports has remained stubbornly low. During WUSA's tenure, for instance, ESPN's *SportsCenter* devoted no more than 2 percent of its coverage to any women's sport, a figure that has not increased substantially since.[63] Media inattention is driven by an a priori belief that women's sports are less exciting than men's sports, draw fewer fans, and are thus less worthy of coverage.[64] This belief, put into practice nearly automatically with little recognition of the crowds that some women's teams do enjoy, ignores the crucial role of media coverage in making fan interest possible in the first place, especially for those who live too far from teams to attend their games. Without consideration of the two-way street that is media visibility and fan attention, assertions that "no one is interested" in women's sports justify the media practices that generate unequal patterns of media coverage. In this broader mainstream media drought, fans of women's sports, including soccer, must hunt for information in the less visible niches of the internet. While social media and other new media forms, such as blogs, do present opportunities for women's teams and leagues to connect with fans, the relative exclusivity of these forms of communication presents a formidable hurdle to fandom for those with little knowledge of or interest in women's sports to begin with. Sport studies scholar Toni Bruce concludes, "The mainstream mediasport message is 'Go ahead and play but don't expect us to pay attention to your activities.'"[65]

Kicking Center

While not all of those who play sports or work in sport organizations would identify themselves as feminists, sport is clearly an important issue for feminism. The "recuperative" repairs through which women's athletic accomplishments are rendered less visible and less valued than men's, while widespread and oftentimes subtle, are never a finished accomplishment.[66] Male dominance is always and inherently "leaky."[67] Scholars, activists, fans, and athletes, among other groups, have taken full advantage of these leaks to contest the status of women in sports. Change, though uneven and often piecemeal, reflects the exercise of "resistant" agency.[68] This agency has successfully poked holes in the long-standing incompatibility of athleticism with femininity such that "the contemporary American sportscape allows for both concepts to coexist, overlap, and at times, even integrate."[69]

Yet it is perhaps most apt to speak in the plural of feminisms, given multiple models of the transformation of sport.[70] For elite women's sports, three variants of feminism have been particularly impactful: liberal (or second-wave) feminism, postfeminism, and third-wave feminism. Although feminisms are often conceptualized as a temporal, linear progression of ideas, encapsulated in the metaphor of "waves," feminisms are more aptly understood as overlapping and ongoing conversations. I use the terms *second wave*, *third wave*, and *post* to represent sets of ideas but understand these as not entirely separate from one another.[71]

Liberal feminism is typically associated with the second-wave feminist movement of the 1960s and 1970s. Liberal feminism sought to open opportunities to women in major social institutions by eliminating discriminatory practices. It championed women's equal rights to men under the law, rejecting essentialism as an explanation for gender inequality in favor of identifying cultural barriers to women's full participation in society.

Liberal feminism has been effective at opening sports to the participation of girls and women.[72] It has successfully challenged many of the barriers that have prevented access and has won legal rights for girls and women. Perhaps the hallmark of this work was the passage of Title IX, which outlawed discrimination based on sex in educational programs receiving federal funding. Liberal feminism has become the dominant model of gender transformation in American society. Its ideas have become so equated with feminism itself that it seems to be the "commonsense" approach to understanding and fighting for gender equality in sports.[73] For instance, the Women's Sports Foundation, the premier U.S. organization for advancing gender equality in sports, has adopted a liberal feminist agenda, championing the expansion of opportunities for girls and women under the rationale of sports' positive effects on participants.[74]

Yet despite its achievements, liberal feminism has limitations, two of which I mention briefly. First, liberal feminism defines equality as women's sameness to men. Women's sports are encouraged to incorporate the masculine norms and structures that already govern sport. Elite sports are often competitive in the extreme and are characterized by high rates of injury and violence to self and others. Liberal feminism asks women to adopt these values and the practices they suggest as the terms of inclusion and equality. One consequence of defining equality as access to and opportunity in male-defined sport is that change is often measured as the numerical representation of women. While gender proportionality may certainly be one important measure of equality, simply adding more women to sport does little to address many of the social problems that accompany existing models of how sport is organized and played.

Second, liberal feminism advocates the "strategic use of the category woman."[75] This means that in seeking access to sport, "women" are presented as a unified group with shared experiences and interests. Liberal feminism has thus been somewhat deaf to the intersections of gender with other axes of social position, glossing over the ways that race, ethnicity, sexuality, and social class stratify sport and shape opportunities to participate between women and men and among women. For instance, the enormous growth of youth development sports programs for girls is both a cause and consequence of liberal feminist thought. As social scientists Lauren Rauscher and Cheryl Cooky argue, these programs posit that sports contribute positively to girls' development.[76] Yet such programs rarely consider how broader social inequalities make sports more available and more positive to some girls than others.

Liberal feminism celebrates the inclusion of women in sport through challenge to normative and legal barriers. However, these are commonly white, heterosexual, class-privileged norms challenged by white, heterosexual, and class-privileged women. White, heterosexual, and middle- or upper-class women are best positioned to gain from liberal feminism, and their inclusion under the banner of women's equality risks reinforcing the normativity and privilege that accompany whiteness and heterosexuality. It is not accidental that many of those women athletes who have achieved the greatest name recognition in recent decades, such as soccer's Mia Hamm or tennis star Maria Sharapova, are white and embody explicitly heterosexual forms of femininity. As cultural studies scholar Anima Adjepong argues, "Although women may be increasingly welcomed to play stereotypically masculine sports, their acceptance into this terrain is circumscribed by the extent to which they adhere to the rules of a heterosexual and racialized social hierarchy."[77]

As scholars note, the politics of gender and sport in the United States grew uniquely complicated with a broader social transition into the era of postfeminism. As sociologists C. L. Cole and Amy Hribar describe, postfeminism emerged initially in the political and economic conservatism of the 1980s.[78] Postfeminism refers to the notion that gender equality has been achieved and feminism is no longer needed. Some scholars have also defined postfeminism as a new gender politic that asks women to assert an empowered sense of self within the ascendancy of a capitalist economy.[79] In women's sports, two linked trends marked the advent of the postfeminist era: the rising popularity of a "fit" body ideal and the corporate adoption of women's sports.

The 1980s and 1990s witnessed the ascendance of an "athletic aesthetic" for women.[80] This aesthetic was a response to critiques of the idealization of the thin body and an endorsement of arguments for the positive health benefits of sports participation for women.[81] This emergent body standard was heralded in some corners for replacing a focus on thinness with an emphasis on strength. There was an upper limit, however, in the extent to which muscle was valued. Strong was sexy, but only if women were not *too* strong. The new ideal was not that different from the old ideal, privileging "the lean, but not skinny, toned but not bulky, white body."[82]

What social scientists Shari Dworkin and Faye Linda Wachs refer to as the discourse of "healthism" tied the display of the strong, slender, active body to the cultivation of heterosexual femininity. Women were encouraged to participate in fitness practices for the *appearance* of a healthy, attractive body. While purportedly about health, healthism turned sports and fitness into projects of conformity to white, heterosexual, feminine standards of beauty. The conflation of the "fit" body with health made adherence almost a moral imperative.[83] Healthism has been accompanied by a barrage of so-called fitspirational images, where visual evidence of bodily power coexists with markers of heterosexual femininity, the duo designed to inspire women to pursue bodily perfection. While athletes have often been used as examples of the new athletic normal, they are by no means requisite, as many "fitspiration" campaigns have used fashion models. The provocative, often highly sexually suggestive nature of many of these images proclaims that the "fit" woman's body is molded and displayed for consumption by a male audience.

Although some fitness regimens today tout themselves as focusing on performance over appearance, they often struggle to escape tensions between fitness, health, and feminine beauty. For example, while the recent physical fitness craze CrossFit is presented as focusing on what the body does instead of what it looks like, in the videos and advertisements released by corporate headquarters, "any and all mention of the athleticism needed to do CF is immediately related back to appearance."[84] Also consider *ESPN The Magazine*'s Body Issue, in which women's soccer stars like Abby Wambach and Hope Solo have featured prominently. At its inception, the Body Issue was positioned as an alternative to the highly (hetero)sexualized Swimsuit Issue released by *Sports Illustrated*. The Body Issue is a purportedly gender-neutral alternative, an equal celebration of men and women's elite athletic bodies. Yet academic research on the Body Issue concludes that gender continues to inform these images, with the athletes' poses suggesting women's greater value in physical attractiveness compared to men.[85]

Also in the 1980s and 1990s, corporations increasingly signed onto the women's sports platform, recognizing that the American sports-playing women's market was untapped and presented an opportunity for growth. Communications scholar Helene Shugart writes, "As a result of Title IX, more than half of all women participate in sports today, implying a huge potential audience for women's sports, which in turn has sparked the interest of the most critical factor in the success of sports today: corporate sponsorship."[86] Foremost among the early corporate adopters of women's sports were apparel companies like Adidas, Nike, and Reebok, which began to use women athletes in their advertisements. In the 1990s women's soccer was a main player in this trend. For instance, in Nike's 1996 "Girl in America" spot, star forward Mia

FIGURE 2 Model Lily Aldridge attends a Victoria's Secret event, October 22, 2013, an example of "fitspirational" imagery. WENN Ltd/Alamy Stock Photo.

Hamm proclaimed, "There is a girl being born in America. Someone will give her a doll. Someone will give her a ball. And someone will give her a chance." While corporate and media attention to women's participation in sports felt like positive, if much overdue, recognition, the messages that these campaigns conveyed were less than progressive considering their goal of corporate profit.[87] These companies "co-opted" a postfeminist language of empowerment through sports participation, positioning themselves as champions of girls in sport.[88] Cultural studies scholar Samantha King refers to this as "corporate feminism," a business strategy meant to spark sales more than to create real social change.[89]

In selling empowerment, Nike glossed over the politicized elements of Chastain's 1999 shirt doffing in favor of using the familiarity of the moment to market its brand. In a 2000 Nike commercial, Brandi Chastain (in full national team uniform) plays foosball against basketball pro Kevin Garnett and several friends. In the ad, Chastain scores a goal and raises her arms over her head in victory. The men look at her expectantly. After a long moment of silence, Chastain asks, "What?" In response, Garnett quips, "What's up with the shirt?" When Chastain does not remove her shirt, Garnett prods his friends back into play with a "C'mon, man." The commercial ends, and the Nike swoosh appears. In this ad, Chastain's shirt removal is not a telling prompt for discussion of societal gender inequality but a lighthearted cultural reference shared between the men playing foosball and the viewing audience. Nike, the commercial suggests, is in on the joke.

These trends complicated the quest for inclusion in sport by channeling women's physical activity into body projects that valued white, heterosexual femininities. Kinesiology and women's studies professor Jaime Schultz argues that these changes reflect a "beauty-myth backlash again women's sports," a countermovement against the gains in participation wrought by Title IX.[90] Together, the twin trends of athletic body ideals and corporate adoption channeled the push for equality into desire for individualized empowerment, achieved via a toned but small body adorned with appropriate clothing and other products.[91] Girls and women became empowered through consumption and transformation of the self instead of through group action toward expanding rights and resources.[92] And this form of empowerment was marketed as a new, more popular feminism that didn't even need the label anymore! Nike, for instance, adopted some of the values of a feminist "politics of positive images" through stressing "appeal to a more authentic, internal self that can be realized through exercise."[93] In taking up a feminist mantle, yet simultaneously individualizing the feminist project and divorcing it from the language of feminism itself, postfeminism became stripped of political edge.[94] Here, "discourses of capitalism and neo-liberalism . . . encourage women to concentrate on their private lives and consumer capacities as the sites for self-expression and agency."[95] Within postfeminist discourse, transcending the barriers that women faced in sports became a matter of the right apparel, the right body, and the right attitude.

Viewed in this light, postfeminist trends are a troubling indicator of the persistence and adaptability of gender inequality in contemporary elite sport. However, these trends receive a somewhat different reading in third-wave feminism. Second-wave and postfeminist arguments presume the marginalization of women athletes relative to male-defined and male-dominated sport. In doing so, these feminisms lack full consideration of women's agency to shape and direct their lives. Women athletes are not entirely "co-opted by a corporate, anti-feminist nexus of domination."[96] Instead, they are sophisticated entrepreneurs and managers of their own image. Third-wave thinkers argue that women often engage in sport beyond male-defined values and practices. In fact, third-wave feminists would likely take issue with my beginning this book with a discussion of male dominance and women's marginalization in sport! From the third-wave perspective, the conflation of sport with masculinity has been dramatically altered through the growing presence of girls and women in sport at all levels of play. Athleticism is increasingly compatible with femininities and in some cases may not be coded with regard to gender at all.[97] Instead of understanding women's sport with reference to men's sport, then, it ought to be understood for itself and on its own terms.[98]

An embrace of fluidity, complexity, and contradiction also characterizes third-wave feminism. Marginalization and empowerment, oppression and equality are not antitheses, but can and do coexist in athletes' lived experiences. The advent of athletic body ideals reinscribes privilege but simultaneously challenges perceptions of women's physical weakness. The corporatization of women's sports channels women away from collective struggle and into the cardio room, but also creates opportunities in the form of visibility, enhancing social acceptance of strong, talented sportswomen. Third-wave feminism commonly takes visual representation and popular culture as its subjects, examining how images of women in sport may be empowering and troubling at the same time.[99] Women athletes are not defined by the binary of beauty or strength, but are increasingly depicted as embodying beauty *and* strength.[100]

My discussion of sports feminisms highlights many of the tensions inherent in varied interpretations of the 1999 Women's World Cup and the advent of U.S. women's professional soccer. From a liberal feminist vantage point, the 1999 tournament and the creation of the WUSA were unqualified triumphs for gender equality, representing inclusion, opportunity, and cultural acceptance in elite-level sport. Postfeminism, in contrast, would tell a more cautionary tale of the corporate embrace of women's sports. Here, the commercialization of women's soccer translated the push for equality into individualism and consumerism. Third-wave feminists would likely argue that the 1999 moment represents both triumph and co-optation at the same time, calling attention to the ways that some women capitalized on the (limited) opportunities that visibility made available. Each of these interpretations holds truth. Collectively, they prompt several questions related to the ongoing, post-WUSA project of women's professional soccer in the United States.

What are the goals of women's professional soccer, and how are they pursued? It is undoubtedly the case that, as sociologists Michael Messner and Nancy Solomon argue, professional leagues in basketball, baseball, and football "occupy the 'center' of the U.S. sports world and enjoy the lion's share of the privileges and resources."[101] As with any newly formed professional sports league, women's soccer looks to access many of these same privileges and resources. Yet to do so it must contend with the systematic construction and maintenance of male dominance in and through sport. In fact, the title of this book refers to the push toward (or perhaps against) the center of U.S. professional sports culture that the existence of fully professional women's sports leagues requires. With few exceptions, however, we don't know how women's professional leagues operate.[102] How, exactly, is the marginalization of women's sports understood and challenged? Is the vision for women's pro soccer in any way a feminist one? And is this vision shared?

Kicking Center analyzes how women's professional soccer in the United States has been built and sold. Simultaneously, I consider what predominant selling strategies and practices, and the tensions embedded within them, reveal about the state of gender (in)equality in contemporary elite women's sport. How, I ask, do those working for and with a women's professional team sport league perceive the environment that they operate in, and how do these perceptions shape their approach to constructing and selling women's professional soccer? What challenges does women's pro soccer face, and how do insiders address these? In answering these questions, I focus on how inequality is both created and contested within women's professional soccer.

Entering the Field

In 2009, I was a twenty-five-year-old master's student living in Chicago. While taking public transportation to campus one morning, I picked up a copy of the *Redeye*, a free city newspaper. Apart from a few recreational games here and there, I hadn't played soccer with any level of seriousness since 2007, nor given much thought to the Women's National Team. My collection of trophies remained at home in rural Iowa, gathering dust. On that day, though, I was surprised to read about the upcoming first season of a new women's professional league, Women's Professional Soccer (WPS). Chicago would be home to a team that would play at Toyota Park, a soccer-specific stadium built for the Chicago Fire, the men's professional Major League Soccer (MLS) team.

Energized by this news, I paid for a season ticket and attended many of that year's home games with my friends and family members. I repeated this again the following year. As an early season ticket holder, I attended small, invite-only events with players, staff, and fellow fans. I began to follow WPS news updates via the league's website and soccer blog sites. I even joined Twitter in 2009 to check in on my favorite players. I stuck a Chicago Red Stars magnet onto my refrigerator and received a team sweatshirt as a holiday gift. My love for women's soccer had returned.

I found Toyota Park to be an exhilarating experience, with the crowd chatter, loud music, and fast-paced play that I expected. But the upbeat tempo to the games was not matched by forecasts for the league's future that I read about in the soccer media. A gloomier tone prevailed here, the focus on low attendance figures and struggles over sponsorship and TV deals in the troubled economic climate of those years. Some of these challenges were also noted informally in my chats with team staff and, less frequently, with players. Through my early fandom, I gained a sense of some of the difficulties WPS faced at its inception. The excitement surrounding the play on the field during game days was almost entirely removed from the difficult work necessary to sell the game.

Over time, I grew increasingly interested in gaining a deeper understanding of the challenges faced by the league. As I had moved on to my doctoral studies, I was also considering possible dissertation topics. In 2010, I decided to pursue research on WPS. As a qualitative and interpretive method, ethnography involves intensive, long-term participation in an ongoing social world. Many ethnographers believe that "doing and feeling first-hand is the best pathway to believing, knowing and theorizing sociologically."[103] Similarly, I believed that to fully grasp the complexities of selling women's soccer in the United States. I needed to directly see and experience this work, getting past the league's public face to see its private, daily operations. I emailed to several teams in the league a proposal for an ethnographic study of a WPS team that offered my services as an unpaid staff member in return for my participant observation. In March 2011, I moved from Chicago to join a team I pseudonymously call the Momentum.

The Momentum was one of six teams in the league in 2011 and was located outside of a large city. After I relocated to the team's suburban area in March, I spent between thirty and forty hours per week volunteering at the team's office. Defined as an "intern" under the supervision of one team manager, I participated in the daily life of the team by completing all tasks that were asked of me. I answered phones, wrote thank-you letters, mailed packages, took photos, made PowerPoint presentations, and worked on the team's e-newsletter, among other activities. In doing so, I observed nearly all facets of the team's operations before, during, and after the 2011 season. I observed routine office work, staff meetings, pitches to corporate sponsors, player media appearances and interviews, community and charity events, practices, home games, and team social events.

As is often the case in ethnographic research, an unexpected event integrally shaped my fieldwork. On January 30, 2012, WPS announced it would be suspending play for the 2012 season. Several months later, the league folded altogether. After the January announcement of suspension, the Momentum office closed. At this point, eleven months after I first joined the team, there was no longer anything to observe. To gain perspective on the league's failure and to get a sense as to whether the social dynamics I had witnessed with the Momentum were similar at other teams, I shifted from observation to in-depth interviews across the league. I had formally interviewed most Momentum staff before the league's failure. Using my existing contacts and publicly available contact information, I requested interviews elsewhere. By May 2012, I interviewed insiders from every team that had ever operated in WPS. Beyond team managers and staff members I included media personnel who covered the league, sponsors of the league, and Momentum season ticket holders. I conducted fifty-five interviews total. Between January and March 2016, with grant support from the Laboratory for Diversity in Sport at Texas A&M University, I conducted an additional twenty-five interviews, twenty of which were with current or retired professional women's soccer players.

Table A.1 in appendix A reports the pseudonyms of my eighty interview participants as well as demographic information. I interviewed more women than men (61 to 39 percent). Participants ranged in age from eighteen to sixty-two, with an average age of thirty-five. The majority (89 percent) of my interviewees were white, although I did interview two Hispanic women, three black women, and four black men. Of those I interviewed, 21 percent ($n = 17$) identified as lesbian, gay, or bisexual. Reflective of my entry into women's soccer via the Momentum, 35 percent of those I interviewed were affiliated with this team, including fourteen fans, eight staff members or managers, and two players. Table A.1 lists the position of individuals at the time of their interview. I spoke to one head coach, seventeen fans, eleven media personnel, eleven managers, twenty-one players, four sponsors, and fifteen staff members. It is important to note, however, that the affiliations of those I spoke to had varied over time. For instance, four season ticket holders had worked for women's professional soccer in the past, while eight other fans had volunteered for the league. Several media personnel had also been previously employed by WPS. Most of these individuals had worked for women's professional soccer at one time or another, although often in unpaid capacity, and all were deeply invested in and knowledgeable about women's soccer.

As part of my study I also collected media data on both the Momentum and WPS. As early as 2009, I began compiling hard-copy and electronic articles that covered the league. I created a Google search alert for "women's professional soccer" that linked me to articles in mainstream news sources. I routinely searched the *Sports Illustrated* and ESPN websites. ESPN launched its online news site for women, espnW, at the time that I joined the Momentum, and this site was a consistent source of media coverage. My personal fandom had familiarized me with popular soccer blog and news sites such as Big Soccer and Equalizer Soccer. The social media platform Twitter was also an important source of information on the league. I first heard about many of the major developments in the league via Twitter, including player signings, game outcomes, and even the league's folding. Prior to the 2011 season, I created a spreadsheet of all staff and players in the league based on information from team websites. Using my own account, I followed all of those who had public Twitter accounts. My attention to social media allowed me to see how players constructed and communicated their professional identities. It also allowed me to see how players, owners, staff, and media journalists engaged publicly with some of the major issues that arose during the season. Finally, as a public social media platform where any member can send public messages to another, Twitter allowed me to see how WPS players and staff interacted virtually with fans, media personnel, and one another.

Kicking Center is an ethnographic study of my experiences within the women's pro soccer community. The study draws on participant observation, interview, and media data to present a picture of the gender politics embedded within the goals and strategies of this league, paying close attention to patterns unique to the Momentum, versus those that were apparent league-wide. Although most data for the study were collected in 2011 and 2012, this book relies on the knowledge of women's pro soccer I have built from 2009 to the present. I also rely on a small number of in-depth interviews conducted in early 2016. My own involvement in women's soccer has changed over time. I have been a season ticket holder, a participant observer and researcher, a beat reporter for a soccer-specific website, an attendee at the 2015 Women's World Cup, and now, again, a fan. My experiences in each of these roles have contributed to this book.

1

Women's Soccer in
the United States

———————————————————●

The question of soccer's cultural position in the United States sparks lively debate in both academic and public forums. This discussion often takes a turn toward the humorous, the juxtaposition of "soccer" and "America" a supposedly tickling oxymoron. Take, for instance, the satirical news site the *Onion*, which has made many a joke at soccer's expense. Mention of soccer on the website in 2011 was located next to headings for football, hockey, and motorsports under the title "Women's Sports/Soccer." The humor here, of course, lies in the suggestion that soccer is somehow "unmanly," a sport more closely linked to women and femininity than to more evidently masculine endeavors like ice hockey. The feminization of soccer emerged also in the site's declaration a year earlier that soccer, at long last, was coming out of the closet. A video of a mock news conference featured an actor playing the part of an official from Fédération Internationale de Football Association (FIFA), the international organizing body for soccer. In the glare of camera lights, the actor declared, "Soccer is not ashamed of what it is. Soccer is a gay sport."

The perceived emasculation of soccer is at the heart of the sport's "ambivalent" status in American spectator sports culture.[1] Those sports at the center of the nation's preoccupation, such as American football, are linked to uniquely cutthroat forms of masculinity that reward the highest levels of force deployed by the male body.[2] Soccer, in stark contrast, is often deemed a less competitive and physically demanding sport more appropriate as a form of recreation than as a legitimate contender for sports fan eyeballs. This denigration of soccer

for its supposedly less-than-masculine attributes also coexists with perceptions of its national foreignness. For example, politically conservative public
figure Ann Coulter published a web diatribe in 2014 that went viral for its
claim that America's pastime was no longer baseball, but "hating soccer."[3] In
support of this claim, Coulter pointed to immigrants: "If more 'Americans'
are watching soccer today, it's only because of the demographic switch effected
by Teddy Kennedy's 1965 immigration law. I promise you: No American
whose great-grandfather was born here is watching soccer." Further, Coulter
argued that the widespread inclusion of girls on coed recreational youth soccer
teams across the nation was evidence of the sport's weakness: "It's a sport in
which athletic talent finds so little expression that girls can play with boys."

While this opinion is certainly extreme, designed to draw online traffic
as much as to spark meaningful debate, it does point to the role that sports
often play in broader cultural controversies. Despite the overlap of sports
with leisure and entertainment, they are eminently social, both a reflection
of the structures and inequalities that characterize our society and a place
where these are actively built and contested. Beyond the formal rules of play,
sports involve complex configurations of cultural meaning that construct
the boundaries of social belonging.[4] Gender, sexuality, race, ethnicity, social
class, and citizenship intersect as core components of the cultural meanings
that sports possess. And the meanings attached to sports are not static but
continually evolve with a sport's development over time, its play across vary-
ing local, regional, national, and global contexts, and the actions of individuals
and groups with particular interests and worldviews.[5]

In the United States, soccer has frequently become a tool to mobilize and
assert political sentiment as part of a national "culture wars."[6] Soccer has
become "a powerful symbol in the struggle between those seeking to define
America in their own image."[7] For some, like Coulter, a dislike of soccer is
underpinned by an assumption that authentically American (and thus most
valuable) sports are those linked to middle-class, white, U.S.-born, heterosexual masculinities. From this perspective, soccer is compromised because of
its links to those outside of this frame as a "foreign, feminine, and adolescent"
sport.[8] Here, the roots of soccer's supposed marginalization in the United
States are its youth, its feminization, and a "residual ethnicity" that derives
from its developmental origins outside of the United States and its popularity
among immigrant and ethnic minority populations.[9]

In the academic literature, soccer's "outsider thesis" explains the sport's
cultural marginalization somewhat differently. In their 2001 book, *Offside:
Soccer and American Exceptionalism*, political scientists Andrei Markovits
and Steven Hellerman locate soccer outside of "hegemonic" sports culture,
which refers to "those very few team-anchored contests involving some kind
of ball-like contraption that have come to comprise a cultural preoccupation

bordering on obsession way beyond the actual contests produced on the field, arena, or rink."[10] Soccer, these scholars argue, was crowded out of hegemonic sports culture in the United States until very recently for three interrelated reasons.[11] First, the much earlier development of baseball, American football, and basketball, as well as the widespread dissemination of these sports through the educational system, meant there was little room for soccer. Second, those who did play and watch soccer (primarily immigrant men) often valued the sport as distinctly *un*-American, a way of cultivating and maintaining ethnic ties.[12] Third, soccer lacked a centralized organizational network.

Markovits and Hellerman's elaboration of the historical roots of soccer's cultural status remains one of the foremost analyses of the sport in the United States to date. However, historians and scholars of sport have also challenged this account on several points. For one, the proposition that soccer is a long-standing outsider gives short shrift to the sport's rich U.S. history, which includes moments of popularity as well as obscurity.[13] Since the publication of *Offside*, the assertion of soccer's second-class status has decreasingly squared with evidence of the "gradual, dramatic rise of soccer in the landscape of American sports."[14] This rise was certainly evident during the 1994 World Cup, which took place in the United States. Despite some uncertainty as to the tournament's reception, the World Cup was a resounding commercial success, with record game attendance. U.S. television viewership has increased for each subsequent World Cup, with the 2014 tournament in Brazil garnering 4.5 million U.S. viewers, up from 3.2 million in 2010.[15] The television audience for the 2011 Women's World Cup "averaged 13.458 million viewers, making it the most-watched and highest-rated soccer telecast on ESPN."[16] In 2012, the Luker on Trends and ESPN study of sports preferences found that "pro soccer" was rated the second most popular sport among young men ages twelve to twenty-four.[17] The number of Major League Soccer (MLS) teams stood at twenty in 2016, with ten of its nineteen teams in 2012 earning profit.[18] While MLS previously paid for their games to be available to a television audience, in 2014 ESPN, Fox Sports, and Univision signed an eight-year contract to broadcast MLS games worth $720 million total, a 900 percent increase on the league's prior contract.[19] These and other metrics demonstrate soccer's rapid and recent growth in size, audience, and financial profile, a growth either ignored or downplayed by those who would continue to claim the sport's total marginalization. In optimistic contrast, political scientist Glen Duerr interprets such statistics to indicate that soccer has definitively broken in to hegemonic sports culture to "become the fifth major team sport in the United States."[20]

The outsider thesis is also limited in centering men's soccer as most relevant to the contemporary cultural position of the sport. Ongoing discussion over whether the United States has or will accept soccer as a full member of its sports culture typically looks to the status of the men's game, often using indicators from the U.S. men's National Team, MLS, or European men's leagues.[21] Women's soccer, in comparison, remains largely on the outskirts of academic and public debate, invoked (as in Coulter's antisoccer screed) only sporadically to argue for the continued marginality of competitive soccer played by men.[22] High levels of media and popular interest in women's soccer, as during the 2011 Women's World Cup, are argued to both reflect and reinforce the effeminate, and thus culturally marginal, status of soccer in the United States.

Within Markovits and Hellerman's analysis, for instance, women's soccer is purported to occupy a space of "exceptionalism," with the U.S. Women's National Team emerging as a global powerhouse because the sport has historically been marginal among men.[23] As their argument goes, if soccer has been outside the powerful, resource-rich, and male-dominated center of American sports culture, then women have had more opportunity and support. One result of the space afforded to women in soccer has been the comparatively early development of the U.S. Women's National Team program and, consequently, the early and ongoing competitive dominance of U.S. women on the global stage. In essence, the thesis of exceptionalism holds that women's soccer has "snuck in" to a corner of U.S. sports culture precisely because, among men, it has often been secondary and small scale in the realm of mass spectator sport.[24]

As a corollary of the outsider thesis, the hypothesis of U.S. women's soccer's exceptionalism is also limited. Exceptionalism posits that women's soccer has somehow "made it," glossing over the inequalities that continue to present challenges for women's soccer players, teams, and leagues. As sports historian Jean Williams queries, "In what ways has women's soccer 'succeeded'?"[25] If professional soccer is the measure of success, then in fact the U.S. men are far more successful, while women "face a quite different set of career options."[26] As Williams argues, "In spite of mass participation and elite success, women's football [soccer] remains separate and unequal in terms of resources, participation, and prestige."[27]

In addition, the thesis of exceptionalism reflects an androcentric bias where the status of men's soccer is believed to be the most influential factor determining the status of women's soccer. Events within men's soccer have undoubtedly shaped women's soccer; for example, the profits of the 1994 World Cup helped fund the 1999 Women's World Cup.[28] However, the women's game also has its own unique story within American culture. As evidenced by my opening this book with the 1999 U.S. Women's World Cup victory, this story includes moments of extreme visibility and welcome reception; rather than understanding these as a function of American apathy for men's soccer, however, they are a product of a far more complex set of social relations. And these runaway triumphs of Olympic and Women's World Cup tournaments not only reflect but also create the cultural position of soccer in the United States, contributing significantly to recent gains in the sport's visibility and popularity.[29]

Beyond outsiderness and exceptionalism, soccer in the United States is no longer the poorer cousin of football, basketball, baseball, and ice hockey. It is a sport on the rise. I hold that women's soccer, rather than playing second fiddle to the men's game, has been central to the sport's growing momentum. In the second half of the twentieth century, organized soccer for girls and women experienced unprecedented growth in tandem with many transformations to postwar American society. These changes included expansion of and increased enrollment in higher education, greater opportunities for women in education and the workforce, feminist activism, advocacy, and policy efforts to advance the equality of women with men, shifting family formation patterns and the expectations attached to parenthood, the racialized and classed geographic reorganization of society, and the formalization of youth sport. Together, these developments contributed to the rapid expansion of girls' and women's participation in soccer. At the same time, the sport became embedded in emergent processes of racial and class distinction among white, middle- and upper-class suburban families. It is these associations that helped move the sport of soccer toward the cultural mainstream.[30] Soccer in the United States took on new layers of cultural meaning, splitting along a youth-amateur/ adult-professional sport divide that was concomitantly aligned with gender, race/ethnicity, and social class. More recent associations of youth soccer with girls, whiteness, and class privilege have not displaced but coexist with earlier linkages of elite soccer to men, ethnic minority communities, immigrants, and the working class, with both constellations of meaning informing the contemporary cultural position of soccer in the United States.[31]

The individuals working for and with Women's Professional Soccer I present in this book had routinely crossed between youth and professional soccer in their social roles as parents, friends, coaches, workers, and fans. Their experiences document the distinct set of cultural associations that operate within each of these soccer worlds in the United States. On the one hand, soccer has emerged as a culturally dominant and top participation sport for white, suburban, class-privileged girls. Today, girls and young women are easily accepted in soccer and resources are rarely lacking, although they may not be equivalent to the resources accorded boy's and men's soccer. In contrast, the women's game remains somewhat more marginal at the professional level, where the sport retains associations with men, ethnic minorities, immigrants, and the working class, and gendered resource disparities are more profound. This firsthand experience with varied meanings across the landscape of soccer generated an acute feeling of uncertainty as to the potential for a stable, long-lasting women's professional league in the United States. The very concept of a *women's* and *professional* soccer league invokes privilege and marginalization, insiderness and outsiderness at once.

Women's Soccer: Historical Development

In the second half of the twentieth century, soccer began to gain cultural associations with white, class-privileged suburban communities. Perhaps foremost among the factors producing these ties was the postwar migration of white, middle- and upper-class families to suburban areas. Between 1950 and 1970, the number of suburbanites grew from forty-one to seventy-six million, composing 37 percent of the U.S. population in 1970.[32] As sport studies scholar David Andrews and his colleagues note, this large-scale geographic reorganization of society "wrought the most profound influence on differentiating the collective experiences of class and race."[33] The swelling suburbs were predominantly, though not exclusively, white and affluent, while cities retained concentrated minority populations that varied in social class. The overwhelming whiteness and wealth of the suburbs resulted from selection out of cities but was also solidified by a host of discriminatory formal and informal practices designed to exclude minority and poorer families, including "legal covenants, real estate practices, federal housing policies, private lending practices, and violent intimidation."[34]

The growth of the suburbs signaled a new set of consumption and lifestyle practices whereby white, affluent families constructed belonging and community through differentiating themselves from what was urban and, by implication, from racial minorities and the poor and working classes. What was suburban was defined in explicit contrast to what was urban, with suburban modes of living communicating and solidifying the confluence of racial and class privilege. Emergent lifestyle practices served to unite "the fragmented subjectivities of America's suburban population into a necessarily imagined normalized community, which underpinned the normality of whiteness."[35]

Youth sports became enmeshed within these practices of racial and class distinction in the suburbs. Sports were uniformly believed to be beneficial to youth development, contributing to the physical, academic, and moral discipline that marked identity and worth among suburbanites.[36] Youth sports participation also aligned with a class-based parenting style that sociologist Annette Lareau calls "concerted cultivation."[37] As Lareau explains, middle- and upper-class parents seek to develop, or "cultivate," their children's abilities through organized activities, thus preparing them for future educational and occupational success. Furthermore, expectations for "intensive" mothering and "involved" fathering also pushed privileged parents toward time and resource investments in their children's extracurricular activities.[38]

However, it was not just sports but *competitive* sports that suburban parents sought for their children. As sociologist Hilary Levey Friedman argues in *Playing to Win: Raising Children in a Competitive Culture*, sports, as with competitive organized activities more generally, are believed to impart skills crucial to the future reproduction of class position among many white, affluent parents.[39] Given widespread perceptions of risk and competition in education and the workforce, competitive activities are believed to give children the edge they need in the quest for achievement. In direct contrast to recreational youth sports programs that embraced an inclusive, "everyone can play" ethic, then, class-privileged parents wanted sports programs where the most talented would rise to the top. Declining financial support for public parks and recreation facilities, in tandem with desires for competitive sports opportunities, pushed suburban parents to organize private sports leagues, clubs, and academies and spearhead the construction of new facilities. Over time, youth sports grew more organized and differentiated, with a growing number of competitive, private options for participation that required substantial familial investments of time and money.

Soccer became the sport of choice for suburban children. Soccer's position outside of the cultural mainstream gave it a "residual indeterminacy" that allowed multiple and shifting symbolic uses.[40] Soccer was not yet established within the public education system when it began to be adopted by increasing numbers of suburban kids, requiring the creation of private leagues and fields on which to play.[41] Expansive suburban youth soccer complexes came to symbolize nature and openness, as opposed to the "locked doors and gated windows of city institutions."[42] Additionally, the U.S. Youth Soccer Association, created in 1974 and officially affiliated with the U.S. Soccer Federation, embodied a "pay to play" structure because soccer at the time was not cash heavy.[43]

In contrast to other sports, then, youth soccer developed largely via a suburban club system accessible to those who could afford it, and the exclusiveness of youth soccer made it ripe for families looking for distinction. The sport quickly became popular as a status symbol, slotting easily into a white, class-privileged lifestyle that stressed achievement and upward mobility.[44] Beginning in the 1970s, youth soccer beyond the lowest level of recreational participation for young children became the purview of white, wealthy communities.[45] Others were left out; Friedman notes that "as these private clubs developed, with their higher participation fees, many children from the European immigrant and working-class families who had previously kept soccer alive in the United States, along with an increasing number of Latino immigrants, were excluded."[46] Ultimately, by the 1990s soccer had become a class-based identity project for white suburbanites wherein upper-middle-class privilege was transmitted and reproduced across generations.[47]

National soccer organizations formed in the second half of the twentieth century picked up on and furthered the redefinition of soccer as a sport
appropriate for white suburban families. For example, the American Youth
Soccer Organization (AYSO) was formed in California in 1964. In his
research on AYSO, social scientist David Keyes shows that its early leaders were explicit in a mission to define soccer as a healthy, safe activity for
native-born white, suburban youth. A host of AYSO rules and practices contributed to this mission: the league restricted the use of "foreign-sounding"
team names and languages other than English, distanced themselves from
existing leagues tied to ethnic communities, and chose American-born leaders. In addition, AYSO promoted an inclusive, "everyone plays" ethic in their
publications.[48] Soccer was constructed in direct contrast to "dangerous" and
equipment-heavy sports such as football as a safe and inexpensive noncontact
sport. By the 1970s, soccer had become quite popular as a youth sport. Soccer
researcher Kevin Tallec Marston argues that "this was the decade when soccer found its place on the national sporting map as a recognized activity for
young people."[49]

Additionally, when the two existing men's professional soccer leagues
joined forces in 1968 to become the North American Soccer League (NASL),
this new organization marketed itself explicitly to white, middle-class suburbanites, a departure from soccer's usual fan base of immigrant and ethnic
minority men. The NASL actively cultivated ties to suburban youth soccer
organizations by hosting youth soccer camps and clinics and discounting
children's tickets, hoping to develop a bigger fan base by promoting "family-
friendly" events.

Soccer's entrenchment as a white, suburban kids' after-school activity was
simultaneously the opening of the sport to girls and the greater association
of soccer with femininity.[50] If soccer possessed an indeterminacy of meaning,
the sport's "gender typing" was somewhat up for grabs. In contrast to those
sports that are firmly entrenched at the core of U.S. hegemonic sports culture,
soccer has not historically been as strongly linked to dominant masculinities.[51]
In short, soccer has never been typed as "masculine" in the ways that other
sports have been, in large part because the immigrant, working-class men
whose play "anchored" the sport in the nineteenth and early twentieth centuries could never attain culturally dominant ideals of masculinity.[52] As sociologist Eric Anderson argues, masculinity is equally about achieved behaviors
and ascribed characteristics, such as race and sexuality.[53] Because soccer was
the sport of national outsiders, many of whom were not class privileged, it
was placed in distinct contrast to sports building "authentic" white, middle-
class, American maleness.[54] Soccer's lack of cultural masculinity, as well as its
emergent association with safety, meant that the sport was more open than
others to girls and young women.

The 1972 Title IX legislation played a major role in the continued development of women's soccer; in fact, the legislation's effect on girls' soccer participation "cannot be overestimated."[55] A 1977 lawsuit won by a high school girl who had been kicked off the boys' junior varsity soccer team helped open the sport to girls and women by demonstrating the legislative "teeth" of the Fourteenth Amendment's Equal Protection Clause.[56] After the passage of Title IX, girls' and women's participation in soccer was less strongly resisted than it was within basketball and baseball.[57] In his study of youth soccer and baseball coaches in California, sociologist Michael Messner found greater acceptance of women coaches in youth soccer leagues, compared to Little League, because soccer has never been culturally associated with masculinity in the same ways as baseball. Women in his study felt they were more valued as coaches in soccer than in baseball.[58]

In an era of rising support for feminist advocacy and policy efforts and growing opportunities for women in education and the workforce, soccer also helped white suburban families pursue gender egalitarianism. For parents looking for greater equality in their marriages, youth sports, including soccer, presented opportunities for men to contribute to their children's development. In coaching their children's teams, men constructed themselves as knowledgeable, capable fathers.[59] For suburban daughters, soccer was an attractive alternative to sports with more clearly masculine, and thus exclusionary, reputations.[60] Messner argues that an ideology of "soft essentialism" enables professional-class families to navigate tensions between support for gender equality and belief in biological gender differences.[61] In contrast to the biological determinism of "hard" essentialist ideology, "this view [soft essentialism] valorizes the liberal feminist ideal of individual choice for girls and women, while retaining a largely naturalized view of boys and men."[62] For many suburbanites, then, daughters choose sports, but sons are destined for sports. Girls' participation in soccer, believed to be a noncontact-oriented and safe (though still competitive) sport, aligned with beliefs in soft essentialism.

Given concerns about compliance with Title IX in the late 1970s and 1980s, soccer was increasingly recognized as a team sport whose numbers could help improve the sex ratios of intercollegiate athletics programs, particularly against the size of football programs.[63] Rates of girls' participation in soccer continued to grow; by the 1990s, soccer had become a top participation sport for girls in the United States. Sport administration scholars Vivian Acosta and Linda Carpenter argue that at the collegiate level, soccer has experienced the greatest growth of any women's sport post–Title IX. In their longitudinal study of gender in intercollegiate sports, they found that "in 1977 there were women's soccer teams at less than three out of a hundred schools. In 2014, women's soccer teams [were] found at more than 9 out of 10 schools."[64]

The acceptance of women in soccer and concomitant growth of the sport among girls and young women through the collegiate level set the stage for the U.S. Women's National Team, formed in 1985, to be an immediate competitor in international tournaments. Strong showings in Women's World Cup and Olympic tournaments from the 1990s to the present would have been unlikely, and perhaps impossible, without the base of talented participants generated through the redefinition of the sport over the past half century and the opportunities provided to girls in youth soccer programs across the nation's suburbs. At the same time, however, this redefinition and the accompanying development of a competitive, private youth soccer pipeline into collegiate soccer has resulted in an overwhelmingly white and class-privileged participant base.[65]

Today, associations of soccer with white, affluent, suburban families coexist with earlier and ongoing links to immigrant and ethnic minority men. However, these configurations of gender, racial, ethnic, national origin, and class meaning inform the sport differently at the youth and professional levels. As I show, the cultural meanings that surround U.S. soccer bifurcate largely around level of competition, with youth and amateur soccer the domain of white, class-privileged women and professional soccer more closely aligned with "foreign" men.

This cultural bifurcation integrally shapes how insiders to the women's professional soccer community—staff members, managers, journalists, fans, and others—perceive opportunity and resource structures for their league and the degree of optimism with which they approach the league's chances at long-term success. A women's professional soccer league in the United States occupies an inherently paradoxical cultural location, caught between the suburban "soccer moms" of the nation and the lingering hints of foreignness and marginality that characterize the professional game.

Girls at the Center: Youth Soccer

Among those in the women's professional soccer community, soccer was frequently described as a youth sport. Among the twenty-one professional players, two had children, but their kids were too young for organized sport. Half of the other adults I interviewed had children. While these children ranged in age from five to midtwenties, all had played youth soccer, with several continuing to play in high school and college. Many reported years of watching, coaching, or organizing their children's youth soccer teams. In addition, several adults who did not have children themselves coached youth soccer teams. As I noted in the introduction, most of those I spoke to were white and all were college educated. Excluding a few players, journalists, and fans, most lived in suburban areas outside midsize or large cities. Located in the predominately white and affluent suburban communities where soccer first emerged as a top girls' sport, the fans, owners, and staff attached to U.S. women's professional soccer could not help but see and experience the suburban youth soccer juggernaut firsthand.

Not surprisingly, then, youth soccer was perceived to be culturally mainstream, and it seemed almost automatic to enroll children in soccer at a young age. For example, David, a staff member for the Momentum, said that when he was looking to enroll his five-year-old daughter in her first organized activity, he was encouraged by family members and friends to sign her up for youth soccer through the local YMCA. As David acknowledged, the Momentum's suburban area was widely considered to be a "hotbed" for youth soccer. Momentum fan Margaret, who lived in the same area, said on enrolling her (now adult) children in soccer, "It was one of those things where, like, in some parts of the country if a little boy doesn't play Little League, you know, you think they can't walk. Well in this area if your kid doesn't play soccer, what's the matter with him?"

For parents I spoke to, soccer had uniformly been the first-choice sport for their young children and both recreational and competitive leagues had been easy to find. Curtis, a forty-five-year-old father of two teens and owner of a company that sponsored the Momentum, had witnessed the historical growth of opportunities for youth soccer firsthand: "Well, there's certain soccer hotbeds in the country. It used to be there were little patches of soccer teams. Now they're all over. It's gotten a lot more. Back when I was in high school, it was considered kind of big, but now it's huge! Now soccer's probably the most popular varsity high school sport in the area."

Soccer was selected for young children because, as a team sport, the game involved cooperation with others, developing kids' social as well as physical skills. Eighteen-year-old budding journalist and girls' youth coach Alicia said of soccer, "It's a very team sport. It's not an individual sport like baseball. It was pretty cool. It was like everybody worked together to achieve one goal." Momentum season ticket holder and volunteer Carl said of his teenage daughter, "When our daughter joined, it could have been something else. It could've been another sport. But she enjoys this. It's something where you learn from a team kinda thing. Social skills hopefully improve. Not hopefully, you *do* learn social skills. You have to deal with people as part of a team."

A second reason many parents liked soccer was because the game's eleven players displaced the need for any individual player to be highly skilled and allowed kids to play without being overly talented. Youth soccer was fun and cooperative, not competitive and hyperfocused on winning. Team sports placed less pressure on individual participants to be superstars. Season ticket holder and Momentum volunteer Dean said of his children, "I've always from day one said, 'Look, they're going to play a team sport.' Not an individual sport because there you really do have to have a level of skill and, you know,

I didn't want the pressure to be solely on them. So soccer is great from that standpoint that as a team sport they can not be good at it and still be part of the team and still get all the benefits and socialization and the camaraderie and whatnot." Even those without children repeated that "anyone" could play soccer. For instance, women's soccer fan Kristy was twenty-four and did not have children. She used the example of her own sports experience as a competitive gymnast to make the case for soccer's accessibility: "A lot of people can try basketball or soccer pretty easily, you know. But few people can do gymnastics, and few people can do gymnastics well."

As sport studies scholars Alan Tomlinson, Andrei Markovits, and Christopher Young argue, soccer's rise as a youth participation sport in the 1970s was enabled by its reputation as an "alternative to the excesses of violent professional sports and, especially, American football."[66] In the same vein, soccer was embraced by many parents I spoke to through an explicit rejection of the "big three" for their kids. The sports that compose the dominant or "hegemonic" center of American sports culture (football, basketball, and baseball) were snubbed in favor of soccer. Soccer was at the center of the youth sports experience, preferred to any other sport. Parents liked soccer the most because it was inexpensive, easy to learn, and involved nearly constant action and minimal risk of injury. Tyrone, a forty-eight-year-old team staff member, mentioned the ease of play: "It's much easier to teach a little kid to play soccer than it is to try to get them to play baseball or to buy all the crap that they need to play football. Soccer is a great game. My son and my daughter, they both like sports where there is continuous action. My son played a couple years of baseball and hated it because you just stand there for half a game." Dean referenced the low start-up costs of soccer: "Because, you know, as a sport, it's cheap. You just need a field and some cleats and a ball and you're pretty much good. Football's an expensive sport to try to do." And Paul liked the continual action of soccer compared to baseball: "You can't really start baseball when you're that young because it's too boring for kids. You stand in right field, waiting for something, you're five, six years old, you're gonna pick your nose and sit down and pluck grass. There's just nothing to do. With soccer, they all get to run and burn energy and they all get to feel like they're doing something, and it's kind of conceptually pretty easy."

Those characteristics that made soccer seem appropriate, even ideal, for youth—accessibility, teamwork, and minimal risk—have over time also made the sport seem uniquely appropriate for girls.[67] What social scientist David Keyes calls the "domestication" of U.S. soccer refers to the simultaneous adoption of soccer by class-privileged, suburban white families and the rise of youth soccer as a popular participation sport among girls. Reflecting soccer's "domestication," those I interviewed enrolled both sons and daughters equally in youth soccer. Girls' entrance into soccer was so easy as to be unremarkable.

Although soccer for young kids was embraced as fun and cooperative, continuing to play into middle school required a jump into competitive, pay-to-play club soccer.[68] While relatively few daughters of Women's Professional Soccer (WPS) insiders pursued the sport at higher levels of play, parents described the move for the few who did as resulting from interest and competitive drive. As in Messner's "soft essentialism," girls were positioned as choosing to specialize in soccer out of passion for the sport.[69] Consequently, the racialized class privilege that foregrounds private club soccer participation became invisible. For instance, Momentum season ticket holder Mary Anne's ten-year-old daughter played soccer on a private club team that routinely traveled across the region for tournaments. Mary Anne said that she and her husband supported their daughter's competitive drive: "I think she is competitive enough. She had the personality where she really wanted something more competitive. The recreational program, it wasn't challenging enough for her. As long as she is gung ho about it we are willing to do it." Similarly, two of Cherish's daughters had played soccer on private club teams, with one eventually playing in college. Cherish also described her daughters' pursuit of soccer as a matter of interest: "We agreed that we wanted sports to be part of their experience as long as they were interested in being involved. We thought that was a good thing."

All the professional players I spoke to had moved from recreational to club soccer between the ages of eight and twelve. For players too, the financial resources for club soccer went unmentioned; class privilege was the unspoken requirement for their mobility in the sport. Crystal, who at twenty-four was the youngest player I interviewed, played one season for a Midwestern WPS team before taking a full-time job at a nearby university. When I asked her about her background in soccer, Crystal said,

> I think I was like eight when I had to make my big decision of what sport I wanted to pursue and put more of my time into, and I chose soccer. So I guess that was kind of the turning point for me, really focusing on it. And I played on my local township travel team I think for two or three years and then when I was eleven, I tried out for the Monarchs [a regional travel team]. Obviously being in the Monarchs' very competitive environment, I loved that and I wanted more of that. It immediately became a priority for me to play in college and all that stuff. It just kind of escalated from there.

From the lowest levels of recreational play to the upper echelons of the college game, whiteness and class privilege surround women's soccer in the United States. As Momentum manager Tanya remarked, "Obviously, soccer is upper- to middle-class and predominantly white." In the middle of the 2011 Women's Professional Soccer season, Momentum owner Steve invited his staff to a local bar for a happy hour to boost morale and provide an opportunity for socializing. My middle sister was visiting me at the time, and she and I sat along one side of a long table directly across from Steve's wife Laura and team office manager Sandra. Laura chatted with Sandra about her interactions with the Momentum players, none of whom were present at the happy hour. Laura said that she always had trouble keeping track of the players' names. "For starters," she explained to Sandra, "they all look alike! Last year it was the blondes. This year, the brunettes." Then, Laura turned to my sister and I across the table, and said laughingly, "They look just like you!" As white brunette women in our twenties, my sister and I did "look like" most of the Momentum players in 2011.

In a postseason staff meeting in September 2011, Momentum owner Steve reflected on the position of soccer as a culturally dominant, resource-rich sport among white, class-privileged women. In his opinion, players' move from college to professional soccer was often experienced as downward mobility given the privileges many had experienced from a young age and often took for granted. Referring to the Momentum players, Steve argued, "They're white, they're middle class. They've had everything their entire lives. College soccer programs spoil them and take care of their housing, their travel, their food, their budgeting. They are not prepared to come into a league where they don't have all of these aspects of their lives taken care of."

Men at the Center: Professional Soccer

For many of those who worked for or with Women's Professional Soccer, including those tied to the Momentum, soccer was also referenced as an occupational pursuit. Soccer played by adults at the professional level was acknowledged to be somewhat outside the core of professional team sports culture in the United States. WPS team manager Amy admitted as much in saying of soccer, "It's not a national sport in our country." Momentum season ticket holder and longtime fan April also invoked this perception when she said to me laughingly, "Soccer's not that big of a thing in America. Well I'm sure you've read all the articles, too, where for some reason Americans think that soccer is a communist plot or socialist plot, or, you know what I'm saying?"

Women's professional and semiprofessional leagues do exist in countries around the world. WPS players, team owners, staff, and members of the media were aware of these leagues; traveling to play abroad in the interim between the Women's United Soccer Association (WUSA) and Women's Professional Soccer (WPS) or in the WPS off-season was a common trajectory for U.S.-born players. Ten of the players I interviewed had played abroad in seven different countries, including Sweden, Russia, and Brazil. However, not a single person I spoke to throughout the course of my research mentioned women's leagues outside of the United States when discussing the cultural status of soccer. Instead, interviewees reported watching European or South American men's professional soccer during international travel or in the context of friendships with those born in other countries. These experiences established adult professional soccer as male and external to the United States. Daniel, one of the Momentum's photographers, said that his soccer fandom was initially sparked through international travel for work. His time outside of the United States made him aware that soccer was "bigger elsewhere." He reported that the people he met and worked with followed the men's international game closely and that he too began to follow European men's professional leagues. Similarly, Dean traveled abroad with the Air Force and discovered that soccer was a culturally dominant sport in many countries outside of the United States: "Soccer was a big thing because they had all these bases overseas and so everybody played soccer."

Jason, a WPS staff member and musician, had worked overseas recording backup for professional musicians. He said, "In Germany that's kind of what they do. You work on music stuff and then the entire studio would shut down because there was a soccer match on. I'm not kidding. You would see, you'd have like thirty people in the studio. All of them would be in the little break room watching the soccer match on like a thirteen-inch TV." And WPS staffer Ronald became a fan of the game in this way: "I started hanging out with a guy who had played professionally in South America, and he was a bartender, and I would go in the afternoon where he was working and they had a satellite dish so we would sit there and watch."

Momentum consultant Sasha was the former manager of a men's professional team in Europe. From his perspective, European men's leagues were the pinnacles of the sport. He often spoke about his work with men's teams outside of the United States and used them as an important point of reference for the Momentum. For instance, one midseason weekday found Sasha in the office room I shared with the Momentum's corporate sponsor and media staff. It was a full house that summer day, each cubicle packed with staff and interns. Standing in front of the seated Momentum staff, Sasha put on a show. He loudly joked from the doorway, "Do you know why Germans have big ears? Because their fathers picked them up by the ears when they were young, pulled them over the dyke to see Holland, and said 'There! That's how you play soccer.'" The Momentum staff laughed at Sasha's teasing voice, but the larger point was clear—the men's game outside of the United States (here, in Holland) was at the top of the global soccer food chain.

Women also reported that their relationships with those born outside of the United States had shaped their perceptions of the cultural positioning of soccer. Invoking professional soccer as male and foreign to the United States was not unique to men, but was a widely shared point of conversation.

For instance, Momentum season ticket holder Carol, who was thirty-one years old, had played soccer growing up. When she was a teen, a player from England had assisted her soccer coach and introduced Carol and her team-mates to European men's soccer: "When I was about fourteen, a coach had a friend who lived in England. This friend was male. He had videotapes of the Bundesliga. At that time I think it was the EPL, I don't know. The Premier League wasn't established at that time. But yeah, he had tapes and we would watch them, and I remember it changed the entire way I viewed the game." Similarly, Momentum season ticket holder Liz said that her West Indian family members exposed her to the fact of soccer's cultural significance outside of the United States: "My ex-husband's family, he's from, like I said, Trinidad and the West Indies. And soccer is much better there because it's a British colony than what it is in the United States. I mean, everything is—in Germany, soccer and football in Germany, you know what I mean? That's—when everybody, all the dual communities, for everybody there's recreational leagues. Children are involved in soccer and they rally around their local teams and it's huge, much bigger there than here in the United States."

Some WPS staff members had worked for men's professional leagues in the United States. These employment experiences also shaped perceptions of the positioning of soccer relative to other sports in the United States. Momentum managers Jordan and Chris had formerly worked for U.S. men's professional soccer teams, and Momentum manager Kendall and intern Dillon had previously worked for National Football League (NFL) teams. In our postseason interview at a local restaurant, I told Jordan about a conversation I'd had with the corporate sponsor manager of the local Major League Baseball (MLB) team, a man the Momentum had reached out to for advice during the spring preseason. I reported that the MLB manager had laughed when I asked him how he sold the team to potential sponsors—corporate sponsors simply came to him! In response to my story, Jordan acknowledged this to be true for baseball but argued that sponsorship would work very differently for soccer, given its comparative cultural marginalization. Jordan's experiences working for an MLS team had shown her that "it's not like that for MLS. They have to go sell."

Professional soccer was tied to a specific configuration of age, ethnicity, gender, and national-origin meanings given the unique history and development of the sport in the United States. Professional soccer was perceived not only as an adult and men's sport but as a sport played explicitly by immigrant men. Culturally, U.S. professional soccer was often coded as Latino. As sports sociologist Sean Brown argues, the association of soccer with men "foreign" to the United States remains an ongoing creation driven by changing demographic and immigration patterns as well as the visibility of immigration as a source of social and political debate in recent years.[70] In several cases, recent experiences had solidified the reputation of men's elite soccer as Latino among interview participants. For instance, I met Nathan at the business he owned, an indoor sports facility that was set up at the time for indoor soccer. As we sat on the metal bleachers encircling the bright green turf field, Nathan told me about attending a game of the local men's semiprofessional team: "I've been to one game this year and the only reason why I don't is because it takes me an hour to get over there. I had a good time watching that game. The announcers in the stadium were speaking Spanish. Everybody around me was Spanish. It was like, 'This is *men's* soccer. Holy cow. This is *men's* soccer.'" And Margaret's perceptions of the relative popularity of soccer across cities in the United States hinged on the ethnic makeup of city populations: "The other reason why Texas is so big, you know, and California has such a huge Hispanic population and that feeds into it too."

Women's Professional Soccer: Margins or Center?

U.S. soccer exists at both youth and professional levels. The age, racial/ethnic, social class, citizenship, and gendered meanings attached to soccer within these locations place WPS in a culturally contradictory space. Those tied to the project of WPS simultaneously acknowledged that soccer was not quite a dominant national sport at the professional level at the same time as they admitted that it was entirely mainstream at the youth level. This complicated positioning has been noted as "interesting" by David Keyes and "striking" by cultural studies scholar Derek Van Rheenen, who argues, "This public perception of soccer as non-American is striking given the sport's long history in the United States and its tremendous popularity among youth and adult amateur athletes today."[71] It is this feature of soccer in the United States, its embrace among privileged girls and women yet lingering marginality at the level of men's professional play, that produced uncertainty as to the likelihood of longevity, visibility, and financial stability for a U.S. women's professional league.

At times, many of those I spoke to invoked the meanings of soccer at the professional level to position WPS as embattled. From this perspective, WPS faced an uphill climb in seeking success. A women's professional soccer league in the United States would undoubtedly struggle due to persistent associations of professional soccer with maleness and "un-Americanness" and the dominance of men's football, baseball, and basketball in U.S. professional sport. This sense of layered disadvantage for WPS was articulated through terms indicating multiplicity. For instance, young journalist Alicia said that WPS faced a "double whammy" of disadvantage in a U.S. context: "I think it's the double whammy because soccer in America already has a hard time. Even the men's soccer, they're having a hard time getting off the ground. I mean I still feel like the world kind of looks down upon the USA as a football [soccer] nation because it's not our sport and we're still a growing sport here. And then if you look at women's soccer, it's even lower, and it's just because of the mentality of any women's sport." In the same way that Alicia described a "double whammy," Momentum intern Dillon referenced the notion of a "double minority" in explaining the league's search for fans. When I asked Dillon why he thought women's professional soccer struggled, he responded, "Because—I mean soccer in general isn't as popular in America as it is overseas. So I feel like it's hard when you're looking for a crowd. You're already looking for the minority in the crowd, then you're looking for the other minority inside that minority with being the women's league. Because it's just not— the women's leagues don't usually draw as much attention as the men's leagues do." Similarly, Jason referred to an "extra hurdle" for WPS: "You're fighting an uphill battle just because soccer's not, it doesn't have the cultural impact that it does over in Europe here. I mean, people just didn't grow up even having it around. They grew up on football, baseball, and that's all they know. And it's going to be really hard to win them over. If you get them hooked on the game, I think that's our biggest hurdle. I mean the women's part might be a little extra hurdle."

Janine, a twenty-two-year-old woman who ran an independent news website that covered women's soccer, used the word "multi" to refer to the problems that a U.S. women's professional league faced: "You know, this is the third time in U.S. history that the men's soccer league has had a league. And now they're finally sticking around. But there were other leagues in the past that failed. I don't think they failed as quickly as the women's league, but they still failed. In the women's league, I think that the problems are multi." Fellow journalist Raymond also referenced the dominance of both men's and big three sports as dual sources of WPS's disadvantage: "So it's not like the NFL or the National Basketball Association (NBA), where the men's version of the sport is already widely successful. So it's still kind of in that very much growth stage, the sport of soccer generally, and then you take it a step further, and it's the women's league." WPS manager Courtney concluded, "Soccer is just a tough sell in the United States. I mean, they'd [U.S. Soccer Federation] had a successful men's World Cup, but this was women's. No one really understood it." WPS staff member Ronald, one of the few African Americans working for the league, said soccer had a "girlie" reputation in the United States. To Ronald, the feminized reputation of U.S. soccer was connected to disinterest in the league: "Especially in the United States as opposed to the rest of the world, ironically it's considered a woman's game. But it's the rest of the world where men won't watch women play because they think that soccer, or football as they call it, is such a macho thing. They don't want women in their sport. Well, I just—I really feel for the women in trying to break into this sport."

For women's professional soccer players, the transition from college to professional play came with new, often unexpected challenges, a fact that Momentum owner Steve hinted at earlier. Shifting upward in level of competition was not accompanied by the increases in status and resources that players envisioned. Instead, moving to the professional level was a shift from center to the margins. Because women's soccer at the professional level takes on a "double disadvantage," some players expressed a sense of disappointment in their experiences as they went pro.

For instance, twenty-nine-year-old Cara played on a Midwestern WPS team and for the Women's National Team. When I asked whether her postcollege transition to professional soccer was what she expected, Cara replied, "I don't know what I was expecting, but I think in my mind once you achieve that status as a professional player then it's like cool, you made it. But it's not like that at all." Twenty-six-year-old Keegan described how a sense of euphoria at attaining professional status gave way as the resource constraints of WPS became clear to her: "I'm a professional soccer player! It was exciting. It was like a dream come true. But when you get the actual scenario of being a professional soccer player—I don't want to say that I don't get treated very well, but in reality you're not treated like you're a professional athlete almost. In college you pretty much are and you have the resources there." In her 2012 memoir, U.S. Women's National Team goalkeeper Hope Solo wrote about being drafted into WUSA, the first professional league for women:

> Professional soccer wasn't turning out to be what I expected. The launch of
> the Women's United Soccer Association in 2001—the first professional soccer
> league for women—seemed to me like a natural evolution, not a revolution. . . .
> When I was drafted by the WUSA, I thought I was joining the big time. I'd been
> in college and wasn't paying much attention to the league's growing pains or
> the dire forecasts. When Philadelphia drafted me, I felt I had arrived—a profes-
> sional athlete, in the same category as Shaq or A-Rod. But by early May, I was
> learning the hard truth—women's professional soccer wasn't anything like the
> NBA or Major League Baseball.[72]

While the "double whammy" made many internal to WPS acutely aware of the challenges of a women's professional league, in other moments the same individuals invoked past successes of the U.S. Women's National Team in wins, ticket sales, fan attendance, and media attention to assert belonging in professional sports and to argue for the potential of WPS. From this vantage point, the on- and off-field victories of the U.S. Women's National Team capped the decades-long growth of girls' and young women's participation in soccer, the triumphant result of broken barriers, expanded opportunities, and more accepting attitudes. Repeated moments of heightened attention and investment evidenced the widespread gender transformation of sport and signaled further change to come. A national professional league could and eventually would carve out lasting cultural space for itself. It was just a matter of time. For some, then, positive expectations for WPS's trajectory were wrapped into a linear narrative of progress in U.S. women's sports, with a stable professional league merely the next in a series of forward steps. As in understandings of young women's soccer careers, however, this forward-marching narrative tended to downplay the role of racial and class privilege in facilitating processes of change.[73]

While men and women were equally likely to point out the challenges WPS faced as both a women's league and a soccer league in the United States, women were more likely than men to feel strongly that U.S. Women's National Team successes were evidence of the viability of women's professional team sport. Optimism for the league's chances was particularly acute among women who were thirty or older. This pattern was partly a function of the personal investment many women expressed in the success of women's sports leagues. Greater optimism on the part of women resulted from a deep sense of identification with the evolution of women's status in sports and, for some, their personal experiences with this evolution in women's soccer. Most of the women I interviewed who were thirty or older had grown up without many formal opportunities for sports participation. They described facing overt biases and discriminatory practices as girls and young women interested in playing sports.

In recalling her childhood, fifty-four-year-old Cherish said that her parents prevented her from playing sports: "Mom didn't think it was appropriate. She was afraid I'd get hurt because I was smaller and she just didn't think girls belonged out there." Compared to their early experiences, moments of heightened visibility and buy-in for female athletes on an international stage were a revelation. Cherish said about women's soccer in the 1996 Olympics, "These were role models. It was exciting to have. Look at the women kick ass in the Olympics!" Alice, a thirty-five-year-old former player in the WUSA and member of the Women's National Team, explained, "So many people, especially boys of my age—I'm thirty-five—I joke about how it must have been. If you were a boy, and you were a decent athlete or you got a scholarship, you must have had that thought of entering college being like, 'Oh, this school, maybe I could be a pro basketball player or football player,' or whatever it is. But that certainly was not the case, I felt like, for really any girls of my generation, because there wasn't a professional league that existed when I started college." Joining the national team for the 2000 Olympics, Alice had seen the growth of the fan base for women's soccer firsthand: "The reality was, at that time, there would be games when we would play with five hundred people in the stands. Or like a hundred people in the stands. It varied widely. There would be games when there would be nobody there." In contrast, later tournaments that drew many thousands of fans bred hope for the continued growth of women's soccer. Alice concluded, "What I'm hoping is as we continue to get generations who are that much further removed from Title IX or that much further removed from not having played the sport as a kid—every girl I know now played soccer at some point, pretty much, as a kid—as we continue to have generations continue to grow and say 'Yes, this is something that I wanna choose to not only go to myself, but now this is something I want to take my family to and my children to,' I think that that can bode well for the league." In addition, only adults thirty and older had firsthand recollections of the 1996 Olympic or 1999 Women's World Cup tournaments. Some Momentum staff members and fans had attended or volunteered at the 1996 Atlanta Olympic Games and vividly recalled watching the women's team earn a gold medal in front of a sold-out crowd. Forty-two-year-old Catherine was so enthusiastic about our interview conversation about women's soccer at the Olympics that she emailed me a folder of photographs she had taken of the National Team's 1996 games. April also emphasized the importance of this event by mailing me a package of memorabilia from Olympic women's soccer after our interview. While these were rare moments of enormous kindness, they also highlight the level of optimism and excitement that moments of international victory created for those tied to WPS. Thirty-five-year-old Liz had also attended women's soccer games at the 1996 Olympics and felt that the team's success led directly to the growth and visibility of the women's game more broadly: "I think when they did really well in the Olympics, it probably did the most for women's soccer because everybody watches the Olympics. It doesn't matter what—curling or whatever, people sit there and watch it. And I think when the women's soccer did really well in the Olympics and got the gold medal, people really started to pay attention."

While the 1996 Olympics was an important marker of potential success for a women's professional league, the major point of reference was the 1999 U.S. Women's National Team, or "the 99ers."[74] The women's victory in that year's Women's World Cup was held up as evidence that women's soccer could attract big-time attention. The tournament was, in fact, a massively popular cultural event and turning point that put soccer on the national map. As Davis, the owner and manager of a Midwest WPS team, said, "After the 1999 World Cup, women's soccer blew up and became cool all of a sudden." With the 1999 World Cup and the birth of WUSA, the first women's pro league, women's soccer "carved out a recognizable niche in the cultural sports space of the United States."[75] Amy, a high-ranking manager for a West Coast WPS team, lauded the stars of 1999 as having "pioneered" the growth of the sport: "Well, think about the team, though. Think about they came off the World Cup in '99, and launched the league in 2001. We had the founding members and the girls—that team we refer to as the girls of summer, there was never a team, and there never will be in my estimation, a team like that. They were the part of American soccer for women in this country and around the world. The Mias, and the Kristine Lillys, and Foudys, and Michelle Akers. I think just, you know, I mean they are the pioneers." Carl, who was thirty-eight, had attended the 1999 Women's World Cup when he was in his twenties. He recalled, "Well I just remember in Los Angeles where it was just the pinnacle for numbers and attendance. Everything else. They beat China. It seems like Mia Hamm, the whole crew, they were playing. It seems like it was really taking off during that period of time." Similarly, Jason argued that women's soccer had gained momentum nationally due to both the 1996 Olympics and 1999 Women's World Cup: "And it started to get a little bit of attention just because of it [Olympics] and then we had the Women's World Cup which we actually won, and I think you just had the momentum of having like an international event here, and then having the women win it, and then they started the league. I think that's why you had the household names because you had the momentum of the World Cup building up." Forty-four-year-old Courtney had worked the 1999 Women's World Cup and recalled the "excitement" of the large crowd: "It was phenomenal. We had a ton of people working in this one trailer and we were totally cramped, but it was so spectacular to see that many people. All of a sudden ticket sales just went berserk. I think we had twenty thousand ticket sales from walk up. And I just remember the whole planning around them trying to deal with twenty thousand people coming for tickets and trying to get them into the game. It wasn't in the day and age of electronic tickets. There was this whole corral, it was exciting." And Erin captured the feeling of many WPS staff members and fans that the late 1990s and early 2000s were periods of remarkable change for women's sports, to the extent that everything seemed to be going "right": "In Atlanta [Olympics], [women's soccer] was so phenomenal and it did seem like it had done so well, and it did have the better attendance. But it was just everything about it was right for us in the early 2000's."

The trope of the 99ers was highly salient not only in interviews but also as part of my observation of the Momentum prior to and during the 2011 season. In fact, WPS as a league was founded within the framing of the 1999 and WUSA legacy. For instance, Momentum owner Steve held a press conference with local and regional media when he announced the addition of his team to WPS after the league's 2009 season. One of the points of the conference was to unveil the team's name. "Momentum" was the same name as the team that had played in the area during the WUSA years. One reporter asked, "Why did you choose the same name as the previous team that was part of WUSA?" Steve listed several reasons in response, one being, "The new team name embraces the previous on- and off-field success held by the WUSA team."

The Momentum's "embrace" of those past "pioneers" of the sport extended to the 2011 home opener in May. It was a chilly, somewhat overcast spring evening, and I wore a long-sleeved shirt underneath my Momentum staff T-shirt. As the electronic scoreboard counting down to the game's start reached zero, I sat in the stands to watch the kickoff. Darius, the team's announcer, led a pregame tribute to the WUSA. Approximately ten former WUSA players were present, and they walked out onto the field to loud applause as their names were called individually. Each held one or two official WPS soccer balls to throw out to the fans, and children jumped out of their seats and lined the stadium's front railing, hoping for a ball. The WUSA players all looked to be in their thirties and were dressed casually in jeans, tank tops, and T-shirts. They strolled slowly along the field's sideline, grinning and waving at the fans.

The glorification of 1999 and WUSA-era players as pioneers forging a path for women's professional soccer was not restricted to the Momentum or even to WPS, but was a narrative repeatedly frequently within mainstream mass media. The supposed triumph of women's sports after the 1999 Women's World Cup had become so institutionalized a story that it was how the current league (WPS) was understood and framed by mainstream media. For instance, two WPS players, both also on the Women's National Team, sat down for a television interview with a local Fox News affiliate prior to the start of the 2011 season. Both players wore jeans and brightly colored team jackets, their long hair straightened. They sat on stools in front of a male interviewer, also on a stool, and the three held microphones in their hands. After joking with the pair about what they had done with their Olympic medals from 2008, the interviewer asked, "I'm curious, too, how much were you guys, when you were younger obviously, at the time, you know the '96 Olympic team, and then the '99 World Cup team with the Mia Hamms and the Brandi Chastains and that group. How much of an influence did they have with you, and can you point to them and say 'Hey, that's the reason I got into soccer?'" The older of the two players, a mainstay of the Women's National Team and captain of her WPS team, nodded in response: "Yeah, they were huge. You know, growing up and watching them, and them being my idols growing up. And then I had the opportunity to play with Kristine Lilly, Mia Hamm, Joy Fawcett in 2003–2004. To play with Kristine Lilly and have her now as a good friend and mentor, I mean, we can't thank them enough for what they've done."

Mainstream media also glorified the 99ers in advertisements for the 2011 Women's World Cup, which took place midsummer, several months into the WPS season. ESPN ran one commercial almost on repeat. The spot featured a close-up on the face and torso of Abby Wambach, star forward and veteran on the squad. As Abby spoke of her disappointment in not yet winning a World Cup title, the camera moved from her to show footage of the 1999 Women's

World Cup final game against China. The ad ends with Abby arguing that the United States was committed to building on the legacy of the 1999 team in the 2011 tournament.

Conclusion

The unique developmental history of soccer in the United States has produced complex configurations of cultural meaning that situate the game differently across age, gender, race, ethnicity, citizenship, and social class. Rather than one set of meanings displacing another over time, however, the game of soccer in the contemporary United States possesses multiple, sometimes contradictory cultural associations. On the one hand, the game has emerged as a top participation sport for youth, especially among white, class-privileged suburban girls. On the other hand, professional soccer has long been perceived as the domain of immigrant men. Associations of soccer with foreignness persist in context of changing demographic patterns, national political debates, and localized team and league dynamics.

Given the layers of soccer's meanings, an organization for women's play at the professional level is caught between both youth and professional sports. Those dedicated to building U.S. women's professional soccer readily acknowledged the tensions inherent in the project of this league and constructed their expectations for the league in relation to the challenges of its presence in dual social worlds. Those who worked for and with WPS felt that the league faced an uphill climb because of soccer's marginal status compared to football, basketball, and baseball and because women's sports are often perceived as inferior to men's. At the same time, many felt that the U.S. sports landscape had changed, with greater opportunity and cultural acceptance for women over time. Women older than thirty had experienced some of this change firsthand. For them, the eventuality of growth for professional women's soccer was "proven" in the enormous successes of the U.S. Women's National Team since the 1990s. The 99ers were glorified not only by the WPS insiders I interviewed but also by local and national media outlets within the dominant liberal feminist framework for making sense of women's soccer. The accomplishments of the 99ers were to be celebrated, as they demonstrated the marketability of the sport and its players, viability many hoped would translate into success for the national professional league.

2

Business or Cause?

————————————————●

Contested Goals

When the 2011 Women's World Cup began in June, the U.S. women's professional league was on something like a hiatus and work inside the Momentum office slowed considerably. One early summer morning, I entered a cubicle-filled office room to find three staff members watching the online live stream of the morning's Women's World Cup game on their respective computers while also browsing the internet. The National Basketball Association (NBA) lockout, where conflict between men's pro basketball players and owners would delay the season substantially, was in full swing. Reading one article online about the lockout, the Momentum's media manager Grace, a tall former college soccer player, laughed loudly. Then, to explain her laughter, she read aloud to the room in a teasing voice: "On this day in history, the NBA lost all its players, the first stoppage in league history." Manager Jordan was also reading news articles online about the lockout. After a few minutes of silence in the room, she announced sarcastically, "I love, love, love this piece. It says the NFL and NBA are on strike. What are sports fans to do? Uh, hello? The Momentum!" She laughed, adding, "We're going to force you to our games!" Jordan waited to see this article posted to the newspaper's Twitter account so she could point out the omission of the Momentum via social media. She continued to lambast the article, declaring, "That's kind of an offensive title. What will we do without sports?" From across the room, Grace agreed: "Uh, duh! There's the Momentum!"

Jordan and Grace wanted Women's Professional Soccer (WPS) to have the cultural recognition accorded the big three of men's professional basketball, baseball, and football. The Women's National Team was excelling in a televised international tournament, and several men's professional leagues had delayed play, and yet WPS was left off a list of sports fan options. This omission was so unacceptable as to be deemed "offensive." Inclusion on this list as a culturally legitimate, valued U.S. professional sports league was obvious to Jordan and Grace but denied by the outsiders who owned the terms of recognition. WPS wanted to be taken seriously.

Legitimacy in the world of big-time professional sports was established through possessing the resources, or capital, valued within it. But the resources most highly sought in professional sports have changed over time. In the same postwar era that saw skyrocketing girls' soccer participation, U.S. men's professional sports leagues became more deeply connected to corporate and market forces.[1] Sports management scholars Laura Cousens and Trevor Slack's study of North American men's professional sport leagues between 1970 and 1997 documents a shift in their organizing logic, from what they term "league dominance" to "corporate dominance."[2] This change took place as the number of cable television networks boomed following the 1970s deregulation. Sports organizations' major source of revenue shifted from ticket sales to television contracts, with concomitant growth in corporate partnerships. Men's professional leagues have increasingly understood themselves as part of a corporate entertainment field revolving around the promotion of celebrity culture, construction of new facilities, and relocation of teams toward wealthier, bigger markets.[3] Sport studies scholar Bente Skogvang holds that professional soccer has a "symbiotic relationship" with both market and media fields, while these links are less salient at the youth and grassroots levels.[4] What this symbiosis signals is that television deals and corporate partnerships have become increasingly important forms of capital for U.S. professional sports.

WPS defined itself as operating within this highly commercialized, corporatized social world. It was difficult not to; "corporate sport" had become the model against which all new leagues were inevitably compared.[5] The goal of recognition among big-time professional sports leagues had existed within women's soccer since the operation of the Women's United Soccer Association (WUSA), the first professional league for women. Sociologist Sean Brown's study of this league concluded that, "WUSA attempted to position itself in the same arena as the three major leagues in American sports."[6]

As WPS got off the ground, playing its first-ever game in 2009, its leaders placed a strong emphasis on ticket sales and attendance, corporate sponsorships, and media coverage as harbingers of success. For example, a 2008 article in *Forbes* described the league's commissioner as "tirelessly pitching sponsors and television executives" in preparation for the first season. The article also referenced fan attendance and ticket sales: "Keeping costs under control is a good start, but there's also the matter of selling the game to enough people." Similarly, a September 2009 article in *Yahoo! Sports* mentioned the league's challenges in accessing these same forms of capital: "Yes, media coverage is difficult to get as newsroom staffs keep shrinking. Sponsorships are a hard sell in this economic climate. And WPS's attempts to tap into the lucrative youth soccer market is tricky business." In a press conference prior to the Momentum's first season, owner Steve fielded a question about how the team would define its success. Perhaps because of a league-wide television deal, albeit a limited one, Steve did not list media coverage as among the team's goals. Instead, he gave three metrics: season ticket sales and attendance, sponsorships, and the team's competitive record.

This understanding of success persisted through the league's folding in 2012. In an interview for the *Sports Business Journal* several months prior to the failure of the league, WPS's then-CEO Anne-Marie Eileraas said, "I look at this year as probably the strongest year overall for the league, in terms of the financials of the league, in terms of sponsorship revenue, in terms of media. What we've seen is that people have fallen in love with the women's game again, and we've tapped into that." In our interview post–league failure, Momentum ticket manager Chris said about the organizers of the league, "They want to play with the big boys." In a similar vein, Keith, a journalist who covered the league, noted of the league's leaders, "They want corporations and business people to run this league."

Despite widespread agreement as to the desirability of recognition among the ranks of big three professional sports leagues and the necessity of corporate and media capital to this goal, however, the individuals whom I met and spoke with were divided as to why they wanted access to the big time in the first place. On the one hand, inclusion in the world of professional sports via media, corporate, and fan capital was necessary to generate profit. Making money was an important return to those owners who were financially invested in the league. At the same time, profit signaled the cultural value of the league. WPS had "made it" when enough people were willing to pay for its product that the league turned a profit.

On the other hand, professional sport was perceived to be an attractive and effective platform from which to advance the achievements of youth soccer players, particularly girls. Corporations and mass media entities had a reach that small organizations could only dream of, one that could be and routinely was deployed in service of social goals. If girls can't be what they don't see, as the saying goes, then access to media and corporate capital worked as a tool for social change by making professional women's soccer visible, thus altering girls' perceptions of the opportunity structure in sport.

Of course, these were not entirely oppositional perspectives; the reach of the league to girls and young women was sometimes deemed valuable for its potential to generate profit through ticket and merchandise sales. For instance, a league-wide corporate-sponsored initiative to raise money for breast cancer research was eagerly embraced for its simultaneous corporate connections and contributions to women's charities. Nevertheless, there were substantial tensions between the business and cause orientations to the work of the league, with a small group of insiders, most of whom were women, who rejected the immediate salience of profit.[7]

While tensions between these orientations had simmered under the surface of women's soccer since the 1990s, they erupted forcefully into the public realm in 2009. The catalyst for this debate, which unfolded largely in the soccer blogosphere, was a June 2009 interview given by Peter Wilt, then-CEO of one WPS team. In the interview, the transcript of which was made public online, Wilt was asked about the differences between men and women's professional soccer. As a former manager with Major League Soccer (MLS), Wilt was uniquely positioned to compare the challenges of professional soccer leagues across gender. In response to the question, Wilt said, "I think in women's soccer there's a sense that it should be promoted as a cause, a social cause for women's rights. Girl Power. That was never the case with MLS or men's soccer. WPS in general . . . made a point of saying no, this is about entertainment. This is a great athletic sport. It's absolutely a good thing for women and a good thing for girls. But we really believe that the product as a sport, as entertainment, is worthy of your investment." With this assertion, Wilt established himself on the business side of the argument by highlighting what he saw as limitations to women's rights as a marketing strategy. While of course the existence of the league was beneficial for girls and women, these benefits should be absent from league efforts at promotion. In a postseason evaluation of WPS's first year in September 2009, Wilt again argued that the league was first and foremost a business and explained why he felt that cause marketing was inappropriate: "I believe WPS needs to succeed as a business based on its entertainment value, marketing and on field performance, not as a social cause. This doesn't mean that there isn't real value or benefit to providing opportunities for women and goals for young girls to admire and aspire to emulate. It just means that as a business, WPS needs to stand on its own legs and not be considered a charity that is supported because it provides the added social benefits." According to Wilt, emphasizing the benefits of women's professional soccer for girls and women would compromise the league's ability to be perceived as a product with entertainment and performance value. By stressing gender equality, purportedly over the skill of the players, such a strategy implied the weakness of women's play. Hinted at in Wilt's narrative are those men's leagues such as MLS that provide the engaging, high-skilled, and competitive atmosphere that professional sports fans and investors expect and against which women's soccer was compared. To engage in cause marketing was thus to stress the difference of WPS from the practices and values of men's sports. Instead, the league needed to emphasize similarity. Furthermore, Wilt contrasted charities, which are given money, from businesses, which earn money. For WPS to exist as a charity, and not a business, meant that it did not fairly earn its investments based on external perceptions of its worthiness.

As an experienced and respected figure within women's soccer, Wilt's opinions were circulated widely on soccer-related blogs and social media. At least one other league manager agreed with Wilt's analysis. In a July 2009 article in the *New York Times*, the Boston Breakers' Andy Crossley was quoted as saying, "We need to get out of the ghetto of being a role model for girls." Sportswriter Wendy Parker also aligned with Wilt. In the same month as his first-year recap, she called cause marketing the "ideological twaddle" of "those who see the world strictly through the prism of gender," writing that "people go to sporting events to be entertained, not to attend a 'Take Back the Night' rally."

However, Wilt's arguments drew the ire of those who did not agree that marketing the league by referencing gender was a mistake. Foremost among these was an anonymous blogger who wrote about American soccer under the name Fake Sigi. After both of Wilt's pronouncements, Fake Sigi published blog posts asserting the utility of tying the league to gender equality. For instance, in September 2009, Fake Sigi wrote,

> In my first response to the [Wilt] interview, I rhetorically asked why there might be the notion of promoting WPS as a social cause. To more clearly answer that question, the notion exists because women are still fighting for things many men take for granted. It exists because women in mainstream media are still largely viewed and promoted as objects and not as people. It exists because women are still fighting for a say in how their bodies are treated in every aspect of the reproductive act. I'm not going to put too fine a point on it, but we don't live in a post-feminist society. There are plenty of good reasons why the notion of promoting WPS as a social cause exists, and why it's wrong to discount that notion out of hand.

Fake Sigi argued that women in sport face a host of inequalities, from beliefs in women's athletic inferiority to low pay and a crippling invisibility in mainstream media. If the playing field onto which women's pro soccer stepped was in no way level, then perceptions of value on which investment decisions were made were never fair in the way that Wilt proposed. From this perspective, social change needed to be a centerpiece of the league's marketing platform because inequality prevented it from being deemed culturally equal to men's leagues. Rather than viewing cause marketing as hinting at women's inferiority, this blogger positioned it as a *response* to perceptions of women's inferiority. Similarity was unattainable when women's leagues were constructed as different from the get-go.

The "blog pong," as one blogger called it, that unfolded around WPS's first season demonstrates the broader clash of business and cause orientations to selling women's soccer that had existed since the 2003 failure of WUSA. Given the troubling legacy of the defunct league, WPS needed to establish its cultural legitimacy and value. To do this in context of the hypercommercialized field of professional sports meant gaining investments in the form of fan, corporate, and media partnerships and communicating these investments to the public. One group, primarily composed of men, prioritized corporate deals as the best way to establish belonging in professional sport. They adopted the quantitative return on investment (ROI) measure of value borrowed from corporate and media worlds. As suggested in Wilt's arguments, this business orientation demands that women's soccer demonstrates its similarity to men's sports within the "fair," meritocratic sports marketplace.

In contrast, a second group of insiders, composed more of women than men, preferred outreach to existing and prospective fans as the league's first step into the center of professional sports. Here, emotional connection, not quantitative return, demonstrated the league's value. Connections to community members were effectively established through stressing the distinctiveness of women's soccer compared to men's sports, especially given a sports marketplace rife with gender inequality.

The Legacy of WUSA

The formation of the WUSA was announced in February 2000. At its helm was John Hendricks, the CEO of Discovery Communications. This was Hendricks's second attempt at establishing a professional league for women in the United States, the first having fizzled in 1995. Since then, however, Hendricks had been championing women's soccer as an untapped "goldmine," as a 2000 article in AthleticBusiness.com noted. Beginning in the 1990s, the growth of women's sports participation was perceived by corporations as an opportunity to expand into the women's market. Women's professional leagues in soccer and basketball, among other sports, were founded to expand the market for corporate interests, an expectation of profit foundational to WUSA's birth. In addition to his own contribution of eight million dollars, Hendricks solicited investments totaling fifty-six million from communications and media conglomerates, leading cultural studies scholars Michael Giardina and Jennifer Metz to refer to the league as "WUSA, Inc."[8]

Given corporate investors' desire to reach a female audience, it should be no surprise that WUSA's marketing and promotional efforts targeted soccer-playing girls and their parents. Yet this outreach was characterized by a focus on empowerment and aspiration that in many instances seemed to escape the bounds of the profit motive. Hendricks himself admitted that his own daughters were a motivation behind his organizing a women's professional league. Amy, a manager who had worked for both WUSA and WPS, said that WUSA investors were interested in a women's pro soccer league because of the inspiration they found in their daughters' soccer participation: "So John [Hendricks] had assembled a few of his friends in the cable industry and I think he told me like within like twenty minutes they had raised about forty-two million dollars. So that league was owned by, you know, Comcast and Time Warner, Fox Communication, Discovery—so they were all cable people who had daughters that played the game and they had a passion for it." League spokespeople stressed the historic role of WUSA as a fully professional league for women and noted the role modeling provided by the players. And players, especially, seemed to view the league as important in nurturing the dreams of younger generations. At the league's folding, for instance, player Shannon Boxx was quoted in the *Los Angeles Times* as saying, "Having this league here is a dream come true and I just feel bad for all the little girls who had a great dream of playing in the WUSA." In 2000, Women's National Team coach Tony DiCicco argued that the players understood WUSA as having a mission to connect with soccer fans: "I'm excited with what we're offering. The members of the U.S. national team really bought into the idea that they were missionaries for the sport. It wasn't a labor for them; they wanted to be role models, to tie in with their fans. I think that's the phenomenon that happened last summer [at the 1999 Women's World Cup]. It wasn't just sport, there was a connection between the fans and players. [WUSA's] job is to recreate that connection, not just with one team, but a league of players."

Within WUSA, financial and social motivations were often entwined.[9] Unfortunately for both its corporate investors and its aspiring change makers, the league was an unmitigated financial disaster, losing far more money than expected through its three seasons. Additional corporate and media partners had failed to materialize, calling into question the viability of women's professional soccer. In the aftermath of the league's folding, Hendricks publicly lamented the unwillingness of corporations to join the league. Marketing efforts, too, came under scrutiny. For instance, sports marketing experts Han Arar and George Foster describe a 2003 meeting of the WUSA Reorganizing Committee during which debate over the effectiveness of targeting families and their soccer-playing daughters was "inconclusive."[10]

The seeds of doubt sewn by the short life of WUSA remained firmly planted in the soil of WPS's development. A March 2009 article in *Sports Illustrated* noted that "credibility is crucial to the women's league, which ... is battling the ghost of the departed Women's United Soccer Association." That same year, *Yahoo! Sports* put it bluntly: "The bottom line is that a professional women's soccer league needs to prove itself." WPS, then, needed to clearly distinguish itself from its failed predecessor.

Reassessments of WUSA's folding at the time of WPS's emergence focused almost exclusively on the league's business model, suggesting that the combination of too much money spent and not enough money generated sunk the league at the end of its third season. With little prompting, multiple interview participants mentioned this narrative of failure. Staff member Joseph noted, "WUSA failed because they thought they were bigger than they were. And a couple of years later, a hundred million dollars in debt, they realized 'Oh my God, we can't do this.'" The notion that significant financial losses spelled WUSA's demise was so familiar that Vincent, manager of an East Coast team, called it the "official story line." He said, "So the sort of official story line of the WUSA, no matter who you talk to, the official line of the WUSA is always going to be that they spent a hundred million dollars in three years, they're so wasteful and they had squandered it." Concern over WUSA's business model was a key point of debate when a new league began to take shape.

At the time of WPS's founding, women's soccer insiders asserted a commitment to fixing the flaws of the earlier generation's business model. In a media interview prior to the league's launch in 2009, one team's general manager made the case that "the WUSA didn't fail across the board. It just failed as a business. On the field the product was terrific. WPS's challenge is to retain that success on the field, but also correct the mistakes on the business side." League organizers created a "slimmed down approach," as one journalist wrote in a 2009 article for the soccer website PitchInvasion.com, a direct comparison between the amount of money WUSA and the new league expected to spend in their early years of operation. In March of that year, the *Washington Post* also picked up on the tweaked business model, noting of WPS, "They've pledged not to spend as indiscriminately as the Women's United Soccer Association, which sunk amid massive losses in just 3 seasons." Brad, a journalist who had covered women's soccer since the 1990s, compared the two leagues by noting, "With WUSA it seemed like the sky was the limit. And with WPS, I think a lot of people felt like, well, with WPS it was all reasonable goals, reasonable expenses, reasonable budgets."

WPS saw in WUSA's failure not an indictment of the goal of inclusion among the big three but an incentive to do better at reaching it. The league was founded amid a (re)articulated commitment to the goal of eventual profit generation through maximizing revenue and minimizing expenditure. WPS crafted an early identity based in part around what it was *not*—a league that would lose large sums of money for owners and investors.

While WUSA's expenditures were rejected by WPS, WUSA's marketing focus was not. Despite some debate in the years between 2003 and WPS's 2009 kickoff, as hinted at previously, the new league maintained the focus on the female and youth markets that were characteristic of WUSA. When Momentum owner Steve publicly announced the name and logo of his team, he argued that the new league would be "fun and affordable for the entire family" while "providing the highest level of women's pro soccer." This continuity was noted in a 2009 *New York Times* article on the league's formation: "Despite efforts to broaden its appeal, the league's core fans remain girls who play soccer and their parents—a potentially large group, since roughly 377,000 girls play high school soccer nationwide."

Curtis, whose company sponsored the Momentum and who was the head of a youth soccer organization, argued that the league's appeal to girls had social importance and was a key reason why he wanted to invest: "A lot of boys have team sports heroes, football, basketball, whatever, and I think it's an important part of growing up, to have people that you look up to and you try to emulate. And I think up until recently, most women's professional sports were individual sports, so golf, things like that. And I think that girls miss a lot of that." Staff member Stephen told me about working with his team's owner and general manager on marketing prior to the league's start in 2009: "I think we all had a strong feeling that we wanted young girls, soccer fans to really have an attachment to the team. When they showed up at the stadium, to really care about the team. We have really marketable players, really positive role models." Certainly, not everyone was on board with the marketing carryover from the WUSA days. For example, WPS manager Vincent felt strongly that the league needed to broaden its fan base beyond youth players: "I thought one of the problems with WUSA was that a lot of adults viewed the WUSA kind of like Chuck E. Cheese. It's like a place that you go for the benefit of your kid, but not for yourself. Like you just have to endure it so your kid could have a good time. I wanted the team games to be a place where like adults would have a good time and maybe even surprise themselves at how good a time they are having, but not feel like it was specifically geared towards kids." Generally, though, the new league emphasized similarity to WUSA in some organizing elements, like the focus on the female market, while downsizing its business model. WPS's simultaneous distance from and continuity with WUSA set the stage for tensions between profit seeking and social motivations. When I asked whether he had heard arguments for marketing the league as a cause, journalist Brad grimaced and called this the "big buzzword," arguing that "people go back and forth, essentially." As I show, these tensions played out in the different emphasis placed on media and corporate partnerships versus fan outreach as the top priority for WPS as it sought the capital necessary to gaining cultural acceptance as a U.S. professional sports league. I argue that the type of capital that individuals felt was most important was aligned with a broader set of assumptions about the nature of gender (in)equality in sports and, subsequently, the ability of women's soccer to exist as culturally similar to or different from men's professional sports leagues.

Getting Down to Business

In 2009, the *New York Times* held that a hurdle to WPS's success was the league's lack of a first-year television deal. This article quoted former head of the Association for Intercollegiate Athletics for Women Donna Lopiano, who called TV and sponsor deals the "keys to the kingdom." She said, "You have an American market where the real big sponsorship money is tied to television deals, because the advertisers will not do anything without television." In this quote, Lopiano argued for interrelationships between the three main forms of capital mentioned earlier: fans, media, and corporations. As Lopiano suggested, television networks commonly air sports programming for its draw in terms of size and demographic composition. Not only are sports popular, attracting an enormous following, but sports fans are the right kind of audience, typically possessing disposable income. Sports programs bring this audience to advertisers who have a large, captive audience.[11]

WPS owners and staff were aware of the tight connections between television exposure, corporate sponsorship, and fans. Almost immediately upon joining the league as a 2009 season ticket holder, I heard the term *ROI*, or *return on investment*, as the definition of value adopted by the media and corporate entities that the league sought to partner with. The concept of ROI suggests that individuals or organizations will buy into women's soccer if they see a clear, quantifiable return to this investment. A June 2009 *Sports Business Journal* article quoted the head of a soccer marketing organization as saying, "For a new property, they [WPS] have to develop that relevancy and value proposition for the corporate world and it takes time to do that." Several staff members who had degrees in sports business or sports management reported that they had learned quantitative definitions of value in their training. Dillon, an intern for the Momentum in 2010 and 2011, was currently finishing an undergraduate degree with a major in sports business. When I asked him about his studies, he emphasized calculating the amount of money fans spend in stadiums: "We look at like the FCI, which is the Family Consumption Index, which is like what the average four-person family spends at a game." In our interview over dinner after the 2011 season had ended, I asked Jordan about her education in sports management: "It was very well rounded. We learned a lot about financial business models, free agency models, the league structures of the big three, the history of it, you know."

Women's soccer employees knew that corporate and media organizations would invest in a team or league only if they deemed the size of the ROI desirable. Jerome had previously worked for a Major League Baseball (MLB) team in sponsorship. When I asked him how he had convinced corporations to sponsor, he emphasized the size of baseball's fan base: "If you're telling me that this campaign has to move Coke Zero off the shelf, then I create something that gives you access to the millions of fans that we have coming in, the print we can reach, the people online it will reach." One company was considering becoming a sponsor of the Momentum in 2011. They contacted the team to ask how many additional units of their product (here, a food item) they could expect to sell because of their sponsorship.

Staff member Michael argued that his team's struggle to sell lots of tickets compromised corporate perceptions of the value of investing: "Really, right now we're not selling the tickets and we can't give them away. So what value does that have? If you're a hedge fund manager, you would say go away." Similarly, after a meeting with one prospective corporate sponsor that I attended with Jordan, the two of us debriefed over coffee. I asked Jordan what she thought corporate sponsors were looking for. In response, Jordan sighed; these meetings were frustrating for her because they rarely paid off in actual sponsor deals: "They want to know how many people see each of our billboards at every game. I mean I can tell you our average attendance, but I can tell you most people aren't going to look at it." Momentum ticket manager Chris agreed: "It's advertising the market is all the same things to the companies. How many people are going to be there, so how many people are we touching? Your stadium holds eight thousand, let's just say you're full, sixteen thousand sets of eyeballs see my message."

If the size of the ROI was what drew corporate investors, the newness and resultant small size of WPS, then, was a challenge to obtaining corporate and media deals. A 2012 article on espnW.com made this connection: "Opportunities don't come along as readily in women's sports. The fan base is smaller and the investors more limited." Manager Amy told me that when prospective sponsors asked about her team's number of season ticket holders, she didn't always have a good enough answer for them: "You know the formula of supply and demand—having too many seats, whereby people would not—we didn't have the—the numbers of season tickets because people could walk up on game day and always get a seat at our game. So that was a downside."

Nancy Nesmith was the co-owner and president of the WPS team FC Gold Pride, which folded in 2010. That same year, Nesmith gave an interview to the online soccer news site Equalizer Soccer. Nesmith made the case that the small size of the fan base hurt the team's financial prospects: "In the end the fans didn't come, the sponsors didn't come and nobody came to support. You know, we have a very small fan base which I love and I love the players and I would have loved to have kept it going because I think we have great players and the fans that came were really supportive and they were great but it wasn't enough to sustain a business."

Despite this challenge, those whom I spoke with throughout the course of my study who represented the "business" approach felt strongly that corporate and media partnerships should be the league's top priority. This group was composed almost entirely of men. Ronald, a fifty-six-year-old staff member, argued that television exposure was of paramount importance to the league: "I think what is holding this league together is the broadcast of one game a week. Of course it's summertime, the European leagues are all done with so they're hungry for any kind of programming, so they pick up WPS, but if it wasn't for the Fox Soccer Channel, I don't know that we'd survive." Staff member James agreed: "You can't start a sport in this day and age without television." Staff member Joseph felt that "corporate sponsorship is nowhere near where it needs to be, and it's not just on a team level. But it's on a league level. When it started out, going after Puma and going after Fox Soccer and Citibank and now they have Playtex Sport and stuff. There's so much more out there on a bigger level." Thomas, a twenty-eight-year-old staff member, also argued for the importance of corporate sponsors to compete in the field of professional sports: "There's so much for them to compete with as far as going back to pro sports as entertainment. The entertainment dollar is what they're dependent on. Unless they can come up with corporate sponsors."

While women certainly understood corporate and media buy-in to be important to the league's financial health, they were less likely to mention these right away when asked about organizational goals. Of course, there were exceptions to the gendered pattern I describe. Jeannette played for a Midwestern WPS team and also ran a nonprofit organization that worked with the league. When I asked for her perspective on the league's goals, Jeanette said that she did not feel women's soccer was adequately focused on "business" due to the backgrounds of those in charge: "It's not necessarily the brightest business minds that are trying to get a league set up. And I feel like a lot of them might not be suited for jobs that they're positioned for, but because we're not able to pay good salaries and what have you, it just ends up being that we don't have the best business people on the business side of things."

What distinguished the group of business adherents was not only the prioritization of signing sponsors and pursuing media exposure but the endorsement of ROI evaluations of value as part of a fair, meritocratic decision-making process. WPS was treated equally to other sports leagues in using ROI as a measuring stick. The gender of the players, then, was immaterial to investment decisions; ROI was key. Despite the small size of the league's fan base, which certainly prohibited charging as much for sponsorship packages as the big three, investment into WPS could be sold as a small ROI–small price package; the league should get the investment proportional to its size. In one staff meeting, Momentum owner Steve said, "You'd think you could sell the league based on a numbers game, asking for little for little." At the Momentum, I spent an afternoon in May 2011 with manager Jordan trying to decide how much to charge companies for placing ads on the team's website and in the team newsletter. Jordan described to me how she did not want a "low" amount that signaled the low value of the team, but did not want to charge an amount that seemed "too high" for the estimated return in fan attention. Jordan and I went through several price point options by compiling recent statistics on website and newsletter views and deciphering the "per click" cost to sponsorship. After we came up with amounts that "sounded right," as Jordan said, she turned to media manager Grace, who was sitting at her desk across the room: "Well, how much would you pay to be on the NFL website?" "Millions!" Grace joked in response. "Yeah, then I think this would be a good amount," Jordan concluded.

To fully believe that ROI was a gender-neutral standard required a simultaneous belief that neither bias and discrimination nor the legacy of these impacted the ability of a women's league to compete for fan attention and accordingly corporate and media deals. The men and the few women I met and spoke with who preferred to target these partnerships believed strongly in the gender neutrality of the market. Those in this group not only embraced meritocracy as the status quo but strongly repudiated what they perceived to be nonmeritocratic processes in sport that worked to women's advantage. Specifically, Title IX was invoked to contrast the operations of intercollegiate sport, where gender was directly taken into consideration, from the supposedly genderless market of professional sports. Tonya Antonucci was WPS's first CEO. In several media interviews, she forcefully delinked Title IX from the league's marketing plans even though the law had never applied. In a 2008 interview with *Yahoo! Sports*, Antonucci said, "There is nothing Title IX about us. It is up to us to prove there is a market for this league. No one is going to do it for us." In 2010, *Forbes* claimed that "Antonucci doesn't plan to play any gender cards to market the league as an opportunity that female players 'deserve.' 'This isn't a cause, it's a professional sports league and will be marketed as such,' she says."

Raymond, who had covered men's and women's soccer for several decades on his popular news website, demonstrated how rejections of Title IX were contrasted with beliefs in meritocracy at the professional level. Raymond told me,

I'm not saying that women's rights or civil rights or any of these causes in the sixties or the seventies weren't important. Title IX gave equal opportunity to women to play sports in high school, in college, in places that were receiving some kind of federal money. And it was certainly a great thing for women's sports, and for women, and it needed to happen. But saying that legally do I have the right to play basketball in high school or in college the same way that boys do is not the same as making a living doing it. You don't have a right to make a living doing anything.

Raymond made the case that while efforts to increase women's participation opportunities in sport were important in an earlier era, these efforts were successful and equality of opportunity had largely been achieved. At the same time, the larger sports marketplace is not (and should not) be subject to mandated equality of the sort legislated by Title IX. Men and women, and the professional leagues they play in, must compete for resources on the purported level playing field of the market. This argument was also made by a popular soccer blogger, who wrote in 2010 that despite supporting girls' opportunities in sports, the "right" to play sports given to girls by Title IX did not extend to the professional arena:

> Being childless by choice, I have little recourse but to empathize and imagine what sort of world I would prefer to raise a child—male or female—into and what sorts of challenges I and they might face. I have concluded that the issue for me boils down to basic civil rights: If my daughter wants to play a sport, I would hope that the opportunity exists. I certainly would not appreciate a scenario where that opportunity was denied to her purely based on gender. But I agree here with Wendy Parker when she says that playing in a league like the WNBA or WPS is not a guarantee or a right.

This group denounced framings of the league that called attention to gender, believing in an equal playing field on which they played by the same rules as men's leagues. In our interview in a soccer bar, manager Davis told me that he wanted his team to be perceived as a product and not a "charity or a social cause." When I asked him why he felt this way, he responded that he didn't want people to be "guilted" into buying tickets out of a misguided sense that they needed to "help these poor little girls." In Davis's mind, selling the league as a social cause was simultaneously to suggest that the players were not able to draw a crowd based on their athletic merits alone.

The belief in the meritocracy of professional sports was strengthened by the public pronouncements of the league's players, many of who invoked hard work as the key to their success, to the neglect of the privileges it required or potential barriers they faced as women athletes. In May 2011, for example, one Women's National Team player said in an interview posted to YouTube,

> Well I think that dreams can come true. And you hear of so many people that are talented over the years, and I've gone through tons of teammates where I've thought, "Wow. This girl is good, she's the real deal." And it's funny to see that, you know, more than 90 percent of those players aren't even playing now. So it's really all about the work. You know, I've been putting in the work day in and day out since I've been younger, kicking the ball up against the curb. Everywhere I went when I was a kid, I always had a soccer ball. You know, whether it's ten, fifteen minutes of juggling each day, or shooting. You know, that's how you make it. You know, everyone has talent, but it's the ones that want to work the hardest that make it there. I think that's a huge thing. It's just putting in hours and practicing daily. Anything is attainable.

Similarly, my analysis of players' Twitter presence uncovered a trend of posting inspirational messages. Besides Bible verses, these inspirational sayings communicated that success was a matter of an individual's will to focus on the task at hand, work hard, and use failure to become better. For instance, one player tweeted in May 2011, "Fear less, hope more. Whine less, breathe more. Talk less, say more. Hate less, love more. And all good things will come." That same day, another player posted, "Failure is simply the opportunity to begin again, this time more intelligently. ~ Henry Ford." A month later in June, one player replied to a tweet declaring a dream to play in WPS: "'Success is liking yourself, liking what you do, and liking how you do it.'—Maya Angelou believe u can & u WILL! go girl :)."

A belief in meritocracy allowed for a creeping of hard essentialism, or the ideology of women's physical inferiority to men, into interpretations of the failures of the league and its teams to gain the investments it needed. If women's soccer was unable to demonstrate an adequate ROI in the eyes of prospective sponsors, this was simply the unfortunate reality of the popular level of interest in women's sports. Due to biological differences between men and women, women's sports were just not as interesting, as exciting, or as competitive as men's. Thus, there was little to no interest in watching or investing in them. As Hampton Stevens, a writer for ESPN and the *Atlantic*, stated in a 2011 online discussion of the Women's World Cup, "The obvious, not especially gracious truth, is that women players aren't as big, strong, or fast as men, so the game is less interesting."

Stan said, "I think one of the big mistakes that the women's leagues have made is in what the ownership, perhaps, perceives is the value of the players. And I don't want this to sound wrong, but if you talk about equal work for equal pay in most situations, they're absolutely not equal." Several men offered high-profile professional male athletes as examples, arguing for their greater skill and value compared to their female counterparts. For instance, Tyrone argued,

> In the context of sports, the job is not just playing; the job is what the value of that playing brings to your organization. So if you look at, for instance, tennis, we're now in tournaments that have both men and woman brackets, like a Wimbledon or a U.S. Open. The participants basically get the same money. We pay money for the same work because they're playing in the same venue, they're drawing the same crowds, Wimbledon's getting the same TV money from NBC or whoever is broadcasting that tournament. When you're talking about women's team sports, you're talking about a different equation because playing in the WNBA for the New York Liberty is not bringing the same value to the parent company that Carmelo Anthony playing for the Knicks brings to the NBA.

Raymond also used a men's player as a point of comparison: "So you could be the best women's soccer player in the world, but the same number of people are not gonna pay to see you because they're gonna pay to see Lionel Messi. And you don't have a right to be paid the same kind of money as Lionel Messi. So we go back to the thing that I said before about equal work for equal pay. They're not the same. So it's the market value." If women's sports lose out compared to men's sports, this was the fair result of lower interest in women's soccer. This lower interest derived from the inferior quality of play, as Raymond asserted that no female player could be as skilled as male star Lionel Messi. Ultimately, explaining the lower returns to women's soccer, compared to men's sports, with the concept of market value portrayed professional sports as a gender-neutral space in which supposed biologically based sex differences in physical ability led to disparate levels of investment for women and men. Essentialism, in the end, legitimized the lack of investment in women's soccer by making it a natural, even expected outcome of women's inferiority on the playing field.

Fighting for the Cause

Organizational scholar Clare Burton has argued that the use of "merit" as an evaluative standard in organizations reflects a masculine bias when "the opportunity to accumulate 'merit' and the attribution of 'merit' are structured along gender lines."[12] Echoing Burton's perspective, a second group of insiders to women's soccer, mostly composed of women, rejected ROI as an appropriate measure of value. These "cause" advocates felt that ROI was not a meritocratic standard because it failed to recognize existing gender bias and discrimination in sports. Hindrance was commonly characterized as emanating from sexist attitudes, or a sexist "mentality" that defined women as less capable than men. For instance, season ticket holder April said, "If you look at women's soccer, it's even lower than men's soccer and it's just because of the mentality of any women's sport. It's usually that it's not worth it, it's a joke, and all these other very derogatory things, which I find ridiculous." When Anne said, "It's that whole mentality," explaining why women's sport leagues persistently struggled, I asked her, "What mentality?" Anne continued, "I think it still stems from that, that it's the holdover from—think about it. My grandmother used to not wear anything but a skirt. My mother still had to wear a skirt to school, can't wear pants to school. Those things like that, women were expected to stay home and not be the athletes. Yeah, they think they're lesser, a lot of sexism."

In addition to arguing for the existence of beliefs in women's inferiority in sport, some interview participants documented practices where these ideas were directly put into action. Multiple people argued that invisibility in mainstream mass media outlets was a result of sexism in sport. For instance, Alicia told a story about contacting ESPN to encourage them to increase their coverage of women's soccer. In an angry tone, Alicia reported,

> The media just assume that people don't want to hear about soccer or just women's sports in general. It's annoying because there is a big market out there. There are a lot of people that really do enjoy women's soccer, and I just feel like a lot of companies and a lot of media just won't bother because they just—it's a very sexist view. It's just people don't really care about women's sports so we're not gonna cover it. ESPN, a couple other fans and I got to email ESPN every day, and they just would not respond. All they did was they had their automatic response and they didn't cover the games.

Strength coach Jerry made the case that pay gaps between male and female soccer players also reflected perceptions of women's inferiority: "It seems like in America they don't want to pay the women the same amount as the men. I'm not really sure why, but if it seems like you can pay David Beckham thirty million dollars and you can't give Abby Wambach x amount? It's like who are the big investors?" Erin agreed, noting, "Women's sports just aren't valued the way men's sports are. I mean the root of it is probably sexism. You look at how much male athletes are paid compared to female athletes. I don't know. People aren't as accepting of women being athletic."

Several participants made the case that there was a lower tolerance for financial loss for women's sports leagues, compared to men's sports leagues. Historically, men's professional sports leagues had lost far more money than women's soccer without owners pulling the plug. Momentum ticket manager Chris said, "They'll show it on ESPN about the NFL and its start and what they went through, how much they lost. They lost billions probably through-out their sports career businesses. A billion easily! And they don't even care." Anne noted, "I mean MLS has struggled for—how many years have they been around? Ten? Fifteen? And they're still not there, you know. How many of those teams are actually in the black versus the red?" Keith also made the case that "the cost of getting MLS to a point where it may be profitable—we think it is. But we're still not sure—takes an enormous amount of investment to get it to be profitable. And I feel that the same is obviously true for women's sports, perhaps even more so. Because you're dealing with a social context where women's team sports are not necessarily valued by what we would con-sider the mainstream media or the mainstream culture unless they're somehow associated with patriotism."

In contrast to business adherents, who reluctantly accepted essentialism as a reality, many in the cause group identified gender essentialism as an ideologi-cal construct that limited women's success in professional sports. Men's and women's athletic abilities overlapped and were influenced by training, with the result that elite female soccer players were more physically capable than many men.[13] For instance, Renee asked me, "Do you think that Reggie Bush could come out there and dribble and juggle and catch a ball, right? Or you know, trap a ball or redirect it or flick it?" In response, I proposed, "Not well." Con-tinuing, Renee said, "I bet you [Women's National Team midfielder] Megan Rapinoe could outrun some people on the football field, you know, pound for pound, size for size. Can she catch a ball? Yes. I bet you she could punt and I bet you she could kick a field goal too." Staff member Jason also argued for women's athletic excellence compared to men: "As far as like the level of play, some of the girls I would feel comfortable putting against the men's team. They're just that talented, that physical." And Mary Anne said, "I guess a lot of time you think of the—you always think of the girls' sports as not being as intense or as physical. I feel like women's soccer is just as physical as men's." Soccer fan Paul argued, "The women aren't dainty. And they're not slow. I see the teamwork. I see the ball skill, the passing, the plan, the break through. And if I'm sitting in the top of a stadium, and I'm looking down at small people running around—because I'm at the top of the stadium, I'd almost have to really watch for a while to see if I could tell whether it was men or women play-ing. If it's a good women's team, from a distance, I wouldn't know. So I like to watch it." The conception of the sports environment as characterized by persis-tently gendered attitudes and expectations explains the low returns on invest-ment within women's soccer entirely differently from the business perspective. Rather than a function of women's inferior play, lower visibility, interest, and buy-in reflect discriminatory practices that emerge from the assumption that female athletes lack value. Ideas about women's inferiority, rather than true inferiority itself, produce the conditions of women's soccer's marginalization.

If sexism prevented women's soccer from meeting the male standards of ROI, then this understanding of value was rejected as both impossible and unfair. Instead, cause advocates adopted a standard of value as emotional connection to fans and to women and girls in particular. Outreach to and engagement with fans needed to be the foremost goal of the league because it was here that women's soccer could excel. The empowerment and inspiration of fans were defined not as quantitative measurement but as emotion, as feelings such as excitement, hope, and confidence were evidence that league goals were being achieved and its value made visible.

A 2010 article on Active.com held that "as WPS works tirelessly to establish itself in the American sports landscape, it's doing so with an eye focused on the future. That means embracing the millions of girls who play soccer at all levels across the United States—getting them familiar with the new league, helping with their skills, and giving them a professional soccer dream to shoot for down the road." The article's focus on girls' "dream" of playing professional soccer was invoked repeatedly by those aligned with the cause approach as an important goal of building connections with fans. Season ticket holder and team volunteer Liz emphasized the league's role in shaping girls' aspirations: "There are professional leagues for soccer and football and baseball and all that, but at least for women there's a soccer league that gives them something to strive for." Christine, who began working in women's soccer for the 1999 Women's World Cup, argued, "I think we always went back to the whole we are great role models for young girls. This isn't actually in the market. There are not any strong female role models. So here's an opportunity to take your daughter and your son to a game to see women in the sport. That was a big piece of what we sold. And I believe in it." WPS was not just about girls' aspirations as players, however, but also worked to open opportunities for women to work in sport. Manager Courtney made the case that the most important aspect of her work during the 1999 Women's World Cup was the opportunity it opened for girls' aspirations to jobs in professional sports:

> To pioneer the Women's World Cup was incredible. It laid a lot of groundwork for giving girls the ability to dream. This now is an opportunity that was not there before. I remember having this interaction with a young girl who asked me for an autograph. And I said "Oh, I'm not a player." And she said, "I know. I know you're not a player, but you work for the team, right?" I said yeah. "That's why I want your autograph." Wow. It's not just that girls can think about being athletes. They can also be women in powerful or important jobs in professional sports. It's important to our society.

Similarly, Jessie, a journalist who had covered the league since 2009, argued, "And in that I think that might be the first time in women's sport history where that has to be the case. Fully professional, fully independent sports league for women that can prove to be sustainable and popular enough to continue. And it provides women opportunities. Not only in the soccer fields but also in management and behind the scenes and coaching. And all the jobs need to be filled."

The few men who embraced the cause orientation, like Paul, Jerry, or Keith, either worked closely with the professional players or had soccer-playing daughters. Renee, a staff member who also coached youth soccer, said, "I read a guy, he was on Twitter, he's like you know what, I have two daughters and I support them and that's why I support women's soccer. I'm like finally somebody gets it! You know?" And David, a thirty-five-year-old staff member, said that his involvement with women's soccer began around the time of his five-year-old daughter's birth. David said, "That's why I do it, for her. And just for girls in general that hope they have something, and when they get older maybe a league to play in."

Beyond Profit

While both men and women noted the league's inspiration of girls, women alone held profit secondary to the role modeling function of women's soccer. As a 2011 *GOOD* magazine article claimed, "Women's sports should be charities, because they will never be financially viable. Still, they hold social importance and value beyond profit." When I asked Grace about the goals of the league, she acknowledged profit, but placed it lower in its significance to "empowerment":

> We see it as women's empowerment. We're about women competing and being competitive in sports. It's about Title IX, there's equality there. The changes Title IX has made cannot be undone. But it's also about the competitive nature of sport, recognizing the positives of sport and creating a model for future generations. It's an idealistic landscape, in that the ultimate goal is opportunity. Well, the ultimate goal is to generate revenue. But ultimately, it's for people who love the game and want to be a part of it, as a player, fan, employee, media person covering the game. We're here to provide opportunity for people to get involved who love the game.

As part of Grace's debate over the "ultimate" purpose of women's pro soccer, Kendall chimed in to support the assertion that the team was about far more than revenue generation: "I get really annoyed when I hear about making money, because it shouldn't be about making money. Maybe we'll break even, at best. Because if we're making money then it really needs to go to our players. None of the players are paid very much; some of them are making ten thousand dollars. So I don't think our focus should be on making money, or at least making money for the owners."

The rejection of profit for ownership was repeated many times by women committed to cause goals. Team manager Tanya had left her job after the league's second season in part out of frustration at league owners' "tunnel vision" around profit. After her departure, Tanya started a nonprofit organization involving many players from the league. When I asked her why she had started the nonprofit, Tanya said, "We have amazing women that are doing amazing things on the field and off and yet we don't do anything to highlight that. So I wanted to do something that could help them in their life and what's next and all of that."

Jordan and I had several conversations about the potential sponsor who wanted a quantitative estimate of the potential sales boost from sponsoring the team. In our postseason interview, Jordan went back to this example to make the case against a quantitative definition of success for the Momentum. Jordan laughed when she told me, "Like I said, the people who were looking for this, like the sponsor, she was focused on how many food items they sold. I mean, it's not about that. It's not gonna change the books. You're helping us change the community. That's the bottom line. You know? You are supporting something we have never had before." Journalist Janine felt that passion for women's soccer rather than expectations of financial gain motivated investment: "Well, I've heard a few of the owners say, 'This is a five-year plan for me. I'm into the second year. I need to start making money.' But honestly, I think in all reality, if you're an owner of a team—of a women's professional anything team, that you're actually in it for the passion and the heart and the game because the notion of making money, to me, is the very last thing."

One Momentum home game in 2011 featured an opposing team with several high-profile players from the Women's National Team. At the end of this game, Jordan was assigned to walk with one Women's National Team star as she signed autographs for fans. At the postgame party at a local restaurant, Jordan told me that a young girl had asked the star, "Can I have your headband?" The player had immediately pulled it off her head and handed it down. Smiling, Jordan said that she had been floored. "It was such a small thing to her," she told me. "Just a sweaty piece of prewrap. But I saw that girl's eyes. It meant so much to her." To Jordan, the meanings that this moment generated were a valuable contribution of the league and one that escaped quantifiable measurement.

Role Models

In March 2011, I attended a Momentum preseason game against a top-ranked regional college team. On that sunny spring afternoon, I sat in a hot plastic seat in the team's stadium. Immediately after the final whistle, the children in attendance ran down to the railings at the front of each section of the stadium and jockeyed for position. The Momentum players lined up to shake hands with their collegiate opponents. They then huddled in the center of the field with head coach Larry. When this meeting was over, the players scattered. Some went directly to the railings to interact with the fans. Some chatted in small groups with other Momentum players or walked to the opposite side of the field to interact with the college players. Some went directly to the bench area at the side of the field to rummage in their bags for a jacket or a Sharpie or to change from cleats to sandals or sneakers. Eventually, though, all the Momentum players appeared along what I came to know as Autograph Alley, signing balls, shirts, programs, and other items presented to them. They also took photos with their young fans. Adults stood behind the children at the railings but rarely interacted with the players themselves by asking for an autograph or photo. The adults took photos—they were not *in* photos. Autograph Alley was repeated at every game at the Momentum's stadium in 2011 and after all the WPS games I watched online that season.

The time that players spent interacting with their young fans after games was widely praised. WPS staff member Rochelle described witnessing a Women's National Team member immediately engage with her young fans after a hard-fought, rain-soaked game: "The next thing I see, there was a group of kids behind the visitor's bench who were yelling at her, and she comes over and spends thirty, forty minutes signing autographs. That right there, when you've got a player of her caliber hanging out after getting drenched, doing the pictures and then signing. . . ." Rochelle trailed off, sighing to express her admiration for the player. Momentum manager Kendall described a similar moment during a postgame team dinner in a local restaurant: "Jaime [player] comes in with her mom and all of a sudden these three little girls rush her and you could see the startled look on her face. It was like she was being ambushed, but she was really so good about it. She took time and she spoke with them, because those girls weren't gonna leave. Matt [an intern] was finally like, 'Hey girls, look, she's gotta eat.' She would not have said anything. I really don't think she would've said anything at all."

Within cause narratives of women's professional soccer, players were positioned as role models for youth. Professional players faced expectations not only for high-level play on the field but also for their availability to young fans off the field. For some, the availability of the players as positive role models set women's soccer apart from men's professional sports. In role modeling, a supposed difference of women from men was made a source of superiority for women's sports. In her 2007 book *A Beautiful Game: International Perspectives on Women's Football*, Jean Williams interviewed former assistant coach of the Women's National Team Lauren Gregg. Gregg explained to Williams that "people can relate to us because we are so available and willing to share our story."[14] Others explicitly contrasted the willingness of women's soccer players to interact with their fans with a perceived disdain for fans on the part of male professional athletes. Ronald argued, "Those women would stay there for hours signing autographs for every fan until everybody left. It's not like they were Barry Bonds and 'Oh, I'm too good and I have an entourage that keeps you away from me.' These women, if you want my autograph, I'm there." In the televised interview with two Women's National Team members mentioned in chapter 1, the interviewer noted, "So this isn't like Spring Training with some of the big-league ball players, like 'Oh, I don't have time.' You sign autographs, you interact with people, you give 'em a day to remember." Laughing, one player replied affirmatively, "Usually they have to pull us out of Autograph Alley, cut us off! Because we'll stay there for as long as we can with the families."

Like this team captain, all the players I interviewed understood themselves to be role models for youth and embraced this work as a meaningful aspect of their soccer careers.[15] Justine, a thirty-two-year-old forward for a Midwestern WPS team, said, "I think that's what at the end of the day kept me coming back and playing season after season. I think that's one of the greatest joys of playing professional soccer is you have these kids that look up to you. It makes you want to be a better person and really get involved in shaping their lives." Twenty-six-year-old Keegan agreed: "I definitely feel like that's one of the best things about my job is that I see myself as a role model. I do get feedback from people who say like 'Oh, you're like such a role model, I love how you play' and things like that. It feels good. It motivates me to be a better player, motivates me to be a better person." Psychologist Andrew Guest and former Women's National Team defender Stephanie Cox also found in their study of Women's National Team players prior to the 2007 Women's World Cup that the majority felt that they were excellent role models due to their hard work, passion, and dedication to their sport.[16]

Related to the rejection of profit among some who believed in the "cause" of women's soccer, players were often expected to provide their time to youth without compensation. While players could sometimes earn money from running youth camps and clinics, without these earnings contributing to team's salary caps, this income was neither guaranteed nor stable. The expectation that players were motivated beyond money is clearly reflected in the title of journalist Tim Nash's 2016 book on the history of the U.S. Women's National Team, *It's Not the Glory*. The message repeated throughout is that players' countless hours of on- and off-field work are less about fame and fortune than about the long-term growth of women's soccer. As Nash described almost glowingly, "The players even seemed willing to do what other professional athletes avoided. They signed autographs, carried on conversations with strangers, made appearances at clinics and games with smiles on their faces, and, believe it or not, they were willing—no, eager—to promote their game with little compensation."[17]

Even when players embraced their status as a role model, a lack of compensation for this work could create stressful time and money crunches. In 2011, the average player salary in WPS was twenty-five thousand dollars, with some players making as little as ten thousand for the season.[18] Apart from the Women's National Team players, who earned salaries with the U.S. Soccer Federation, most of the Momentum players, as well as other WPS players I interviewed, held second jobs, their pay with the league inadequate to make ends meet. These jobs were ubiquitously described as a necessary but unfortunate distraction from the demands of professional soccer. Largely, however, players did not overtly challenge the expectation that they inspire others for free; commitment to the forward movement of the sport they loved overrode more immediate concerns about money. For example, twenty-nine-year-old Raina acknowledged the financial difficulties she encountered as a WPS player. Yet she argued, "The reality is that's what it takes when you're part of a growing league in the professional ranks. I think that it speaks to how much people want to be able to participate in something they love."

During the first weekend in April 2011, the Momentum lost a home game after what was reported in several popular soccer blogs to be truly terrible play. In a postgame cloud of disappointment, the players arrived at a local restaurant filled with waiting fans only to retreat to a separate back room. The Momentum staff members I was seated with exchanged concerned glances, unsure how to respond to the players' absence. After thinking a moment, manager Jordan announced, "They're good girls. They'll come back out and talk to the fans." And they did, emerging shortly afterward to pose for pictures, sign autographs, and chat with the crowd. Near the end of the evening, defender Meg approached team manager Chris, seated at my side, and asked to speak with him privately. In response, Chris asked Meg to speak to him publicly at the table. Meg seemed hesitant, looking around her at the remaining fans. At Chris's insistence, she spoke in a near whisper to ask for clarification of the upcoming schedule of community appearances. She explained that she needed to arrange another job: "I really need this money." Meg's hesitance to reveal the conflicting demands of role modeling and external employment in front of the team's fans highlights the downside to constructions of women players as inspiring figures. This player's economic position became invisible, hidden within feel-good constructions of "good girls" who willingly sacrifice for the greater good of their sport and the young girls who play it.[19]

A Feminist Organization?

In 2009, an article in Equalizer Soccer featured Dr. Bob Contiguglia, former president of the U.S. Soccer Federation and advisor to WPS. Bob, the article noted, "understands the type of folks who are willing to invest in women's soccer." He was quoted as saying, "Anyone who is going to invest in this is passionate about the women's game. They are passionate about what it will do not only for women's soccer and for young girls having role models but for what I call 'the cause of women.'"

The frequency with which terms like *empowerment* and *inspiration* were referenced within the women's soccer community made me wonder: was the "cause of women" a feminist one? I began asking those I interviewed whether they understood empowerment and role modeling to be feminist goals, and the league a feminist organization. The responses I received expressed a high degree of ambivalence about feminism and its application to women's professional soccer. Some argued in favor of rules that gave women opportunities to work in sport, labeling these explicitly feminist practices. For instance, April was in favor of a policy of hiring only women as referees: "I think they [WPS] should be feminist on some aspects. All of the referees should be women. Period. Everyone should be female. If you want to give somebody opportunities, give them that opportunity because the men are never going to give them the opportunity ever." In my interview with Momentum staff members Grace and Kendall, the two also felt positively about this practice. Kendall explained, "The whole women ref thing, they brought it up in the World Cup and made a big issue out of it, that they only hired women referees. I mean, they made it this big deal in the World Cup, how the women were refereeing and they were less experienced." At this, Grace chimed in to ask, "But how can they gain experience?" And Kendall nodded emphatically, "Right, if they don't get the chance!"

On the other hand, so-called feminist practices were not always supported. For instance, manager Courtney did not support providing child care to players who were also mothers:

> I think there were some things that to me were not feminist. The example, one of the things we had to do when we negotiated creating the contract with WPS with the players, one of the things they had to have was the players who had children, that when they traveled or had to be at training, the team had to pay for child care. It had to not just pay for it, but find it, too. And I thought wow. For me as a mom, the last thing I would expect would be my employer being responsible for taking care of my child. And as a woman in the workplace, as important as day care is, that's my responsibility.

Beyond formal policies, there was a good degree of uncertainty as to whether the feminist label applied to WPS as an organization. When I asked Grace if WPS was a feminist organization, her response was essentially "maybe." Grace said, "It could go both ways. We see it as women's empowerment, whether that lies on the platform or not." Christine, too, expressed ambivalence when asked this question: "I've never thought of it that way. I just haven't! I think that if somebody's definition of being a feminist is to demonstrate strength in women and showing the importance of the role of women in society, then yeah, I'd say it's a feminist organization. Or there's some feminist prevailing in there. There are definitely a lot of women who would say they were feminists in the organization, who are supporters. So maybe you can't separate it."

Others who embraced the inspiration and role-modeling functions of women's soccer nevertheless rejected a feminist label for women's pro soccer. Journalist Janine, for instance, felt that a feminist label would unnecessarily complicate the work of the league:

> I think doing something like that would be—I mean, at least, as far as I know, a little bit out of the ordinary. I don't know for sure that any other professional sports have done that, but I'm not sure that that would be helpful to do something like that. I think sometime, you have to—in order to overcome things, that the best thing you can do is simplify it. And the simple truth is that we are women. We're good at what we do, and we're ready to go out there. So why shouldn't you support us?

Dillon argued that a feminist label would alienate people due to its negative connotations. He said of WPS, "I mean I definitely think it's promoting a positive female image. And I don't know if I would classify that as feminist. Because I feel like when you say feminist it definitely has a negative connotation to it, so people would think of anti-male or pro lesbian or something like that. I think maybe attaching the feminist, it might be too soon to do that or it might be too strong a word. I don't think it's necessary to actually attach feminism to it." Journalist Jessie argued that feminism was perceived to be too extreme for WPS: "I think they still have this idea that that is really radical." Keith, too, felt that the league shied away from feminism due to fear: "It makes people scared."

Business or Cause?

WPS was explicit in its mission to exist among the ranks of the big three of U.S. men's professional basketball, baseball, and football. Given the cultural omnipresence of these leagues and their commercialized, corporatized model of operations, it is perhaps difficult to imagine any other goal for a nascent professional sports league in the United States. Cultural studies scholar David Andrews argues that "the normalized and indeed normalizing blueprint for commercial sports organizations" is the model "against which established and new sporting entities are measured."[20] In order to penetrate this social world, WPS needed to acquire the forms of capital most highly valued in this social field—fan numbers, corporate partners, and media attention. Yet a previous women's professional league had failed to garner much of any of these, at least for the long term.

In the aftermath of WUSA's 2003 failure, Sean Brown concluded, "What is left is why the league had such a difficult time building an audience that would satisfy the corporate sponsors that were funding it. The answer to this question leads to the tautology that the league organizers could never get around."[21] The tautology Brown references is the chicken-and-egg problem that WPS also faced as it got off the ground. As a new league, WPS was not going to immediately have the fan base needed to convince TV and corporate executives that they were worthy of investment. Yet without this investment there was little chance for the league to permeate a social world in which these forms of capital were imperative for survival and growth.

Those working for and with women's professional soccer came at this issue from opposing sides. One group oriented around what I refer to as the business model for the league felt that WPS ought to go after big-time commercial partnerships, which required them to demonstrate an adequately sized ROI to convince partners to sign on. This is a top-down approach to gaining capital, seeking to stress to outside entities that the league possessed the same types and levels of value as men's sports. The men and few women in this group did not feel that gender inequality existed or that past inequality continued to shape the league. The market was meritocratic. If women's soccer played the same game as men's leagues and lost, this result was not a function of bias or discrimination, but reflected low levels of interest in women's soccer. Often, this perceived lack of interest was interpreted as evidence of the inferiority of women's physical prowess compared to men's.

In contrast was a ground-up approach adopted by cause-oriented adherents who felt that the league ought to prioritize building its fan base. This was a direct response to the historic and ongoing bias and discrimination that hindered the league from being perceived as equal to men's sports and thus from gaining capital. Rather than emphasize a similarity that was not possible, this group used difference strategically to gain supporters. As I will describe more fully in chapter 3, girls were particularly valued as fans. Outreach to girls derived in part from a desire to rectify the gender inequality that limited girls' aspirations and opportunities in sport, but was also an attempt to translate the enormous suburban population of affluent, soccer-playing girls into butts in the seats at the league's games.

3

We're Taking Over!

━━━━━━━━━━━━━━━━━━━━━━━━━━━●

Constructing the Fan Base

In the early evening heat of July 2011, several hundred fans milled around behind the tall iron gates in front of the Momentum's soccer stadium. Adults scrolled through their smartphones alone or chatted in small groups, while children kicked soccer balls back and forth in spontaneous play. One hour before the home game's scheduled start, the gates opened and a stream of people flooded the main concourse, a stretch of white concrete wrapping around the stadium above the playing field. From my position in front of the Momentum's information tent, I watched four young white girls in matching royal blue soccer jerseys sprint to the railing overlooking the carefully manicured soccer field below. They peeked down at the field, looking for early signs of action. The summer's pop anthem, Adele's "Rolling in the Deep," blasted throughout the stadium and the girls nodded their heads in time to the music.

Walking down the concourse past concession stands, a corporate sponsor tent offering free plastic noisemakers, a face-painting station, and a brightly colored inflatable bouncy house, I entered the shaded underbelly of a section of general admission seating. A white, middle-aged man with buzzed blonde hair walked in front of me slowly, holding the hand of a young girl in a flowered romper. Pop star Ke$ha's song "Blow" began to play, its bass line amplified underneath the stands. "Cool!" the girl yelled out, excited by the music. Three tall, thin teenagers, all with long side ponytails, short jean shorts, and white T-shirts, slunk across the floor from behind me. They, too, were enjoying the music. "Go insane, go insane, throw some glitter, make it rain!" they sung loudly in unison, and one threw her hands in the air. Hearing their voices echo, they waited to shout the lyrics, "We're taking—over!" along with Ke$ha and giggled at the loud sound that resulted.

The omnipresence of white girls and their parents in the stands at women's professional soccer games made it easy to conclude that families with soccer-playing daughters were quite literally taking over, overrunning the spaces in which women's soccer operated. The visually dominant presence of girls became clear to me at the first Momentum preseason game I attended in March 2011. Waiting for the game to begin, I watched the fans dotted in small groups across the single open side of the stadium. Later that evening, I elaborated on my observations: "There were many young girls in attendance. About half of them were sitting with adults and half were sitting in clusters with other girls, with adults at the end of the cluster or in the row behind. In fact, there were so many girls (and more than a few boys) that there were no adults present who were not obviously with a child. There appeared to be several girls' soccer teams in attendance, all wearing matching jerseys or t-shirts." Such a scene was also acknowledged in a 2009 *New York Times* article: "Many of the 3,000 or so fans at the recent match between the [Boston] Breakers and the [Washington] Freedom were young. Groups of girls, some in their soccer club shirts, jumped around in the aisles while their parents sat nearby. Others ran to the first row to snap pictures with their cellphone cameras. Many stuck around afterward to get autographs."

The fact that soccer-playing girls and their parents made up the overwhelming majority of the fan base at games was often understood as evidence that youth players and their parents were highly interested in women's professional soccer, a seemingly natural result of girls' love of playing the sport. Consequently, girls and their parents constituted the "market" for Women's Professional Soccer (WPS) as a league. Momentum manager Jordan gave a clear example of how the experience of a home game crowd translated into beliefs about interested fans when she contrasted attendees at Momentum games with those at the games of the MLS team she had previously worked for: "We see mostly families of four. It's interesting! I've worked for other soccer teams before and that wasn't the case. It's because it's women's soccer. This is our market." Referencing the age categories in youth soccer, Momentum ticket sales manager Chris explained to me, "I think the whole league as a whole said the market is U8 to U12 girls and their parents."

As I mentioned in chapter 2, WPS's "missionary zeal to teenage and preteen girls" and parents as the target fan base for women's professional soccer had carried over from the Women's United Soccer Association (WUSA).[1] Christine, who had managed a WUSA team before later working for WPS, jokingly called the fans of this second league the "ponytailed bandits." When I asked her whether the fan base had been similar in the WUSA era, she laughed and replied, "Mia [Hamm] and little girls. That's what it was all about. Although now it's Abby [Wambach] and little girls. Sometimes Alex Morgan and little girls!" For many, being surrounded by these jersey-clad "ponytailed bandits" and their parents at WPS games proved that this was, indeed, the most appropriate fan group for the league to go after. There were so many girls and their parents in the stands because girls and their parents were the most interested in the product! And this already-interested group was a big one given the number of youth soccer participants across the nation. If women's soccer could just tap into this already constituted group of soccer-loving fans, the league would easily draw the numbers needed to make prospective corporate and media partners take notice.[2]

An Active.com article around the time of WPS's emergence in 2009 quoted the league's director of communications as saying of soccer, "It's the biggest team sport for women in the country. The numbers have grown incredibly over the last two decades. The goal now is to make them fans. And that means giving them incentive to watching the world's best. There's no question that the demographic we want to reach out to are those young soccer fans and the young girls that play. It's very important for this league." The article went on to elaborate the league's efforts to "reach out" by establishing affiliations with youth soccer organizations such as American Youth Soccer Organization (AYSO) and U.S. Youth Soccer and by holding youth playing camps and clinics.

Similarly, in 2008, WPS commissioner Tonya Antonucci penned an article for the news site Soccer America: "As the league operations come into full swing and with the season less than six months away, we can't and won't lose sight of one of our most important core constituents: America's youth soccer players and their loyal and supportive families. The youth soccer community is an absolute priority for us." While the description of youth players as only "one" fan constituency acknowledged other prospective fans, the article's title, "Pro Role Models Return for U.S. Girls along with Top Level Soccer," equated fandom solely with girlhood. After asserting the new league's priority focus on youth players and their families, Antonucci detailed the league's efforts to build partnerships with youth soccer organizations. Similarly, scholar Timothy Grainey concluded in *Beyond* Bend It like Beckham, "WPS teams associated themselves with local youth programs."[3]

Undoubtedly, many girls and their parents did buy tickets to women's professional soccer games out of interest in the league, an interest piqued perhaps by their own experiences playing or watching soccer. Yet the interest in women's pro soccer signaled by the presence of soccer families in the stands at Momentum games neither predated the league itself nor was divorced from team efforts to build awareness and visibility. The Momentum actively worked to grow interest among their "market" of soccer girls and parents. As should be clear from the opening scene of this chapter, for instance, the entire game-day experience at the Momentum, from the location of the team's stadium to the activities available for fans and the music selected, was arranged explicitly to welcome kids and parents. The league-wide efforts to partner with youth soccer organizations described by WPS's early leaders made the league's very existence more visible to these groups than to others, and opportunities for fandom more readily available. While women's professional soccer reached out to youth soccer organizations assuming that youth players would con-stitute the majority of their fan base, in the very act of doing so the league ensured the outcome it presumed. The gaggles of "ponytailed bandits" in the stands were not necessarily the most highly interested in watching women's soccer. Instead, they were the most sought after and idealized, those whom the league most wanted to come to their games. In their fan outreach work, WPS selected their fans as much as their fans selected them.

In this chapter, I describe how the Momentum constructed its fan base and explore the racial, class, gender, and sexual meanings embedded in the team's processes of fan base cultivation. Through their use of space and geography, marketing campaigns, public event schedules, and game-day operations, the Momentum sought to draw a predominantly white, class-privileged audience of heterosexual suburban families with soccer-playing children. The team's efforts at building a fan base routinely excluded those outside this group as less than desirable fans, subtly downplaying or ignoring existing fandom among lesbian women and heterosexual adult men who did not have children. While the team targeted an audience based in part on perceptions of its size, its afflu-ence, and its uniqueness compared to audiences for big three competitors, these were not the only considerations. These metrics did not require white-ness, heterosexuality, or children. Pursuing white, heterosexual, nuclear fami-lies with soccer-playing children was not simply the "natural" result of these families' existing interest in women's soccer. This strategy was also concerned with creating a public image for women's professional soccer.[4] Maintaining a "family-friendly" image distanced women's soccer from the lesbian sexualities feared to alienate some fans and, perhaps more importantly, the prospective corporate and media partners for whom a safely white, feminine, and hetero-sexual image was most desirable.[5] White heterosexual femininity also served to repair lingering discomfort with the presence of strong, assertive women's bodies in the public sphere.[6]

In contrast to league-wide tensions between business and cause goals for WPS, the process of constructing a fan base was far more team specific. In large part, this was because of one element of league organization that did not live through the WUSA years. WUSA operated on a single-entity model where all teams and player contracts were owned by the league. In contrast, WPS was marked by a franchise structure where teams and players operated independently, albeit with some oversight from the league. This change gave each WPS team freedom to decide on their local marketing and fan outreach efforts.[7] As I will show, the Momentum cultivated a white and affluent fan base of suburban youth soccer players and heterosexual families, at the same time minimizing the presence of others. While other teams followed this model, there were notable exceptions.

Most, though not all, WPS teams assumed that girls' play would translate neatly into interest in their league, with girls the core of their fan market. As I show, however, girls were not as interested as imagined. White, suburban families were often too pressed for time to attend games, community events, or playing clinics, especially if these conflicted with the stringent demands of club soccer. And even when they did attend games, girls were as interested in music and peer group dynamics as in the play on the field. In contrast to this halfhearted, sporadic fandom, I witnessed a group of childless adult women and men who were marginalized in marketing campaigns but who persisted as highly involved, passionate fans of WPS.

Soccer Space

Perhaps first and foremost, the Momentum cultivated its desired fan base in deciding where to operate. The team's office, practice fields, and game-day stadium were in the suburban town of Bankworth. Excepting several public appearances, all practices, home games, community appearances, playing clinics, and private team events in eleven months took place in and around Bankworth. While this decision was convenient given that team owner Steve lived there, it would also have been possible to operate out of the city. In fact, the WPS team stood in distinct contrast with the earlier-era WUSA Momentum, which had played games in the city. Team managers, staff members, and fans frequently contrasted the city with its suburbs. Although the distance between the two was easily traversed by car in under an hour, the perceived social distance was far less navigable.

Tanya had been with the Momentum in 2009 and 2010 and described a reluctance to visit the city: "When I first moved here, [owner] Steve was like, 'We don't go downtown.' I'm like, we're an hour from the city, how do you not want to go downtown and grab dinner or whatever it is downtown you do? It's like, now that I've been here, I very seldom go in there. I think there's some sort of force field that's up that says don't go to that attraction." Similarly, team photographer Daniel said that it was "hard" to travel between the city and its suburbs, jokingly calling the road where the city ended and suburbs began the "great divide." Daniel said that based on the number of residents alone it was "odd" that the WPS Momentum was not located in the city, "unless you're trying to be an explicit alternative to the city."

This city is one of the fifty largest in the United States. As of the U.S. census of 2010, the year before I began to study the Momentum, the city was 54 percent black. The city is regularly recognized for its large gay and lesbian population, with several gay neighborhood enclaves. WPS staff member Stephen reported, "The city has the second largest gay and lesbian population. So when you go downtown, it's very evident." In contrast, the suburb of Bankworth was 59 percent white and 22 percent black. In 2010, Bankworth's median household income was sixteen thousand dollars higher than in the city. In the mid-2000s Bankworth was chosen by *Family Circle* as one of its Top 10 Best Towns for Families. The accompanying article praised the town's small size, quality schools, and "sense of community."

Contrasts between city and suburb often contained implicit recognition of social class, racial, and sexual orientation differences in residents. Among the predominately white and suburban-living individuals whom I interviewed, stereotypes of black, urban, low-income communities were often expressed indirectly through the linking of geographic space with safety/danger. For instance, several of those I interviewed who had attended the WUSA Momentum's games in the city recalled perceptions that the team had operated in a "dangerous" area. Black WPS staff member Ronald said, "You know, a lot of people felt threatened going into that neighborhood. Now I never did. I thought it was really kind of a cool stadium because it was more intimate and smaller as opposed to a Class 1A football stadium." Mary Ann said that she preferred the Momentum's suburban location to the city: "I do think more people in the suburbs would come more here than they would downtown. They're not familiar with downtown, and they're not really comfortable or feeling safe. I just feel like this is a good location." The perception of the city as particularly prone to crime was as much a function of its racial and class makeup as of any direct experience of crime. Momentum manager Tanya felt that the WUSA team had been in a crime-ridden part of the city, but said that she had never felt unsafe personally. She said of the earliest iteration of the team, "It was actually in a bad area. Violent city. There's a lot of crime that goes on down there. But you know something? There was never any problem for us. We'd take public transit down, and we'd have to change a few times."

The city was also understood to be more welcoming of gays and lesbians and to contain more sexual-minority residents compared to the suburbs. This perception was true not just for the Momentum, but for several WPS teams that operated in the suburbs of large urban cities. In 2011, the lesbian pop culture and news site After Ellen interviewed two publicly "out" lesbian WPS players. The site's interviewer asked, "You have a good contingent of lesbian fans. Is there anything that the WPS is doing to reach out to those fans?" In response, the two players noted that the lesbian fan "could be and is" devoted to women's professional soccer. However, they also argued that "it is a difficult situation for the WPS because they can't necessarily afford to operate in the large cities where most of the GLBTQI community resides." Despite this challenge, the players recommended that WPS have a "stronger presence" in cities, at gay bars, and at public LGBT events such as pride parades.

Politics were sometimes invoked to compare the social acceptance of gays and lesbians across geography for the Momentum. Suburbs such as Bankworth were described as religiously and politically conservative, and thus unwelcoming, in contrast to the open-arms liberalism of the city. As Carol described, "I think their location is a very conservative area, as opposed to being in a more urban environment. If you're inside, you know, it's more liberal. It's the city." Erin described the Momentum's suburban county as "right-wing," homophobic, and racist: "And the county is more right-wing as far as antigay, antiblack. That's just what it's been as far as I can remember. And Bankworth is just some extension of that. There is some, I don't know, kind of Christian right-wing atmosphere that goes along with Bankworth."

Conscious of existing class, racial, and sexual orientation segregation in its broader metropolitan area, Momentum ownership located the team near their self-defined "market" of white, heterosexual families with kids in "safe" communities and away from "dangerous" urban racial minority and lesbian and gay communities. Team manager Grace described the Momentum's switch from city to suburbs as a direct appeal to families. "Family," in the context of the team's geographic location, did not refer to all families, but was code for white, heterosexual suburban families. Grace said, "Yes, the Momentum is here because they wanted it to be family opportunity. And there are a lot of families here, and many here don't want to drive down to the city and struggle with parking, pay twenty dollars. They wanted an experience close to home where they could come to their own backyard."

The Momentum was successful in drawing a largely suburban crowd of white soccer-playing girls and their parents. In running the team out of Bankworth, the Momentum drew fans largely from Bankworth and its nearby suburbs. When I asked ticket manager Kendall the proportion of game attendees that came from the city, she paused. "Oh, geez," she said, thinking. "I could get you hard numbers. From the city? Only 10 percent are coming from far away." Intern Dillon, who had spent the 2010 season working with ticket manager Chris, confirmed this: "Yeah, definitely I think most of the first season, most of those people lived in Bankworth or their [soccer] clubs were located in Bankworth. It was in close proximity."

The spatial location of the team, nestled within a predominately white, suburban community, made it seem both natural and expected for white suburbanites to be at the games. The team's geographic location contributed to what sociologist Anthony Kwame Harrison calls "racial spatiality," or "the perception that certain racialized bodies are expected to occupy certain social spaces and, complimentarily, that the presence of other bodies creates social disruption, moral unbalance, and/or demands explanation."[8] This "racial spatiality" was simultaneously classed and sexualized, as the bodies the team expected were not only white but also class-privileged and heterosexual. Those who didn't visibly fit the Momentum's "target market" often seemed hypervisible and were spatially segregated in the team's stadium.

At the Momentum's 2011 home games, nearly the only visible people of color in the stadium were staffing the concession stands. All the employees who sold food and drinks during Momentum home games were black, while the crowd was almost entirely white. During one home game in April, my attention was drawn to a middle-aged black man who walked the stands selling frozen lemonade cups out of a silver tub strapped to his chest. His uniform of black pants, black collared shirt, and money belt marked him as working the event and not attending it. He was not having much luck selling and seemed at a loss for things to do. I watched him pause on the stairs between sections and watch the game, the only person of color cheering on the Momentum in a stadium filled with white children and their parents.

Fans who were obviously outside the norm of the white heterosexual family also commonly sat in unique areas of the stadium, whether due to self-segregation or social exclusion. This pattern included people of color and those in wheelchairs, but most commonly involved white, able-bodied gender-nonconforming fans. Due to the small size of typical crowds relative to the stadium's capacity, almost all game tickets were general admission and fans could decide where to sit. The Momentum always dotted a few wicker tables and chairs along the concourse above the stadium seating to accommodate eating and drinking before the game. Once home games had started, however, few fans remained in those seats. At one mid-June home game, I stood at my usual post in front of the Momentum's information tent as fans entered the stadium, jotting notes here and there on my cell phone and answering fans' questions. I watched one white, masculine-presenting woman walk in alone. She rolled up the sleeve of her T-shirt to reveal a multicolored triangle tattoo, a visible symbol of LGB affiliation, and went to sit at a wicker chair overlooking the field. This position put the maximum distance possible between herself and the stadium seating while still allowing her to watch the game. Although I joined the fans in the stands as the game began, a text message request from a Momentum staff person brought me up to the concourse before halftime. The fan was still there in the wicker seat, sitting alone. Beyond these spots at the top of the concourse, I also saw visibly gender-nonconforming fans sit isolated at the top of sections of seating or closer to the middle or front, but with far more space between themselves and others than was true for heterosexual families. I noted patterns of seating segregation to a greater or lesser extent at every home game in 2011 except for the one immediately following the

Women's World Cup; for that game the stadium was sold out, with many fans purchasing standing-room-only tickets the day of the game.

In the Community

The Momentum also cultivated their fan base through a robust schedule of community events. These events included youth playing clinics, meet and greets with youth soccer teams, speeches to school groups, and appearances at road races, food festivals, charity fund-raisers, sporting events, and holiday parades, among other events. As noted previously, most events took place in Bankworth or other nearby suburbs. By locating their events in the suburbs, the team made the predominantly white and class-privileged families who lived there aware of their existence, their roster, and their schedule. The team also frequently gave out free tickets at their public appearances, making attendance at games most possible and likely for local suburbanites. Beyond just the location of their events, however, the team also selected certain types of events over others. The Momentum preferred events with youth, particularly girls who played soccer, as well as those tied to charities or nonprofit organizations. These events crafted a "family-friendly" and civic-minded image of the Momentum as a team with excellent "role model" players active in the local community.[9]

One weekday in May, team manager Jordan called Coach Larry to discuss an upcoming event at a local hospital. As Jordan described, the players were scheduled to take a tour of the facility and would then color and "hang out" with some of the patients. After Jordan ended the call, manager Grace asked from her cubicle across the room, "How old are the patients?" Jordan sighed in response. She said that "they had really wanted kids, but these are adults." Two months later in July, Jordan held a meeting of the team's interns to brainstorm future events. Jordan instructed the team assembled around her to "look for a girl's organization like the Girl Scouts." During one in-season week, the team attended a catered dinner with an elite local girls' club soccer team and an end-of-year soccer banquet at a local school. The following Monday I was asked to write thank-you letters to the school and to the family who had hosted the dinner. When I asked about the tone of the letters, I was told to emphasize how the events built "community." I was praised for the resulting letters, which read in part, "The opportunity to come together and to meet and socialize with you and some of the next generation of young players was one that helped us to build and solidify the sense of community that we so cherish at the Momentum. The connections that we have made through social events such as this one are key to our successes as a team this season."

The Momentum wanted to appear to be an upstanding and engaged member of the Bankworth community. As with "family," "community" was a frequently used code word, signaling a sanitized, limited form of involvement with soccer groups or health-related initiatives designed to boost the team's public image. Consequently, the Momentum was hesitant to engage in events that would compromise the safely white, heterosexual, and depoliticized image it had crafted for the imagined politics of its suburban fans.

One sunny Saturday morning, I attended a local charity five-kilometer race with the Momentum. Several staff members and a handful of players helped set up the team's tent among a long row of tables and tents in the grassy post-race "party" area. We arranged stacks of game tickets and team merchandise inside the tent and set up a miniature soccer field with two small goals and a ball. While we waited for the runners, Jordan announced to the group that she was not looking forward to the team's next event, which was "very controversial." One player asked in response, "What do you mean?" Jordan stumbled over her words. "Well," she said, "it's Juneteenth." She paused and raised her eyebrows. "Juneteenth commemorates the emancipation of slaves," I added, saying what it felt like she could not. "Oh," the player responded, and then, in a low voice—"So there's like going to be a lot of black people there." Jordan nodded a yes. She said that she and Steve would not have chosen this event, but the team's primary sponsor would be there and so "the Momentum have to be there, too." Hearing this, the player shrugged and turned her attention to the soccer ball.

The Momentum also declined an invitation to participate in the city's annual pride parade. David said, "When it was brought up as they need to have a gay and lesbian type event, be in the parade, Steve said no." Manager Chris told me that he had supported participation in the parade, but that several others had argued against this event, as well as the possibility of hosting a pride-themed game. "It was odd," Chris said. "My entire family was there, my eight-year-old son skateboarded in the gay parade. We all went down there, but not the team. There were a few people in our office that said 'We're not going. You can't make me go.' I don't get that. Then I said hang on, we can have a pride night. 'Absolutely not.' They fought it like crazy."

Marketing the Momentum

A league-wide budget and staffing contraction between 2010 and 2011 meant that the Momentum, among other teams, had a nearly nonexistent marketing budget and no staff devoted solely to marketing.[10] Journalist Jessie described this change in the league: "I mean the league cut its entire marketing and it let go experts in marketing. Now it's basically taking this scattered approach and there is no recognizable marketing." The Momentum did not create billboard, newspaper, or magazine ads, television commercials, or other marketing campaigns that required substantial financial investment. Instead, marketing was on a small scale and creatively mediatized, largely comprising a social media presence, YouTube videos, and a weekly e-newsletter. Halfway through the season, media manager Grace became too busy with preparations for the Women's World Cup to produce the newsletter and the task was handed off to me.[11] I used a template already established for the newsletter but created each week's content myself with input from Grace and several media interns. The team's videos and newsletter items relied heavily on the buzzwords "family" and "community." Through its visual and textual marketing materials, the Momentum further solidified its image as a civic- and youth-oriented entertainment option, an image believed to attract the white, heterosexual families of the suburbs.

One video released at the end of March featured footage of a Momentum preseason game against a highly ranked college team. From the vantage point of the stands, a voice said, "This is a dad who brings his kids to the games. Dad, let me ask you—Masters tournament or Momentum home opener?" The camera panned to a middle-aged white man sitting with several children. Looking at the camera, the man said, "Saturday, we're gonna go to the home opener with my little girls. We're gonna go see the Momentum. We're very excited about it." The voice applauded, "Now this is a five-star dad. The kind of family event we like to see." Another video, titled "Momentum in the Community," showed footage of players juggling and kicking soccer balls with children at a food festival. A staff member joked with two players sitting on the ground eating pulled-pork sandwiches that they needed to energize themselves to beat the kids. The players were shown handing out tickets and cheering kids on as they juggled. Except for one black girl, all the children in the video were white.

On one occasion, a city newspaper had interviewed a former Women's National Team player about her charity work. I was asked to include this media coup in the week's e-newsletter. Above a link to the article, I included a photo of the player in her Momentum uniform. When the newsletter draft was sent back to me, this photo had been exchanged for one of the player out of uniform, seated and smiling next to her husband. In this instance, community involvement was juxtaposed with white heterosexuality, the photo a textbook example of the type of family the team hoped to draw.

Game Day

The Momentum also worked to attract a crowd of suburban children and their parents through its game-day operations. The importance of stadium space to fan cultivation has been recognized by sociologist Tiffany Muller Myrdahl, who argues that "game spaces are material articulations of league self-image; thus, they provide insight into the strategies intended to cultivate enduring support for women's soccer."[12] As Muller Myrdahl notes, WPS teams centered normative gender and sexuality through the explicitly "family-friendly" atmosphere at games, communicated in the types of companies that sponsored teams, the campaigns these companies ran, and the "fan zones" that created a "playground environment."[13] Through the organization of space, WPS welcomed children and their parents.

The Momentum's game-day experience was organized around the interests of children. For example, the music played before each game, during halftime, and after each game included only top-forty pop songs without swearing or explicitly sexual lyrics. During the hour before one home game, I listed the songs played in the stadium. These included the Black Eyed Peas' "Where Is the Love?," Adam Lambert's "Whataya Want from Me," Miley Cyrus's "Party in the U.S.A.," Justin Bieber's "Baby," and Cupid's irresistible dance invitation "Cupid Shuffle." Upon entering the stadium, fans immediately faced a bevy of child-friendly activities. A woman spray-painted colorful designs onto kids' faces and arms. A rainbow bouncy house attracted lines of eager children. Concession stands sold sodas, chicken sandwiches, pizza slices, and Dots ice cream. Several tents announced the presence of local and regional youth soccer associations. Sponsor tents attracted fans with raffles and giveaways—one had a large white wheel that fans could spin to win prizes.

The Momentum also held theme nights accompanied by ticket discounts and special events. In 2011, two of the team's five themed games celebrated children, with ticket discounts available to adults accompanying children. For the Father's Day game, the Momentum also held a free ice cream social for fathers and daughters. Other home games honored teachers and local police officers and firefighters. Manager Kendall, in response to my question about how the Momentum decided on these themes, replied simply, "Ideas have to match demographics."

When purchasing game tickets, fans could choose VIP seats in the stadium's suites, individual general admission tickets, or the Family 4-Pack, which included four general admission tickets, four hot dogs, four drinks, and four bags of chips. General admission tickets were inexpensive at fifteen dollars apiece, but concession items were comparatively pricey, which made these packages attractive to fans. Although any foursome could purchase this ticket package, in practice only opposite-sex couples with children did so. The Family 4-Pack was coded as appropriate for the heterosexual nuclear family. Multiyear Momentum intern Dillon noted, "I guess the Momentum, the image we kind of drew for ourselves, it's a family game. Like it's a family event that you could come to, a great way to spend the evening with your family. And if that's the image that we're gonna go after then that's something we need to really incorporate. I thought the Momentum did really well, you know, each game we'd have like a family four-pack thing." The team also gave out two awards at halftime that further linked women's soccer to "family" and "community." The "Mom of the Match" award was given to a local mother who most embodied the team's "spirit." As fan Cristina described, "They're always like, 'We recognize the Mother of the Game.' And that's nice and all, I suppose. They think the moms will bring the kiddies and it will put butts in the seats." Similarly, an e-newsletter column seeking nominations for the "Champions in the Community" award read, "Star athletes, tutors, academic all-stars, charitable go-getters and volunteers are examples of the types of Champions we need! The Momentum has the best fans in WPS whether they are cheering in the stands or helping out in their community. That's why the Momentum has created 'Champion in the Community,' a program that honors everyday youth who contribute to the development of others and their community or display mental/physical excellence."

Lesbian Fans: Left Out

The Momentum worked to attract heterosexual married couples with soccer-playing kids. Their inclusion of some was simultaneously the exclusion of others, particularly lesbian women and adults without children. Yet lesbian women and heterosexual adult men and women without children were also in the stands, albeit in smaller numbers compared to heterosexual families. The Momentum staff was highly aware that lesbian fans made up a sizeable minority of game attendees and an even larger minority of season ticket holders. I asked the Momentum's ticket sales managers about the demographics of those who bought tickets. In response, Kendall said, "Hmm. I would say families, families with girls who play the game. And a lot of single women. They get together and come to games together." Chris was more direct: "They're thirty-to fifty-year-old dads of daughters who think they are the next Mia Hamms. They're the gay and lesbian community. Out of season ticket holders lesbians are probably close to like 40 percent. I thought for sure that was a huge market we were going to tap into." Manager Jordan summarized the crowd accurately by saying, "It was young girls. I think we were surprised by how many dads we had. I would say definitely not a lot of diversity. Predominantly white, upper-middle class, or fairly well off, very well educated, and older women. [By] older, I mean like thirty-five-plus, not teenagers." Momentum player Marie had noted the same demographics from the field. She said, "I mean, you do see this sort of two main areas. You've got the families who come and then you've got eighteen to thirty-five, mostly white women. It is mostly white. It might be a little more diverse."

Despite this recognition, the heteronormativity and child centrism that pervaded the Momentum's marketing materials, game-day promotions, and schedule of community events made the team's lesbian fans invisible.[14] This was not due to lack of interest on the part of lesbian women or their scarcity at home games. Instead, the presence of lesbian fans was minimized to uphold the "family-friendly" (read: heterosexual) image of the Momentum. Team staff member Joseph believed that gay and lesbian sexuality drove heterosexual families away from women's soccer: "You do get your same-sex couples that are at the game. And a lot of people my age that are conservative like me are not going to take their ten- and twelve-year-old girl to a soccer game where it's just no big deal. To that ten-year-old girl or to that parent, it's a big deal. There are parents of kids in the league that would freak out. It's the perception of women's sports and some people do not want to be subject to that." Former staff member Anne argued, "I mean, think about this. You're appealing to the little girls and you're bringing them in with the parents. Then there are the large numbers of gay and lesbians. I think Steve, at this point, is trying to get one fan base first and hopefully he will not ignore the other fan base. But I think if he tried to enter both at the same time, he might have some problems because you're going to have some very narrow-minded folks." Curtis, whose company sponsored the Momentum, suggested, "Organizations are afraid of anything that would alienate families, and to focus on gay and lesbian marketing and crowd is something that they're going to worry, 'Oh, it'll put off the families.'"

The team thus assumed and enabled homophobia on the part of white, suburban, heterosexual families. Within the Momentum office, lesbian sexuality was never discussed openly. Journalist Hannah, who had worked for WPS and attended multiple Momentum games in 2011, said of the league, "There's like just a general silence. Like an unspoken code of silence about that entire issue. It's still too much of a taboo subject. It's not necessarily discouraged but it's also not encouraged either. I think when you talk to people who know women's soccer at all, just like softball, they're associated with lesbians. Just like in athletics, they have that perception or that stereotype around it."

In our postseason interview, I asked Momentum manager Jordan her opinion on the recent "coming out" of several lesbian WPS players. Jordan argued that while she personally didn't care about players' sexual orientation, neither she nor anyone else working for the league was likely to publicly mention lesbian sexuality: "I've been asked this whole question before about the girls coming out. No one's ever gonna comment. I just said it. You're really asking for it asking about lesbianism in sport. No one's gonna talk about it."

"Sometimes the players talk about it," I prompted.

Jordan agreed, "The players talk about it. But only them. No one will ever speak on their behalf. Not on behalf of the league. I mean, it's not a big deal to me. Honestly, you can choose to sleep with whoever you want as long as you're performing on the field. I don't care as long as you're winning."

The Momentum's 2011 roster included one lesbian player who joined the team partway through the season. This player was accompanied by her partner, an amateur soccer player, who was granted permission to train with the team. One weekday in July, media interns Carolyn and Samantha were huddled in one cubicle, talking about their experiences filming the players at that morning's practice. "Grace," Samantha queried, "who's the new player on the Momentum? She's so nice."

"Oh," Grace responded, "she's just a practice player. She's not on the roster."

"What? How can you just be a practice player?" Samantha asked, confused.

"She's so nice. I like her," Carolyn seconded. "She's the one who came the same time as Abigail!"

Grace paused and then said, "I'm not going to explain it. I'm just saying." There was clearly something that Grace was *not* saying.

"What, are they girlfriends?" Carolyn asked somewhat incredulously.

Grace replied "Yes" to this softly, but Carolyn had already begun laughing so loudly that she didn't hear the reply.

Fans Talk Back!

Lesbian fans were acutely aware that they were somewhat less than welcome with the Momentum, their presence a source of silence and discomfort. During our midseason interview at a coffee shop, lesbian fan and team volunteer Erin acknowledged that the Momentum was afraid that homosexuality would alienate their core fan base: "The only thing that I know is that it doesn't go along with the image of what the league would want. I don't know if people are specifically told never to discuss sexuality or partners or anything like that. But it does make me wonder whether that's a specific message to people. Yeah, avoid it specifically. It's all about image. It wouldn't be family friendly, kid friendly, so they don't want to have sexuality involved." While recognizing the anxiety that drove the silence around sexuality, lesbian fans pushed against the heteronormativity of Momentum marketing, arguing that the team limited the potential size of its fan base by celebrating some fans while ignoring others. For instance, season ticket holder Susannah said, "It seems like all the marketing is geared towards families and kids and there's this whole audience that you're completely missing. The gay audience, but I wouldn't just say the gay audience. Adults who don't have kids, too." And Carol commented sarcastically, "What do they want to do? Market to the myth of the American nuclear family? Hah! It's an elusive beast. Why wouldn't you adopt a 'by-any-means-necessary' attitude toward survival?"

On several occasions, lesbian fans' "push" went public. Throughout the Momentum's 2011 season, I collected survey data from those attending home games, an initiative designed by several team managers to measure fan demographics, sponsor brand recognition, and anticipated game attendance. During the second half of one midseason game, I surveyed a particularly crowded section. About twenty fans actively filled out paper surveys from their seats while I zipped back and forth between the rows handing out pens and collecting completed surveys. I wore navy shorts and a white Momentum T-shirt that read "Staff" on the back in black capital letters. My hair was tied up in a ponytail and I was sweating profusely. Four white adult women sat together one section over. They were some of the only adults present without children, and two of them were masculine in their self-presentation. These women were seated in the middle of the section, with a large oval of empty seats separating them from other fans. They were literally surrounded by adults accompanying children. I heard them yell at me, asking to take the survey, and I nodded in their direction. I was not able to get to them quickly. Impatient, one of the women, who had short blonde hair and glasses, yelled loudly, "Come over here, you little dyke! We want to talk to you!" The reaction from the crowd was instantaneous. There was loud murmuring. Heads whipped around to see who had said this, and some adults glared at the group of women. The adults immediately surrounding me looked up anxiously to see how I would respond. It was a highly disruptive comment and surprised me. Thrown off guard and more than a little uncomfortable, I burst out laughing. This was not the reaction many in the crowd expected, and several adults exchanged sidelong glances and grumbled to one another.

Several WPS players also disrupted heteronormativity through their social media posts. For instance, in May 2011, Women's National Team midfielder Megan Rapinoe tweeted a link to a YouTube video titled "How Many Gays Must God Create before We Accept That He Wants Them Around?"[15] The video showed footage from C-SPAN of an elected official speaking in front of Congress. The official argued that sexuality was innate and thus that God had created gays and lesbians. We are, the speaker noted, on the losing side of history if we oppose gay rights, and our children will look back on our actions with shame.

Lesbian fans also resisted the explicitly heterosexual child- and family-focused environment of Momentum home games in the ways they took up space in the stadium. Kinesiologist Cathy van Ingen argues that while "inequalities are reflected in the way space is designed, occupied, and controlled," we can interact with space to challenge the meanings embedded within it.[16] Research on the Women's National Basketball Association (WNBA), for instance, has found that lesbian fans construct game sites as spaces of "lesbian community," defining these against the heteronormative environment in which their identities are erased.[17]

At a late-season home game, I spied Catherine and April, two of the lesbian women I met among the group of four who had called to me. They stood at the rail in the front of a section of seating, blocking the view of the families sitting behind them. Catherine had a large black camera at her shoulder and was snapping pictures furiously. Her attention was focused entirely on a U.S. Women's National Team star who was walking on the field directly in front of her. At the end of the game, I saw April and Catherine again defy the usual spatial order of the stadium by placing themselves directly along Autograph Alley. They were the only adults asking for autographs from the players. One Momentum player signed April's game program and thanked her for coming. The two women spotted the National Team star walking across the field toward the locker rooms and yelled loudly to her, "Can I get an autograph?" Catherine nearly hung off the railing offering up her program. The player was too close to pretend not to have heard them. She looked up into the stands and said with a shrug and a smile that she had a plane to catch. She quickly disappeared underneath the stadium. April and Catherine were clearly disappointed but were happy to be acknowledged at all. "At least she didn't ignore us," nodded Catherine. April said to me, "The worst they can say is no!" Later, at the team's postgame party for fans at a local restaurant, I asked Catherine whether she ever felt out of place as one of the few adults to seek autographs from players. "Oh, the devil take them," she laughed, referring to other fans. "But they don't make being a fan easy."

Suspecting the "Superfan"

Heterosexual adults without children were also left out of the team's promotional efforts. Childless heterosexual women were easily accepted as fans, in no small part because many of the women who worked for the Momentum fit into this group. Heterosexual women without children were an admittedly small percentage of game attendees, but their fandom could easily be made comprehensible through narratives of women's empowerment in sport. And, given the deep investment of many older (thirty-five and up) women in the gender transformation of sports participation (described in chapter 2), feelings of inspiration did often motivate childless women's interest in the league. Like Andrei Markovits and Emily Albertson's "sportistas," or devoted women sports fans, most of the childless heterosexual women fans I interviewed had played soccer, their experiences on the field translating into interest in watching other, more elite women play.[18] For these women, the doing and following of sport were connected. For instance, Donna described how she became a fan of women's soccer in this way:

> I guess I just liked it and my parents never discouraged me from anything I
> wanted to try. And I was good at it. I was a natural athlete, came from good
> athletic teams, and I just remember from a young age I was kicking the ball

around and I got into soccer. That was it. I played through high school and then I coached because when I graduated—I graduated high school in the eighties and the college programs were just about starting then. But the women's game, probably around that era, started and I went to the '96 Olympics and went to a couple of matches including the gold medal match. I mean I have known about [Julie] Foudy and Shannon McMillan and Kristine Lilly I think probably just from reading like *Sports Illustrated* or something. But that was it for me, I'm like whoa, on the highest level. That was the specific reason to go.

Childless heterosexual men, though, were another story. Unlike lesbian fans, childless men were not ostracized within the stadium. Yet they faced a different reception among Momentum staff. Lesbians' presence was tolerated, if rendered invisible by the team's refusal to acknowledge lesbian sexuality. In contrast, straight men that were not accompanied by children were treated by Momentum staff with suspicion, believed to be interested in the players' bodies and not their athletic abilities. Heterosexual men's fandom was positioned as inherently and inappropriately sexualized.

At the restaurant party following the Momentum's home opener, I met three white male fans at the bar, members of the team's fan club. Two were in their thirties, while the third was somewhat older, his hair completely gray. All three men wore Momentum jerseys. Over the course of an hour, these men told me repeatedly how much they loved the Momentum. When they discovered that I was a graduate student doing research with the team, they regaled me with stories of the team's 2010 season.

The oldest man was particularly eager to interact with the players. Arriving from the stadium on a bus, the players grouped at two long tables lined with pizzas, breadsticks, and large bowls of salad. The informal norm was that fans let the players eat before asking them for autographs or pictures. On this occasion, the gray-haired fan approached each player as she left the table. He variously complimented the players' game performances, told them how much he enjoyed watching them play, referenced statistics on their soccer careers, and made jokes. The players were gracious in the face of such enthusiasm and thanked him for his support. Following each conversation this man returned to the bar side of the restaurant, exclaiming things like "I can't believe I just talked to Abigail. It's Abigail!" After this pattern repeated several times, he looked at me with concern. "This isn't sexual or anything," he explained. "I mean, they have great bodies and are very beautiful, but it's just that I appreciate their play so much. They are just such amazing athletes. You know?" I nodded that I understood. At one point, the man saw that a player he had not spoken to was in the parking lot about to leave. He sprinted from the bar to the lot to catch her for a quick hello. He returned a few minutes later, heaving from the run but with a grin on his face.

In a nod to the importance the team placed on children's connections with the players, men and women without children ubiquitously sat in the bar section of the restaurant at postgame parties, separated from the players, children and parents, and Momentum staff members. I did not know this before the first home game of the season. Arriving at the restaurant before other staff members, I selected a seat at the bar to wait for the people I knew. The restaurant's tables filled while I was drawn into conversation by the three fan club members. When I joined the Momentum's staff table some time later, Jordan gave me a sympathetic look, said that I looked "stuck over there," and passed a basket of breadsticks as if to comfort me. Kendall described the oldest of the men sneeringly as a "superfan." She said to the table, "He is a fifty-year-old guy. Why is he asking twenty-four-year-old soccer players to be his friend? He's not their friend. That's where there has to be some kind of an ethic." Manager Chris agreed, saying that the man was "inappropriate."

Through the derogatory label "superfan," heterosexual childless men's motives for fandom were called into question. Authentic fandom of women's soccer was motivated by appreciation for the player's athletic abilities or for the league's inspiration of girls and women. Such "pure" motivations for fandom were tainted by the imposition of (hetero)sexual desire on the part of adult men without children. Similarly, sports studies scholars Katelyn Esmonde, Cheryl Cooky, and David Andrews found in a study of women fans of the National Football League (NFL) that attraction to players was devalued as a motivation for sports fandom.[19]

Men's public expressions of sexual interest in the players were few, restricted to often anonymous communication via mail or social media. Rare though it was, men's attention to the sexual attractiveness of the players was treated with derision. On a weekday in July, intern Carolyn read aloud a letter addressed to a Momentum defender and former Women's National team player. Carolyn and other media interns were responsible for reading and responding to fan mail. This letter was from a married couple in Hawaii. It praised the player's soccer talent and "work ethic" and mentioned how much the duo enjoyed watching her play at defense. The letter requested an "autograph or keepsake if it isn't too much trouble."

"Aw, that's sweet," intern Samantha commented in response to Carolyn's reading.

"At least it's not creepy fan mail," Carolyn said.

"We get creepy fan mail?" I asked from my desk in the adjacent cubicle.

"Oh yeah!" Samantha chimed in. "Mostly from guys, older guy fans." She described one letter from a man in Italy or "some foreign country" that gave a glowing review of one player's beauty. Another man had printed out the Momentum players' headshots from the team's website and mailed them, asking for them to be signed.

Carolyn interjected, "Maybe we shouldn't knock them. Maybe they're not all creepy." She paused, and then added, "Well, they probably are."

Like lesbian women, childless straight men were highly aware that they didn't fit the Momentum's ideal fan demographic. Jared likened his fandom to a strenuous sporting activity, saying, "I mean, the league is totally geared to like teenage soccer players. That's kind of what they're going after. I just—nothing. Don't care. I swim upstream. I like what I like. No one can tell me any different."

And Jim noted, "Yeah, I'm not the typical thing. It's like, well one, I'm a guy. Two, I don't have kids. Three, I'm just that weird demographic. You would expect me to be at the baseball game and expect me to be at the football game and here I'm at the Momentum game."

Like the older man I met at the Momentum's first postgame meet and greet of the season, heterosexual men who did not accompany children to games denied sexual interest in the players, separating themselves from the stigma of the "superfan" label. Jared said that he loved the players' talent. "I mean, it's not like we're sex offenders!" he said to me, referring to his attendance at one home game with several male friends. At his request, my interview with Carl took place at his home. Carl was a season ticket holder and volunteer trainer who organized group runs and weightlifting sessions with the Momentum's players. As I removed my shoes in his doorway and accepted his offer of a glass of water, Carl made sure I knew that none of the players or women staff members had ever been to his home: "You are literally the first woman from the team who has been in my house. And it's funny because you're just like, 'I'll just come!' And I'm like, 'Okay.' I don't think they should, and no one has ever come over."

Limitations and Variations

Limitations

The Momentum's efforts to cultivate a suburban family audience of young soccer players and their parents were not just limited in their symbolic exclusion of lesbian and childless heterosexual adults. The team's fan outreach was also of limited effectiveness due to the time crunches characteristic of affluent suburban families with children. In fact, the very fans the team most hoped to draw were those most pressed for time, stretched thin by the demands of paid work and the extensive "concerted cultivation" of their children through organized activities.[20] Club soccer gobbled up much of families' free time, limiting their availability and generating a feeling of soccer burnout. Chris, who worked for the Momentum and whose children played club soccer, was intimately familiar with the time, money, and energy demands that competitive soccer placed on parents: "Youth sports, competitive soccer, is a business. They don't need us. They don't want us. It's tough because you drive so far to play the games. You drive an hour and a half for a game that lasts fifty minutes. So your whole day's gone. The last thing you want to do is come back and go, okay, let's go to soccer. Kids don't want to do it and parents don't want to do it."

Most WPS teams hoped to attract substantial numbers of youth soccer players and parents. Yet the reality was that soccer families simply didn't come to as many games as imagined. This pattern was evident during the WUSA years; sports marketing scholars Richard Southall and Mark Nagel's study of this league concluded that "the vast majority of WUSA fans were parents and young soccer-playing girls who, on average, only attended one to two games per season and attended games in insufficient numbers to generate ticket revenue to either meet league expenses or justify continued sponsorship investment."[21] This pattern was also true for the Momentum. My survey of four hundred fifty adult fans at Momentum games throughout the 2011 season, while not representative of all game attendees, showed that 12 percent had attended most (six or more) or all of the team's 2010 home games, while only 18 percent planned to attend most or all games in 2011. Table A.2 in appendix A reports the demographics of the fans I surveyed.

Those who had worked in women's professional soccer for any length of time had seen the limitations inherent in defining the league's "market" as youth soccer players and their parents. Momentum ticket manager Kendall recalled a former staff member who had argued that the team could expect most members of a regional youth soccer association to be season ticket holders. Kendall argued, "You're thinking 75 percent of [a youth soccer organization] is going to buy season tickets? That'll never happen; 75 percent of the people might attend a game, but not season tickets; 10 percent might attend multiple games; 1 or 2 percent are going to buy season tickets. No, no, no." Similarly, staff member Rochelle said, "Obviously, you're gonna have a certain number of families and that kind of stuff. But I don't know that you're gonna get repeat customers or season ticket holders. They're going to go to a game or two but they're not going to ten games." Manager Vincent had worked for both WUSA and WPS. Vincent acknowledged that families' wide-ranging interests and options for entertainment made it unlikely that they would regularly attend women's pro soccer games: "Yeah, well for us it was they want to do different things. They didn't want to do the same thing every weekend, so they want to go to the beach. They want to go to the symphony. They want to go see the baseball team. They want to do different things. So that's one of the biggest challenges."

Scheduling issues could generate tension between WPS teams and youth soccer organizations. Club soccer organizations' schedule of practices, games, and tournaments sometimes conflicted with women's professional soccer's schedule of games, appearances, and playing clinics. While teams could work to avoid these conflicts, and the Momentum certainly tried, overlap with at least some youth soccer functions was inevitable. When this happened, club soccer commitments won out. WPS manager Christine recalled that when her team was playing for the league's championship one year, many fans chose to attend their children's club soccer games over the WPS final, held locally. She chafed at this prioritization, feeling that a men's sporting championship would have taken precedence over youth soccer:

> I just remember when we were in the finals. And television dictates when your games are played. And they had picked 11 am. And this was going to kill us because youth soccer happens then. And so we went around to the clubs, even the adults. We said, "We're in the championship, this is awesome." And it was, "I have a game. My son has a game; my daughter has a game." I just thought wow. Why can't you miss the game? This is the championship! If the baseball team wins the World Series they have a parade in the middle of the day. Forget work, forget school.

When I asked her who made up the WPS fan base, manager Amy concluded, "It's families, families with young girls. That's the obvious answer, the one everyone goes to. But it's hard to build a fan base with a lot of families. It's hard for them to commit all the time with kids. Game time, it's really sensitive. The facility might not be able to have a game at four o'clock on a Saturday. And suddenly you're in a lot of trouble if you have a seven o'clock Sunday game."

At one Momentum preseason game, I sat in the stands several rows behind eight white adolescent girls. Perhaps because of their age or because they were grouped, there was no adult sitting with them. Half of the girls sported side ponytails, and all wore soccer T-shirts or jerseys. The girls paid little attention to the game as it unfolded. Instead, they talked, gossiped, squirmed, and laughed their way through the action, attracting my attention by the loudness of their voices and the silliness of their interactions. They seemed engrossed entirely with one another. The concession stands were a major topic of discussion, their trips for food necessitating substantial planning. The dyads and triads who left together to visit the concession stands clearly reflected the peer group's status hierarchy. At halftime, a Momentum intern on the field came up to the stadium's railing and asked one of the girls if she would like to be a ball girl for the second half. The girl looked around at her friends and shrank down in her seat in embarrassment as she shook her head no. The intern then shouted out the request to the section at large. After long seconds of silence, the intern smiled and pointed to a girl high up in the stands who had jumped out of her seat in excitement and threw her arms into the air furiously. This girl, who had been sitting between two adults, bounded down the stairs with a wide grin and hastily threw on the neon yellow pinny handed to her as she climbed over the railing.

The volunteer ball girl's enthusiasm was an exception to the rule that girls demonstrate disinterest in women's professional soccer. Over the course of the 2011 season, I witnessed kids' preference for socializing with friends over watching soccer again and again. WPS staff members and fans who brought their children to games readily admitted to their apathy. For instance, James admitted that his son would go with him to WPS matches but was rarely interested in the game: "Kids don't want to watch. He'll go, but he'll only go because his friends are going so they can run around and play in the bounce house or play video games. He could care less about the game. The game just isn't exciting enough to kids to make them want to come back." Players, too, had noticed that kids' focus was often in the stands, rather than on the field. As Corrine explained, "Soccer for them is social. And that's what makes it so difficult to sell. Just because you play doesn't mean you want to watch it."

Diane was a retired professional player who was raising two children. Diane acknowledged that while "families" were targeted as fans by the league, many families, including her own, were pressed for time, her kids largely inattentive when they did go to games. When I asked her who WPS fans were, Diane explained,

> People want to say people with little girls who play. But as a parent, I take my kids and they don't watch it. They hang out with buddies, roll down the hill. But really the people who were at our games, they marketed to families but they didn't buy season tickets because that's too many games. They don't watch that, they're not attentive. Even me as a former player, I'd go to one game but my primary focus is my children. You got to find a sitter or we both have to go. There are forty-eight other things I gotta do.

Given the challenges of time and kids' attention spans, some WPS insiders concluded that the league was off base in targeting youth soccer players and their parents above other groups of adults. In November 2012, WPS midfielder Joanna Loman wrote a guest blog post for the news site Soccer Wire titled "How to Market Our New Women's Professional League." Post-WPS shutdown, Loman argued,

> I am convinced, after significant research, investigation and personal experience, that the "soccer mom" is NOT who we should be marketing to. With all due respect to her, she is too busy, too distracted, too overloaded and too disinterested in sports to hear our plea. She just doesn't have the time, energy or desire

to come out EVERY weekend to cheer on the team in a passionate and sophisticated manner. Sure, she could bring her screaming daughter and her friends once or twice a season—but you don't build a team or a league on people who come once or twice a season.

Instead, Loman suggested that the league seek out an "eclectic" group of twenty-one- to forty-year-olds from diverse racial, social class, and sexual orientation backgrounds who appreciated the beauty of soccer rather than the spectacle of a stadium "event." Journalist Derrick agreed: "Well the market has been trying to sell it to young kids, which is not sustainable. And I think there's been people who pointed that out, other people think that it works. It's clear that it doesn't work. I mean you have to have the young kids there, you have to give them something to look up to, but I mean you need to tap into a serious soccer fan, too." Player Helen also argued that the league should market to adults:

> You're talking about little girls who don't even watch when they are there, you know? You go to play with your friends and make noise and yell. But you're not an educated fan. And if you don't get those educated fans you don't create the dialogs and you don't get people who keep coming back because that's what they want to do with their Saturday or Sunday or that's their weekend plan. They actually watch the game and care. If you appeal to those people and you attract adult fans you have a much better chance of getting people to come into the stadium. I just don't think appealing to dads and little girls is the way to go. And if that dad isn't going to come on the weekend that his daughter is away or sick or whatever, then you've failed.

Variations

The Momentum targeted white, heterosexual suburban families whose kids played soccer almost exclusively. With a small and shrinking staff, owner and general manager Steve took on an outsized influence in directing the team's marketing, limited as it was.[22] And, as manager Chris noted of Steve, "He doesn't front that category," referring to gays and lesbians. Steve and his staff defined suburban youth soccer players and their opposite-sex parents as the most desirable fan base. In doing so, the team subtly neglected adult fans without children. In contrast, other WPS teams' fan base cultivation included outreach to multiple possible constituencies. As Muller Myrdahl noted in her analysis of WPS, some teams' advertisements to white middle-class families coexisted with direct appeals to childless and lesbian adult fans.[23] One team owner argued in an August 2011 article in the *New York Times*, "We've got to transition beyond just suburban families. We need more mainstream soccer enthusiasts."

Other teams did engage marketing materials, community events, and game-day activities meant to welcome childless adult fans, including gay and lesbian fans. For instance, several WPS teams participated in pride parades and reported these events in their self-created media. Manager Courtney said of her team, "We went to the pride parade and we publicized our team there which people thought was really cool." Susannah had traveled to several WPS games and said, "I know that there have been some other teams that had events. Was it for lesbian breast cancer or something? They did something that was reaching out to the lesbian community. And I remember thinking when I read about that, 'Wow, they actually get it, you know!'" And staff members with several WPS teams argued that game-day beer gardens and game viewings and meet and greets in bars attracted young adults without children to women's soccer.

Team managers, journalists, and players routinely traveled between WPS team locations and frequently highlighted variation in fan demographics. Manager Davis said, "The demographics were very mixed. I mean, you would come to a [team A] game and it was very family-oriented. There were a lot of families there with their kids. And at [team B] then you had young professionals. You'd go to a [team B] game and there would be beer lines. You come to a [team A] game and beer would never sell. So it was a whole different type of an atmosphere." Journalist Janine commented, "I would say that [team A] had a family feel but also, you know, thirty-five- to forty-five-year-old women. And at [team B], it was a lot more family-oriented where you'd usually see like a Mom and a Dad and the younger type of kid." Journalist Brad compared the Momentum with another team. He said of the other team, "They were way, way out in the suburbs so they appealed, essentially, to maybe a harder core audience, maybe people who didn't want to drive with their kids. Also they had a beer garden, which was lovely. So it seemed a little bit more adult. And certainly you had kids there, I saw kids running around, but it did seem like it had a slightly older audience." As player Robin concluded, "Each club seems to be different. [Team A] can target everyone and anyone, kids and families as well as young adults who would like to have a beer or two. [Team B] focuses more on the youth, especially with the youth academy. I think the audience is different based on location. I don't think there is one target fan base."

Conclusion

WPS hoped to capitalize on the growth of youth soccer participation in the United States in building up a sizeable fan base. Like sports apparel companies and its predecessor league, WPS believed that soccer-playing girls and their parents were an untapped, affluent sports fan market who already loved women's soccer. The commitment to the sport required by expensive, time-consuming club play was assumed to easily translate into attention to a women's league at the highest level of play. That this preexisting interest could be shared by adults already invested in women's soccer, but without involvement in youth soccer, was largely unconsidered as the league formalized partnerships with youth soccer organizations early on.

Soccer girls and parents were not quite as interested as imagined. While they did constitute most fans at WPS games, attendance was not always the same as attention. And attendance itself was inconsistent, as overextended suburban families faced time and energy limitations and often chose to invest both elsewhere. The Momentum recognized some of the drawbacks to targeting families with soccer-playing kids. Nevertheless, in their geographic location, community event schedule, marketing materials, and game-day promotions, they pursued white, suburban, heterosexual families with a single-mindedness out of proportion to the meager reward in these fans' ticket purchases and event attendance records.

What I came to realize was that suburban families were perceived to be the ideal fan demographic not only due to their size, affluence, and supposed passion for soccer. Heterosexual families were also sought to communicate the team's desired image. A stadium full of smiling white girls sitting with their opposite-sex parents was evidence of the safety, friendliness, and community-mindedness of women's professional soccer. The youth, whiteness, femininity, and heterosexuality of this highly cultivated crowd stood in for qualities believed to make an elite women's sporting league unthreatening in the public sphere. These cultural linkages distanced women's soccer from the stigma of homosexuality and from the challenge that strong, muscled women pose to ideologies of women's physical weakness and inferiority to men. The Momentum was playing it safe, both relying on and solidifying associations of women's soccer with white, affluent heterosexual families in their fan outreach efforts.

In doing so, the team's attraction of some came at the expense of others. Families were pitted against lesbian and childless adult fans as if multiple constituencies could not, or perhaps should not, coexist inside the team's stadium. Ultimately, the Momentum acceded to what they perceived to be a homophobic environment. As one consequence, adult fans not accompanying children were made invisible and unwelcome. Childless lesbian and heterosexual men's fandom, which was far more consistent than that of the suburban families I met, unfolded despite the Momentum's fan outreach work, and not because of it. Other teams in the league departed from this model, creating more inclusive marketing campaigns and event schedules.

Esmonde, Cooky, and Andrews's study of American football fandom found that men's heterosexual desire, as for cheerleaders, was widely accepted as a routine part of NFL fandom.[24] In contrast, sexual desire for women's soccer players was defined as outside of authentic WPS fandom. Fandom motivated by the sexual appeal of the players was decried as inappropriate, an imposition of sexuality where it didn't belong. One result of the team's constructions of "pure" fandom was a complicated relationship with media. As noted in chapter 2, WPS wanted media attention and in fact needed it to survive. The bigger the outlet, the better. Yet the platforms with the widest reach were also those most likely to sexualize the players, compromising the family-friendly and community-minded image that the Momentum strove for.

4

Image Politics and
Media (In)visibility

━━━━━━━━━━━━━━━━━━●

As Women's Professional Soccer kicked off its first season in 2009, its apparel sponsor Puma held a public event to reveal the team uniforms designed by *Project Runway* winner Christian Siriano. Photos and video footage from the event documented the show's setup, with a green, fake-grass runway lined on either side with folding chairs. Several players and a fashion model were shown having their hair and makeup professionally done in preparation for the event. Smiling, waving, and dancing, players walked the runway to energetic music, showcasing brightly colored jerseys and matching soccer shorts and socks. Toward the end of the unveiling, several players strode down the runway wearing jerseys and team-logoed skorts. While the skort was little more than a footnote in Puma's video coverage of the day, this new item of soccer apparel quickly generated controversy for the fledgling league.

The unveiling of the WPS-branded dual skirt and shorts created immediate confusion; the function of the skort was unknown. Was it supposed to be worn during play? After games? Only by fans? One blogger who attended the event described even the players as "bewildered" as to the skort's purpose. Bloggers, fans, and WPS staff members decried the skort as sexist for its purported emphasis on femininity above athleticism. As sociologist Tiffany Muller Myrdahl summarized, "According to these fans, the skort and the accompanying fashion show hoopla drew exactly the opposite kind of attention to the one the WPS sought: rather than requiring that their athletes be taken seriously *as athletes*, the league and its key sponsor emphasized the beauty of its players

FIGURE 3 Women's Professional Soccer (WPS) players show off the Puma skort, February 24, 2009. WENN Ltd/Alamy Stock Photo.

and the feminine design of its uniforms; indeed, the unveiling highlighted everything *but* soccer skills."[1] Several commentators likened the skort to the feminized, skirted uniforms of the long-defunct All-American Girls Professional Baseball League. In an interview published online, WPS team general manager Ilissa Kessler said of Puma, "The skort was a personal fight with them. I refused to have my players wear them—here I was trying to legitimize women as strong, athletic, professional athletes, and they wanted them to play in a skort. Not on my watch."

The following year, Puma held a similar event to reveal each team's home and away game uniform. The detested skort was nowhere to be seen. Still, YouTube videos featured players getting their hair and makeup carefully done before again strolling down a green carpet as part of a mock fashion show. With few exceptions, all the players' long hair was down and neatly curled, their faces bright with mascara and lipstick. In one brief camera shot, a wall tagged with the phrase "Recognize Awesome" popped into view, a reference to a Puma ad campaign for the league.

The commercial and print advertisements for "Recognize Awesome," as well as a similar "See Extraordinary" campaign, took on a distinctly different tone compared to the uniform unveilings. Here the styled hair, neatly made-up faces, and fashion tie-ins were gone, replaced by the active performance of soccer skills. One commercial featured slow-motion footage of a uniformed player sprinting past two defenders toward goal in front of a cheering stadium crowd. As the player ripped a hard shot toward goal, a young girl mimicked this motion from her bed, leaping into the air to blast an imaginary shot. The selling point of Puma's video advertisements was the players' "extraordinary" and "awesome" talent and not their physical appearance.

Juxtaposed against one another, Puma's uniform reveals and advertising campaigns conveyed a mixed message, sometimes celebrating the athletic talent of WPS players and in other moments emphasizing their (supposed) heterosexuality and femininity. This sponsor, perhaps uncertain as to which image of women's soccer would be most appealing to prospective consumers, moved between soccer prowess and femininity in its publicly released media. This back-and-forth between athletic talent and (hetero)sexual appeal was not restricted to Puma but took place internally within the professional league as well.

WPS league- and team-produced images, videos, and media texts escaped many of the gendered and sexualized themes scholars of media and sport have documented for decades. Women's professional players were almost always depicted in uniform and in action, leaping up to win a header or celebrating a goal with teammates. Their athleticism was front and center. If you looked only at the public face of the league, then, it seemed that the selling point was clear—the players were strong, hardworking athletes who deserved recognition and reward for their skills on the field.

Infrequently, however, WPS did emphasize an explicitly heterosexual femininity in its media, highlighting players' feminine attractiveness or relationships with men off the field alongside their strength, persistence, and athleticism on it. For instance, the Momentum released one YouTube video showing players having their hair and makeup done at a local salon before a preseason photo shoot. These depictions went largely uncontested. Not only were they a minimal presence in league-produced media compared to illustrations of talent, but they also enhanced the image of WPS as a feminized, heterosexual, and youthful sports league that many desired. And the display of (hetero)femininity aligned with class-specific constructions of "professionalism" for women working in sport and was often taken for granted as normal and expected.

Although WPS did sometimes produce media focused on feminine beauty or heterosexual relationships, what they decidedly did *not* do was create so-called softcore images where "female athletes are sometimes photographed in poses similar to those of women in soft-core pornography, where the camera lingers on the signifiers of sexuality."[2] Not a single team- or league-generated image of its women players placed emphasis on sexual availability by, for instance, featuring a player in skimpy clothing or focusing on sexualized body parts such as the breasts or buttocks. Refusal to go the "heterosexy" route stemmed from its perceived undermining of the players' talent.[3] Sexuality took the focus off soccer and compromised the legitimacy of women's professional soccer. This imagery hurt the league's ability to be taken "seriously" by fostering perceptions of athletic incompetence.[4] If WPS had to sex up the players to gain attention and investment, this must be because the play alone had failed to do so.

There was also tension between overt sexualization and the charitable, "family-friendly" image that the league cultivated. Good role models for young girls engaged in community volunteering simply did not appear in bikinis, gazing suggestively at the camera. Rather, as in Puma's "Recognize Awesome" commercial, the players' value as role models lay squarely in the "awesomeness" of their soccer. Despite recognizing drawbacks to "hypersexualization," however, most WPS employees I spoke to nevertheless believed that emphasizing women's bodies could be an effective advertising tool, particularly if the goal was to gain media, fan, and corporate attention.[5]

The sense of being both pulled toward sexualized imagery and pushed away from it cannot be understood outside of the mainstream mass media invisibility of women's sports and the gender ideologies that support it. WPS, as all profit-seeking professional sports leagues, needed mainstream mass media coverage to reach existing fans and make new ones, especially those whose geographic location made it difficult for them to attend games. Mass media coverage also facilitated new corporate sponsorships. Unlike its men's counterpart leagues in high-profile sports, however, it received little to no exposure in mainstream media, with some exceptions during the 2011 Women's World Cup.

Images that the league produced were consumed primarily by those fans already invested enough to visit websites, subscribe to newsletters, and buy tickets. WPS chose athleticism as the predominant image of their league. Yet they were communicating mainly with their small, existing base of fans, their internal image choices doing nothing to expand recognition. One Momentum manager, Chris, laughed ruefully over this conundrum in our interview, questioning, "If no one knows that you're here, does it matter how good your product is? If a tree falls in the woods and no one sees it and no one hears it, did it really fall?" No matter how women's pro soccer opted to depict its players, did these images matter if few people saw them or knew the league existed?

In contrast, mainstream media outlets with enormous reach did sometimes sexualize women athletes, a willingness to strip down often a seeming prerequisite to attention. It appeared that a sexed-up image could sell, if not to fans, then to the very media whose platforms could generate greater public awareness of and investment in women's soccer. But was trading the league's preferred image of athletic competence for greater visibility worth it? And who got to decide?

Importantly, social media platforms such as Twitter and Facebook were adopted quite early in WPS's existence in response to the league's need for media exposure but absence from most mainstream mass media outlets. Social media proved something of a double-edged sword. These platforms enabled the league to communicate quickly with both existing and prospective fans, at least those who also used social media. At the same time, some players chafed at what they saw as an onerous responsibility, preferring to focus on training over marketing themselves with a Facebook page. Social media also brought the balance of power between players and team owners and staff into question. As players were ultimately responsible for the content of their accounts, they had more control over their image on social media.

Media and Women's Sports

Professional sports could not exist without the mass media outlets that enable fandom for geographically dispersed individuals. At the same time, mass media need sports programming to bring large numbers of consumers to advertisers. Media and sport exist in a reciprocal relationship to one another, this dynamic described by scholars as the "media sport cultural complex."[6] Yet despite the exposure and cultural legitimacy that mainstream mass media provide to professional sports leagues, women's sports lose out to men's in both quantity and quality of mass media attention. Women's sports receive substantially less mainstream media coverage than men's sports.[7] For instance, a recent analysis of ESPN's flagship program *SportsCenter* found that a mere 1.3 percent of airtime and 2.7 percent of ticker time was devoted to women's sports.[8] During the Women's United Soccer Association's (WUSA) 2001 to 2003 existence, coverage of women's sports on *SportsCenter* declined.[9] Sports networks even neglect in-season women's sporting events to include stories on out-of-season men's sports or human-interest stories on male athletes.[10]

Low levels of coverage are often assumed to reflect higher levels of interest in men's sports, and thus audience demand, as media act to "give the people what they want."[11] And, in fact, "the dominant philosophy in journalism remains largely that the media should cover the events and issues that have the widest public interest."[12] Yet this standard for determining what to cover puts women at a disadvantage when the leagues they play for are young, are small, and have few resources. Compared to their larger, longer-standing, and more resource-rich men's counterparts, women's leagues will always come in second in the number of fans based on their comparative newness. Additionally, media organizations often assume that their audiences prefer men's to women's sports without having done the research to know this.[13] Standard work routines in many news groups, including the assigning of regular beats and a heavy reliance on wire organizations, further entrench inequitable amounts of coverage; doing what has "always been done" privileges the (men's) leagues that have been around the longest. And gender bias among sports journalists also contributes to the erasure of women's sports, though it is often obscured by the rhetoric of journalistic "objectivity."[14] As sport studies scholar Toni Bruce concludes, "Sports journalists' decisions appear to be based on historical precedent and tradition (thus privileging established male sports), anecdotal evidence and intuition (based on their own experiences and ideological beliefs rather than critical public feedback or research), and their belief that a predominantly male audience is not interested in women's sport for its own sake."[15]

More than simply reflecting preexisting audience preferences, media coverage also builds audience demand, increasing awareness and interest. Low levels of media coverage not only reveal but also suppress interest in women's sports.[16] In some cases, media entities' neglect of women's sports may harm their own bottom lines. For instance, ESPN televises Women's National Basketball Association (WNBA) games but fails to routinely include the game highlights on *SportsCenter* that would help build an audience for its own broadcasts.

Women's sports have received more attention from sport-specific and online sites such as espnW. Increasing media fragmentation has opened opportunities for media coverage for all women's sports and men's sports outside football, basketball, baseball, and ice hockey. At the same time, many of these outlets are decidedly out of the mainstream and are visited primarily by existing fans. Mainstream outlets remain the gold standard of sports media coverage because they enjoy more public recognition and have a far greater reach. When women's sports are persistently relegated to minor online media sites, espnW and not ESPN, what message does that send about their value? Sociologist Michael Messner has argued that women's sports are made second-class through this media "re-ghettoization," even if committed fans can find more information about them than ever.[17]

Also in quality of coverage, women's sports tend to get the short end of the stick. Production values are often lacking in mainstream media coverage of women's sports, with fewer camera shots, poorer quality video footage, and less of the vocal enthusiasm typical of coverage of men's sports.[18] Even when women do appear in mainstream media, lower production values communicate to viewers that their sports are less exciting and less worthy of attention than men's sports.[19] Sociologists Michela Musto, Cheryl Cooky, and Michael Messner argue that the "lackluster, matter of fact manner" in which women's sports are often covered reflects a "gender-bland sexism" through which the greater worth of men's sports is subtly created and upheld.[20] Media engage in an "aggressive and celebratory audience-building for central men's sports" while positioning women's sports as less interesting and less exciting than men's.[21] While often justified as the result of supposedly lower levels of interest in women's sports than men's, gender-bland sexism in fact denies women's sports the public recognition and audience they deserve.

Women athletes are also often framed quite differently than their male counterparts. Decades of research on gender and media has found that women, more so than men, are presented as though their value lies in the appearance of their bodies and not their bodily capacities. Sports philosopher Paul Davis argues for a distinction between "sexuality" and "sexualization" in sport.[22] Sexuality is inherent to sport, as athletes develop and use their bodies in very public fashion.[23] The sexual meanings and desires we attach to bodies are always and already present in sports contests. Sexualization, in contrast, is the decontextualization of athletes' bodies from their sporting endeavors and the reduction of athletes to sexual objects. Davis argues that sexualization is a troubling trend because it separates women from their autonomy and minimizes the significance of their athletic accomplishments.

What Davis calls sexualization, or what other scholars have referred to as "hypersexualization," has declined in media coverage of women's sports, a response in part to persistent critiques of "overtly sexist media practices."[24] Women athletes are less frequently presented as sexual objects or as sexualized body parts than in the past. Yet at the same time as media coverage has grown more respectful and less graphically sexualized, women athletes' sexuality has been brought into media in more subtle ways. Today, sexuality is often invoked in the form of heterosexual relationships or normatively feminine gender presentation; "professional women's sports are frequently framed by commercial interests and media in ways that highlight women athletes' heterosexual attractiveness and/or roles as mothers."[25] For example, communications scholar Helene Shugart's study of media coverage of the 1999 U.S. Women's National Team identified a trend of "passive objectification," where players were depicted off the field and out of uniform in so-called beauty shots with their hair and makeup done.[26]

In critique of this media trend, scholars argue that heterosexuality and femininity are evidence of enduring homophobia in women's sports. Such images repair lingering associations of women's sports with lesbian sexuality, assuring onlookers that despite their strength and competitiveness on the field, athletes are still "normal" (meaning heterosexual) women off it.[27] And although heterosexual and feminine framings may appear less objectionable than overt sexual objectification, these depictions fail to dislodge the presentation of women through the male gaze equally true of hypersexualized imagery. In emphasizing marriage, motherhood, and physical attractiveness, women athletes are presented for the imagined interests of a male audience, their familial roles suggesting "vulnerability and dependence on men."[28]

Media Matters

Among WPS insiders, mainstream mass media coverage was ubiquitously acknowledged to be vital to the league's health. Reflecting media's audience-building function, mass media coverage was believed to increase public awareness of the league and boost its ticket sales. For instance, in an Awl.com article prior to the 2011 season, one former team general manager said, "I would sell my soul to ESPN to get the coverage that they would provide. If we had the breadth of ESPN, we would instantly have a huge foothold." Journalist Joshua agreed that media coverage would help to establish a "foothold" for WPS: "Give them the same kind of coverage that baseball gets, that football gets. They need to cover football during the off-season? It's like nothing's happening, why are you talking about this? I think what media need to do is take a chance and they just need to invest in women's soccer and they need to grow it because it's not gonna get big if you don't market it and grow it."

Ashley was a thirty-three-year-old midfielder with an East Coast WPS team who used to play on the Women's National Team. She argued that mainstream media coverage would generate greater appreciation of her play by exposing more people to it: "You're not getting on television. Any news at this point is good news for all the league. The more people are going to come to our games and then they'll see me play and they might not have known about me before, but they come to the game, they'll see me play and they'll appreciate me as an athlete." Another player, forward Marcy, concurred: "I really think it's that media coverage. You know, what's on TV is what you're going to watch and know. So I definitely know that not having much TV coverage is something that is hard."

A few players and staff members were familiar with academic research on media coverage of women's sports and used it to support their arguments for the importance of mass media in expanding recognition. As I discovered during our interview, general manager Leslie had read the longitudinal study of *SportsCenter* mentioned earlier in this chapter. She argued, "When people argue, 'Well, women's sports aren't covered because nobody wants to watch it,' I'm sorry, but that's bullshit. When it's talked about, people watch it. If we start dedicating, you know, more than three to four percent of our coverage on ESPN on women's sports, and we start talking about the leagues and the teams, it will have a dramatic impact. So imagine if we could just have five percent. Imagine what a leap that would be, and how dramatic that would impact our ticket sales."

The Momentum's media specialist Grace kept a list of local and regional publications on her desk. Grace sent out weekly rounds of email inquiries to these outlets, asking for coverage of the Momentum. On one afternoon in June, the office room Grace shared with team manager Jordan and a cadre of interns, including myself, was silent except for the clacking of computer keys. Then, Grace broke the silence with a loud "Wohoo!" She announced to the room that a citywide lifestyle magazine had returned her email and was willing to feature the team in their upcoming July issue. We all congratulated Grace on this accomplishment. The magazine feature was heralded by team owner Steve at the beginning of the next staff meeting, the free exposure a coup for the team.

One college student intern at the Momentum was tasked with "archiving," compiling articles on the team in local, regional, and national media into a black three-ring binder. After the season ended in August, Grace went through this binder to calculate what she called the "marketing value" of the team's presence in media, measured as the size of each article and its estimated cost if purchased as advertising. During this process, Grace announced to Jordan and me, "Did you know that the value of our *USA Today* article is fifty thousand? That is amazing!" Jordan replied in a surprised tone that this seemed like a high figure, even though "they have a really high circulation." I joked, "We should be in *USA Today* more often!" In response, Grace exaggerated a sigh and said, "Someday in our perfect world, Rachel."

Several fans made the case that televised women's games were crucial to making fandom possible for those who didn't know that professional women's soccer existed. The evidence was often personal. Anne had worked for the Momentum but admitted that she would not have become a fan without accidentally stumbling onto a broadcast of the 1999 Women's World Cup. Anne said, "I watched it on TV. You didn't get it otherwise, you just didn't hear about it. Women's sports do not get the press that men's sports do." Paul, too, described his fandom as a "happy accident," recalling, "I didn't go looking for it. I mean, I didn't pursue women's soccer. I didn't even know about it. So it was just pushed onto us by the media that I finally heard about it. Oh, the Americans are in the World Cup. Oh, they won a game. Oh, hell, they won their division. So then you start following it because they start writing about it." Nina, a thirty-seven-year-old former Women's National Team member, argued, "I think in the earlier years of women's soccer, they hadn't reached that pinnacle until probably '99, where they're on TV and everyone all of a sudden was like 'Hey, we've got women's soccer in our country!' So you know I think that it definitely put women's soccer on the map, having a little bit more consistent visibility."

Media (In)visibility

Prior to its start in 2009, WPS signed a three-year agreement with Fox Soccer Channel (FSC) to air live games on Sundays and to broadcast the league's all-star game. Fox Sports Network was to air playoff and championship games. Additionally, apparel sponsor Puma produced print and video advertisements, including for a "Make (Football) Anytime" campaign in 2011. These were the known, guaranteed sources of mainstream mass media exposure for WPS as it got under way, but they were not always the boon they appeared to be. The partnership with FSC was not a rights deal; as scholar Timothy Grainey reported, "They signed a three-year agreement with Fox Soccer Channel for a game of the week, but no rights fees were paid. Advertising revenue would be divided between the network and the league."[29] Televised games were accessible only to those with subscription access to FSC and were criticized for their poor production values and uninspiring commentary. Puma campaign images and videos lacked much national circulation. And despite a publicly announced goal of signing five corporate sponsors prior to league kickoff, WPS headed into 2009 with only Puma and one other, smaller scale deal. Reflecting back on the start of the league, team general manager Davis asked, "Were the Coca-Colas of the world throwing large sums of money at it? No. Did we have a TV contract? No." The *New York Times* struck a similarly pessimistic tone several months into the 2009 season, noting, "The seven-team league has no television rights deal, a meager media budget and just a handful of major sponsors."

Despite unanimous agreement that mass media coverage was vital to reaching fans, WPS and its composite teams were infrequently covered by mainstream outlets and struggled mightily to gain their attention. The *USA Today* and lifestyle magazine articles were such highly lauded achievements at the Momentum in part because they were rare. Those I called business and cause adherents in chapter 2 understood the causes of mainstream media invisibility somewhat differently. Dean, reflecting the cause approach, argued, "Well, you know it's basically capitalism at its best, right?" In contrast, others saw this pattern as resulting from gender bias and not market principles. However, everyone I spoke to recognized the league's near total absence from mainstream outlets and the challenge this absence presented for a young women's professional sports league. Looking back at the league in 2012, Equalizer Soccer concluded, "WPS always faced the uphill battle of making a women's sports league succeed, which includes garnering attention from mainstream media mostly interested in debating the attractiveness of players."

Journalist Brad had written for several national newspapers and had covered women's soccer for more than twenty years. He acknowledged that WPS lacked a mainstream media profile: "They really struggled to get any sort of attention behind it. The national media ignored them for the most part. I mean, I wrote about them!" High-ranking managers from multiple WPS teams told stories of being shut out of media coverage, even when their teams were winning or when local men's professional leagues were out of season. Forty-four-year-old manager Courtney told an impassioned story of being refused space in a local newspaper:

> I get a paper on my doorstep every Thursday for free, the local times for my area. They never would run stories on us. Sure, they had a sports section. I called. I had my PR person do it first. No response. Then I did it. "I actually live here, I'm a general manager of a pro sports team, and I expect you to cover us." "Well you're not close enough to our area." "Well, you cover the NFL team and they're not there, either! It would be great if you could cover women's sports. Listen, we'll make it easy for you. We'll write the articles. You don't even need to send out a reporter. We just need you to publish them." It just kills me. The freebie doesn't even think we're worth coverage.

Christine shared a similar story:

> A TV station, when we pitched to them that we were playing a championship at home, they told us we needed to come up with a hook for them to cover us. I was like, "*Okay*. We're a championship team in the area. What kind of hook do you need? You cover all of the other professional sports." Fuck. So you have

that disparity in coverage between men's and women's sport. Not to say that we didn't get some coverage. But we still had those attitudes prevailing. It was still a struggle every day.

Players witnessed a scarce and inconsistent media presence at practices and games. When I asked her how often she spoke with media, former Women's National Team midfielder Cara said, "It's not what you would think of for a professional athlete, that's for sure. It's really spotty in terms of that and sometimes I have no interaction with mainstream media for months and months." Forward Justine agreed: "I think there wasn't a lot of media coverage, or at least access that we had. It would kind of be more of the high-profile players too, would have interviews with bigger media outlets. But yeah, it didn't really seem like there was a ton of people there to really talk to the players, in my opinion." Among the four WPS players interviewed by researchers Elsa Kristianson, Trygve Broch, and Paul Pedersen, "the invisibility of women's sport accomplishments in the media" was a main topic of discussion.[30]

At the Momentum, ticket manager Kendall told me that the biggest challenge the team faced was "staying relevant in people's minds, being out there and keeping visible." During the first week of June 2011, Grace read aloud a fan's Facebook comment decrying the lack of coverage of the league on ESPN. The room's response was immediate. "Amen!" shouted Jordan from her swiveling desk chair. "Oh my God, seriously," seconded intern Samantha. In our lunchtime interview, Grace admitted, "It's a constant struggle to keep our name out there."

This "constant struggle" was apparent to several Momentum fans. Carl noted, "They're getting zero coverage. It doesn't make any sense to me." Liz agreed: "You don't hear anything. I don't hear anything on the radio stations that I listen to. And you don't read anything or see anything really on TV." Several fans and journalists had become so fed up with the lack of media coverage that they had emailed outlets in protest. For example, Paul had written a lengthy email to Fox Sports requesting more broadcasts of WPS games. In the email, Paul described his frustration when the WPS team within driving distance folded: "Before the World Cup my college soccer playing daughter developed a renewed interest in soccer. Her interest and invitation led me to drive over 3 hours to go to a game with her. You know the history of the team; they're history. So how to follow another team? You know the answer: they're not on TV."

Everything changed during the Women's World Cup, held in late June and early July 2011. Inside the Momentum office, media outlets were calling us, instead of us calling them. The week before the Women's National Team departed for Germany, two regional newspapers and three local news stations sent staff to the Momentum's practices to interview the players who

would shortly feature in the tournament. The week after the team's star players returned, they were again interviewed by a major newspaper and traveled
into the city to appear on four television programs. Other teams saw similar
media interest. Vincent, general manager of an East Coast team, said, "After
the World Cup, our media increased like 200 percent, it was crazy." The
league's average attendance doubled after the tournament ended. The *New
York Times* reported, "To be sure, the World Cup bolstered women's soccer.
Since the tournament, average attendance has increased to 5,164 from 2,741 at
W.P.S. matches. Television ratings are up 18.5 percent. Social media traffic has
soared. Inquiries are being fielded about adding teams and corporate sponsorships." But this newfound attention didn't last very long. After a sold-out,
standing-room-only game immediately posttournament, attendance at the
following Momentum home game fell to pre–World Cup levels. The phone
quickly stopped ringing.

The Push and Pull of Sexualization

Given the frustrating invisibility of women's soccer in mainstream media,
hypersexualization was appealing as a strategy to attract notice. Yet women's
professional soccer teams did not produce or circulate hypersexualized images
of their players. As many acknowledged, sex would certainly draw attention,
but it was the wrong kind of attention. Staff member Ronald said of "taking
it off," "Would it help? Yeah. Would it hurt? Yeah. Objectifying women is
always a bad thing. I think if you highlight their sexuality just to get people to
watch, even if the women are okay with that, I think it's still not forward, but
backward stepping." Similarly, Michael argued, "Would it get more exposure?
Yeah. Would it be good exposure and positive? Probably not."

Momentum manager Chris made the case that sexualization would be
particularly effective at attracting adult (and presumably heterosexual) men to
women's soccer. Chris said, "If you want to reach an audience that you're not
reaching, the men, you have to show them what they want to see. I know that
they talked about this years ago as maybe they should dress them differently."
Chris assumed not only that adult men uniformly want to see women as sexual
objects but also that the league wanted men as fans in the first place. As should
be clear from chapter 3, however, the Momentum did not unless these men
were accompanied by children. The role of father desexualized men enough so
that their presence in the stands was uncontroversial, the "family-friendliness"
of women's soccer uncontested. Although a highly sexualized image for the
league would draw more men to women's soccer, it would also turn off
the "family" crowd. Reflecting this perspective, Rochelle said, "I think everybody who thought about bringing their family would just stop. And the eighteen to twenty-five-year-old guys would go one time. But when they saw that

they're playing with their clothes on they won't come back. I think the sexuality is a dead-end street. You go that route you're gonna kill yourself. You're not a sports team anymore. That would not work." And James commented, "I don't think you need to go that route here and it would turn people off. I don't want people's daughters thinking that's the only way that they can get ahead is to somehow sexualize their sports experience."

Overtly sexualized imagery was also deemed problematic because it at best took the focus off athleticism and at worst denied its existence entirely. Rochelle spoke to this idea when she said that sexualization meant "you're not a sports team anymore." Sexiness delegitimized WPS as a "real" and "serious" sports league. As Dean argued, "I don't think that they should go that route because I think it would make it cheap. You know, you're trying to make this a real sport." Journalist Hannah felt that U.S. Women's National Team forward Alex Morgan was often appreciated for her looks and not her skill: "You have people who are out there only because the players are pretty. Alex Morgan gets marriage proposals! It's like are you here because she's pretty or because she's a good player? You do see the comment about women's sports. Not just women's soccer, but women's sports, that they are lesser than the men's sports." Margaret had seen young men with the letters A-L-E-X painted on their chests at a game Alex Morgan played in. Like Hannah, Margaret felt that this attention was motivated by appreciation for Morgan's appearance over her soccer: "I don't know how she feels about it, but I think it's demeaning. It's, you know, it's not appreciating her as a player. They're appreciating her because she's a pretty girl." And twenty-six-year-old forward Elizabeth felt that the design of her team's training shorts was more feminine than functional. Elizabeth critiqued what she saw as an attempt to sexualize women's soccer: "The training shorts had pockets. What is this? This isn't the first time soccer has been played by females. Our value is beyond sexuality. Yes, I am going to be sweaty and not have makeup on and you should still come watch because we are professional athletes."

My interview with Momentum managers Grace and Kendall was instructive on the issue of sexualization. I asked Grace, as the staff person who both dealt with media and selected most of the team's media images, what she made of those who critiqued the way that women athletes were sexualized in media. In response, Grace echoed Paul Davis's distinction between "sexuality" and "sexualization" but made it clear that she rejected sexualization: "I think it's a fine line. It's one thing to say here is a female athlete who is very attractive and we recognize that. These are all pretty women with fit bodies, so it makes sense. But it crosses that line when you're explicitly trying to use sex and sexiness to sell the sport. We need to be taken seriously as athletes. This means emphasizing toughness and athleticism and strength." Kendall then joined in, contrasting the Momentum with the other WPS team she had worked for.

To Grace, Kendall said, "But I think we are different than some of the other teams. I mean at the other team, they tried that. Some of the players did this photo shoot and their outfits, they were dressed skimpy. One of them was in this short black mini dress. And the ownership group squashed it, but it happened. They were always throwing around this idea, the idea of calendars." At this, Grace nodded thoughtfully and added, "It's really about the sport, it's not about sex. We can never lose that message."

Momentum manager Jordan told me that a player had joked to her that if the games were played in sports bras, more fans would show up. Jordan laughed while telling this story and said about the proposition, "No, it will never happen. I mean you can't. You can't! Sex sells, we have sexy players. But we'll never choose to display our players as sexual objects." At this, I asked, "It wouldn't be worth it?" Jordan said in response, "I mean, it would boost attendance. The lingerie football team, they sell out every game! But it's a joke. If you ever put that on your resume, someone will laugh in your face. It's not respectable. It makes you a lot of money, but as a woman you can't actually think that this is okay to do." Like Jordan, many women's soccer players, staff members, and fans recognized what scholarly research on women's sports has concluded: sexualized imagery sells sexual appeal, not women's athletic talents.[31] Images of sporting competence do more than pin-up images to increase interest in women's sports.[32]

Although WPS didn't create explicitly sexualized images, mainstream mass media outlets occasionally did. Only players from the Women's National Team whose normatively gendered self-presentations could be easily translated into "sexy" received this treatment. Despite a generally negative sentiment toward sexed-up images, when these were produced outside of the league, they were considered positive publicity. For instance, although Grace forcefully decried sexualization, she also told me, "One of the first media requests I got last year was for a player for *Stuff Magazine*. They wanted to do a photo shoot with her as one of the sexiest people in the city. Of course that helps. It attracts the nonfans to a game or two." Halfway through the 2011 season, Grace called the team's head coach, Larry. She had heard a Momentum and Women's National Team player mentioned on the radio while driving to work that morning. Grace said excitedly on the phone, "She was voted third sexiest athlete. Were you listening to the radio this morning? I heard that, too! It was just kind of one of those out-of-the-blue things."

In October 2011, espnW published an article titled "Hope Solo, Abby Wambach Take Different Paths." The article discussed differences in the public profiles of two stars of the 2011 Women's World Cup. Since the World Cup, Solo had been more successful in gaining resources and attention, signing with Gatorade, appearing on the television show *Dancing with the Stars*, and posing nude for ESPN's yearly Body Issue. Solo's greater success was attributed to her sex appeal. And Wambach, the article noted, supported using (hetero)sexiness to sell the sport. Wambach was quoted as saying,

> I think they'll be successful in that genre of marketing. I think Hope and Alex [Morgan] both bring that level of sex appeal, if you will, to the sport. I think Mia [Hamm] brought a level of that as well. She'd probably be the first one to say that's not true, but I think you have to take advantage of the things you have. To be part of the "DWTS" cast, I don't understand anybody who thinks that could be wrong because she's doing more for the game than maybe any of the men have even done in terms of popularity and getting the face out there and our team's name out there.

U.S. team forward Alex Morgan appeared in *Sports Illustrated*'s 2012 Swimsuit Issue. In the photos, Morgan is clearly an object of sexual desire, posed suggestively in a painted-on bikini, her long brown hair blowing over her shoulders. Several staff members mentioned these photos in interviews. Amy's response was typical: "We come at it to portray these women as professional athletes. You try to treat them like it's any other professional sport. And if they do things on the side, like the Swimsuit Issue that Alex did or photo shoots or fashion shows, that will bring more people to the game."

While it may seem incongruous to both deride and accept sexualization, the underlying issue was control. Amy's distinction between how "we" (WPS) portrayed the athletes and their depiction in "side" projects is illuminating. In the eyes of Grace, Amy, and others who worked for WPS, the league could and should not undermine itself by sexualizing the players. However, when these images popped up externally, their production was out of WPS's control. And if WPS could do nothing to prevent these images, the league could at least approach them positively. And although sexualization was perceived to harm WPS's status as a "serious" sports league, it was hard to fault individual players whose "decisions to appear nude and/or semi-nude are based on their desire to increase public awareness, boost media coverage and enhance their own and their teams' financial standing."[33] Sometimes, it was okay to acknowledge and even to applaud sexualization's contribution to enhanced visibility.

Glamming It Up

I met David at a coffee shop early in the 2011 season to talk about his experiences as a member of the Momentum staff over the past two years. He brought up sexualization without being asked. Like many others I spoke to, he didn't feel positively about it: "I'm not a fan of sex sells. I think there's other avenues, so I do not like that avenue one bit. Do I think they need to glam it up a bit to bring a little something? Yes. But not that way." To David, selling sex was distinct from selling glamour. And while the former was a bad idea, the latter was needed. Cherish also suggested that the league emphasize "glamour": "Women are about things like beauty and appearance and glitz and glamour. Is there some way to make women's soccer more appealing in that sense? The best thing you could do is get a beautiful woman who women idolize or admire that they just kick ass out there. You need a female David [Beckham]. Somebody that's just amazing and also could be a model. Tough situation, and is it right? Is it fair? Is it correct? I don't know. All I do know is that I think it would work as well as anything."

David and Cherish both distinguished between sex and glamour. To them, obvious sexual objectification of players was inappropriate, but highlighting feminine beauty was an acceptable way to "bring a little something" to the public image of women's soccer. In moments like the Puma uniform unveilings, feminine attractiveness was communicated league-wide. At other times, an emphasis on glamour seemed unevenly distributed across the league, with the Momentum peddling physical attractiveness more than its sister teams. However, my position as an insider to the Momentum made me more familiar with image dynamics at this team than at others.

The overwhelming majority of the Momentum's publicly released images and videos featured players in uniform, on the playing field, and in action. Yet when players were depicted off the field, they were often presented in traditionally feminine ways. Grace openly admitted as much, acknowledging, "I mean, we do want the players to present themselves in a certain way. With headshots and team photos, we mandated that they go to a sponsor and have their hair and makeup done so that they all looked feminine and attractive. But it has to be classy." The YouTube video of the pre–photo shoot salon visit released by the team, mentioned earlier in this chapter, was titled "Primping with the Ladies." To the sound of upbeat pop music, players were filmed having their hair and makeup done, and, as a superimposed title declared, being "just like the rest of us." Two players joined the Momentum after the season had begun and had to have headshots taken. Grace reminded the first player to "make sure your hair looks nice." For the second, Grace asked Coach Larry to have the player "wear her hair down and a splash of makeup, but nothing too major."

Momentum employees Grace and Kendall were skeptical of another team's effort to produce a player calendar, perceiving this as an attempt to present explicitly sexualized images of women in soccer. Yet this very idea was discussed inside the Momentum's office several weeks before the season's end in August 2011. In this moment, a calendar became acceptable if the pictures emphasized beauty but not sexual availability. As Kendall argued during the discussion, if the team wanted a player calendar to circulate in the off-season they would need to hold a photo shoot for it before the players left town.

FIGURE 4 U.S. Women's National Team forward Alex Morgan "glams it up" while unveiling her spread in *Sports Illustrated*'s Swimsuit Issue, February 15, 2012. WENN Ltd/Alamy Stock Photo.

Brainstorming out loud, Grace said that the players should pose in "pretty, nonrevealing clothes." Jordan offered that she already had a stylist and makeup artist lined up for the shoot. Grace then asked to see examples of this person's work. "I trust you," she said to Jordan, "but it's always better to see." And "if any of the players try to dress themselves, I will scream." Jordan seconded, "They can be pretty *and* covered!"

Scholars have argued that emphasizing femininity in off-field representations of women athletes is a response to the discomfort many continue to feel with the public presence of women whose bodies and actions seem to escape the norms of womanhood.[34] Importantly, though, only explicitly heterosexual forms of femininity can serve this purpose. That is because the anxiety over women's challenge to normative gender is rooted in homophobia.[35] The role of homophobia in driving constructions of femininity was evident in the importance placed on hair. Hair lengths and styles communicate cultural messages about gender, sexuality, and race.[36] For instance, while the ponytail is a functional style for holding back longer hair in sports competitions, it is simultaneously a potent symbol of white, heterosexual femininity. That a ponytail has featured in the logos of all U.S. women's professional soccer leagues to date constructs symbolic boundaries of belonging in the sport, with whiteness, femininity, and heterosexuality at the center.[37] Similarly, Grace's insistence that players have their hair "down" for photos both referred to and reasserted the whiteness, femininity, and heterosexuality of women's soccer. Following this instruction was possible only for players who had hair the right length and texture to be "down" at all.

On June 28, 2011, Momentum owner Steve ordered pizza and invited his staff to watch the United States' opening game of the Women's World Cup on the flat-screen TV in his spacious office. An hour before the match began, I filled a paper plate with slices of pepperoni and took a seat in the crowded room. Some staff members sat in folding chairs arranged in a semicircle around the television, while others sat on the carpet in front. Everyone was excited for the tournament, the break in routine, and the free lunch, and the room buzzed with conversation. The chatter slowly died down as the American and North Korean teams emerged from underneath the stadium. At a close-up shot of U.S. forward Abby Wambach, several staff members in the room gasped. "Her hair!" one whispered loudly. At the start of March's WPS preseason, Wambach's brown hair had been long enough to pull back into a small ponytail. Since then, however, it had been cut above the ears, a ponytail no longer possible. For the tournament's opening, Wambach's cropped hair was slicked tightly against her head, a thin black headband holding it off her forehead. This distinctly masculine style elicited substantial conversation in the room. Questions about "why" Wambach would have cut her hair before the global gaze of the Women's World Cup revealed an assumption that players should want to be read by the public as both feminine and heterosexual. In removing the longer hair that "deflects lesbian suspicion by signaling hetero-sexuality," Wambach had opened herself to public interpretation as lesbian.[38] The potential for this interpretation was met with surprise and more than a little anxiety.

The expectation that players be good role models for girls extended beyond their skilled play, unlimited availability, and inspirational outlook to their own presentation of self. In some contexts, players were also expected to be tradi-tionally feminine, a look that for some players, regardless of sexual orienta-tion, clashed with their preferred self-presentation. While players could and did defy gender expectations, their resistance was met with concern among the very group of people who held their public image, and oftentimes their careers, in their hands.

Professionalism

In contrast to hypersexualized depictions, off-field images of feminine beauty were perceived not to hurt but to enhance the "family-friendliness" of women's soccer. "Glamour" distanced the league from lesbian sexuality while simulta-neously reinforcing its youthfulness, whiteness, and heterosexuality, and in ways understood to be compatible with (and not opposed to) appreciation for players' on-field talents. Additionally, heterosexual femininity presented a "professional" public image of WPS. As in sociologist Nancy Theberge's study of an elite women's ice hockey team, the Momentum sought "professionalism" in their quest to be taken "seriously" as a sports team.[39] Professionalism meant not just paying the players, winning games, and releasing a regular e-newsletter but also communicating a unified, highly gender-normative image through the visual presentation of players and staff. Joseph argued, "There needs to be a professional approach to women's professional soccer. They're not in sweat-pants and cleats. They're not in shorts or jeans. At the end of the day, we want to sell this to someone else. Someone else has to buy into it as a product."

For men, like owner Steve and head coach Larry, a "professional" image required a suit or dress clothes such as slacks, a collared shirt, and a tie. For women, expectations for "professional" self-presentation overlapped with an exaggerated form of (hetero)femininity, with high heels, skirts or dresses, styled (long) hair, and makeup the norm. To successfully pull off this version of femininity required the hair type and texture, body shape, and financial resources most available to white, heterosexual, and class-privileged women.

Consider the example of women sportscasters. Women who have broken in to the masculine, male-dominated world of sports media are more often than not white, thin, and conventionally (and heterosexually) attractive. Their function is sex appeal as much as sports commentary. In fact, rather than primary analysts, women disproportionately occupy sideline and supporting roles, leading communications scholar Jamie Skerski to label them "sexy sideliners."[40] To make it into these ranks, women must perform not just in sports knowledge but also in fashion and beauty. Similarly, if women in pro soccer became the public spokespeople representing their team, they needed to look the part.

Women at the Momentum typically wore casual clothing such as jeans, sweatpants, and T-shirts to help set up for each home game and then changed into dressier apparel before the stadium gates opened. Momentum fan Erin remarked that she had never seen any "Marla characters" at Momentum games, referring to a decidedly unfeminine female baseball player from the movie *A League of Their Own*. For one April home game, I joined Chris, Grace, Jordan, and a number of team interns and volunteers to haul boxes onto the main concourse. For this task, we all wore T-shirts, shorts or jeans, and tennis shoes. Later, at halftime, I saw Grace on the field, microphone for the upcoming entertainers in her hand. She had changed into a bright purple-pink, form-fitting dress and high heels and had taken her hair out of its ponytail. In the Momentum office the day before one home game, two newly arrived women student interns asked Jordan what they should wear. Jordan told them that they would be given a team staff shirt but should wear something "nice" on the bottom in order to look "professional." "I usually wear a skirt," she told the students, "and Grace always wears a dress."

As sociologists who study gender have argued, women can, of course, break with gender expectations, but they are still subject to evaluation according these norms.[41] Women who worked for the Momentum did sometimes deviate from "professional" attire, but they knew that doing so risked others' disapproval. For instance, I witnessed one male manager tell Grace that she looked terrible and needed to dress up more when she wore jeans and no makeup to the office. Raymond criticized the appearance of the Momentum staff who wore casual clothing to a league event that was streamed online: "You look at them and they're slobs! And they're representing your club? Oh Lord. And I'm thinking of the draft. And the people sitting at the Momentum table looked like slobs. It was commented on Big Soccer, how unprofessional they looked." For women whose very jobs seemed unstable, the risks associated with breaking appearance expectations were sizable.[42]

At the same time, meeting expectations for "professional" feminine self-presentation was not always easy. "Glamour" and "sexy" could bleed into one another quite easily, the distinction between the two less one of presence or absence than a matter of degree. What skirt hemline was adequately feminine without being slutty? What made player headshots "classy," as Grace desired, but not classless? Women players and staff members were forced to navigate between these two poles, both establishing and policing the boundaries between acceptable and unacceptable invocations of women's sexuality. In doing so, women defined culturally white and class-privileged styles of femininity as "classy" and "professional" in contrast to "trashy," hypersexualized, and lower status femininities.[43]

Social Media

WPS was an early adopter of social media, particularly the microblogging site Twitter.[44] I discovered quite early in my own women's soccer fandom that Twitter was a key communication medium and created a personal account in 2009 as a way to follow the league. Social media had been on the table even before WPS's first season; more than one early contributor to the league's development was well versed in social media and saw the potential of Twitter as a marketing tool. Thinking back, general manager Leslie recalled, "So, way back in early '08, we were kind of early on Twitter because we had somebody in the room who was saying, 'This is the next big thing. We need to be having a conversation. This is a way to talk to fans.'" Journalist Brad agreed: "That's one thing WPS did very well, was they adapted to the new media landscape well."

Brittany was a thirty-five-year-old goalkeeper who had played for both the WUSA and WPS. Like Leslie, Brittany remembered conversations about social media that predated 2009. While she was skeptical of social media at the time, she was happy to be proven wrong:

> I remember the first time I heard of Twitter I was at a meeting with basically the strategic marketing partner of WPS when they were in the ramped-up period of 2006–2007. And I was sitting in this room and this guy started talking about this new thing called Twitter and how you can say something in 140 characters and people follow you. And I remember looking at the person next to me, my business associate for these trips, and I was like, "Who the hell would want to say anything in 140, like who cares?" Like this is gonna be a total fail. And boy was I wrong about that!

WPS was remarkably successful in gaining followers on social media. In November 2009, Equalizer Soccer wrote,

> The ever-growing power of social media is undeniable, and its enormous value to developing grassroots brands such as Women's Professional Soccer cannot be understated. As of 12 a.m. on Nov. 20, WPS has 93,513 followers. That has certainly created some buzz, as WPS has shot up the charts in comparison to other sports leagues. Currently, the league sits in fifth place among major American sports leagues in number of followers, behind the big four of the NFL, NBA, MLB and NHL.

Goal.com interviewed Tonya Antonucci in 2010 as she stepped down from her executive position with the league. After describing the "effort and creativity" needed to bring women's soccer to the fans, Antonucci concluded, "But we've also made strides in our coverage, particularly in new media, and with our 250,000 fans following WPS on Twitter. You have to start from the ground up."

Social media use was a way of circumventing mainstream media outlets to communicate with and expand the fan base. It was a way of combatting women's sports' invisibility in mainstream media.[45] In *Beyond* Bend It like Beckham, Timothy Grainey quoted league operations head Mary Harvey as saying, "We're not at the mercy of mainstream media anymore because we're the wrong sport or women or whatever."[46] And social media were free to use, an important consideration given small, even nonexistent team marketing budgets. As Leslie acknowledged, "At that time, you know, we weren't working with a large marketing budget, but hey, this is free. We can go on social media and have a pretty dramatic impact with very little money. Now the game on social media is changing a little bit with all the paid advertisements. But you know, even at the end of the day, that's still so dramatically cheaper."

Among the twenty-one women's professional players I spoke to, social media were perceived to be valuable in expanding awareness of WPS and enabling quick, often intimate communication between athletes and fans. At the same time, not all players were equally comfortable with the time and effort required to maintain an active social media presence. Players often expressed both appreciation for and frustration with Twitter. For instance, midfielder Sarah lauded Twitter: "I think it's fabulous how many people you connect and get the word out, and I think that's one way it's been helpful to build the game. It allows young players to feel like they're connected, see inside what it takes to get to the highest level." But Sarah also described a "love-hate relationship" with Twitter. For Sarah, responding to all of the tweets and direct messages she received was a time-consuming, often overwhelming task: "I think it also sucks the life out of us now. I'm like thinking about all our time connecting. With a lot of the young athletes I coach, they're so shy and, for lack of a better word, a little awkward when it comes to face-to-face connection. And you're like, 'Okay, did they take anything any from this session?' Then you get home and you have a thousand tweets from them!"

Like Sarah, other players described how the expectation of their availability to young fans extended into the social media realm; "two-way" interactions between players and social media users was the norm for professional women athletes.[47] Thirty-three-year-old midfielder Ashley argued that social media were an "asset" because they enabled WPS players to be "accessible" to fans:

> The more they know about an athlete, the more they want to watch them. I
> think social media is a huge asset to that, so the more that each player can get

involved, to their own comfort level, to be accessible. I think that's why some people really love women's sports, because the athletes are so accessible. We all play a game, you can meet me after the game, I'll talk to you, we'll have a conversation and you can't really do that in a lot of men's sports because they're just so popular. So that accessibility is an essential part of who we are, so I don't want to lose that.

Yet Ashley also described some of the drawbacks to accessibility on the internet. Fans could be demanding of her time, their requests blurring the boundaries between fandom and friendship. As Ashley explained,

> People think they know who you are. You really don't know someone through social media, so that can be frustrating at times. One of the drawbacks of being accessible is that people really come at you a lot and they can expect a lot of your time. You know, they think that they're your best friend. With all due respect, you're not my best friend. I value the part you play in my life, I value the support you give to our league, but you're not my best friend. It's really hard sometimes to draw those lines between a fan, a friend, and a stranger.

Twenty-six-year-old midfielder Keegan said that she "didn't mind" social media and understood interaction was a "number one priority" for the league, but felt she had to censor herself for her young fan base. Keegan did not feel she was able to be herself through social media: "I think it's fun for girls to see what a professional athlete is doing. But I'm obviously only putting things that are appropriate. Because there's probably more young kids, like young girls, following me so you have to watch what you're putting up." And midfielder Robin said she could "see the value" of Twitter, but felt stressed out by its demands. Like Keegan, Robin did not feel authentically herself on Twitter: "I see the value in it but it's not something that I like doing. I find it really annoying. I think just how you're supposed to be witty and original and that I find rather stressful. I feel like I'm forcing it a lot."

Each WPS team had Twitter and Facebook accounts. At the Momentum, Grace tweeted at least once per day, often consulting with other staff members to determine what to post. Players were encouraged to have their own accounts but were not required to do so. Players from several WPS teams told me about social media trainings with staff members. These trainings were about more than teaching players to use social media. In fact, most of the players already knew how to use social media and had existing accounts. Instead, these trainings were designed to communicate what the team deemed "appropriate" use of social media. Cara argued, "I feel that WPS brought to our attention kind of the dos and don'ts. Like don't really say negative things, you always say how proud you are of your team. All the go-to media things that we learned, mostly for interviews, I kind of carried over to social media." Teams felt that players represented them to the public on social media and that, therefore, they could exercise some control over the content of their accounts. Some players, like Keegan, did monitor their accounts as the team suggested, but others did not agree to these terms. At the Momentum, players' social media posts became points of contention several times during the 2011 season.

On one occasion, the team's backup goalkeeper Anastasia tweeted her cell phone number to another player. When the Momentum managers discovered this, they quickly asked her to remove the tweet, seeing it as an inappropriate release of personal information. As Grace recalled to me after the fact, "I saw Chris and Kelsey and I was like, 'Anastasia's got her phone number on Twitter!' And they said, 'What?' I pulled it up and was like, 'See!' I've told those girls." As several staff members recounted later, Anastasia had bristled at what she felt was unwarranted intrusion into her life off the soccer field and had refused to take her number down.

Defender Meg also drew the ire of the Momentum by repeatedly posting to Twitter suggestively posed photos of herself in bikinis or underwear. Meg was admonished for these pictures several times throughout the season but continued to post them. On one afternoon in the team's office, six staff members huddled around a computer to check out the latest photo. Kendall commented teasingly that Meg should play for the lingerie football league instead of WPS. "Is this how you want to portray yourself?" she asked rhetorically. "Your owner has access to it. You might want to rethink your privacy settings." A minute later, owner Steve walked down the hallway. Seeing the group congregated around the single computer, he entered the room and asked what was going on. "Oh, man!" he yelled after seeing the photo. Again, Meg was asked to delete material on social media that Momentum staff members found objectionable. In the postseason, Steve admitted, "Do I like Meg? Love Meg. Do I think she plays off her sexuality more than she should? Yes."

During a team appearance at a local food festival in the summer of 2011, midfielder Amber approached manager Jordan. "Can I tweet this?" she asked. She wanted to respond to a friend with an insult about being a "fat loser." "I mean, it's just a joke, but I don't want other people to think I'm serious," she said. Jordan asked her not to tweet the insult and Amber acquiesced.

U.S. Women's National Team and WPS goalkeeper Hope Solo's use of social media brought the balance of power between teams and players into acute focus. Solo was the highest-profile and best-known player to eschew team and league control over her posts to social media. Throughout her professional career, Solo had challenged expectations that women soccer players be "nice," uncritical of the status quo, and uniform in the front they presented to the public.[48] For instance, she generated controversy in 2007 when she publicly criticized National Team coach Greg Ryan for benching her for a World Cup game in favor of Briana Scurry. In this case, the backlash was swift; Solo was banished from the team the remainder of the tournament, including for the plane ride back to the United States. Yet Solo was undeterred from breaking the unspoken norms governing player conduct. During WPS's tenure, Twitter was used as a public forum for Solo to air grievances. In August 2010, she had taken to Twitter to berate an opposing team, accusing their fan club of racist chants. And on June 15, 2011, immediately prior to the Women's World Cup, Solo tweeted her obvious annoyance with the U.S. Soccer Federation's commercial advertisements for the Women's National Team: "We do more than color and look at rainbows. We also prepare for that little thing called the World Cup!"

Solo's Twitter posts were hotly debated among players, staff, and fans. While some acknowledged the legitimacy of Solo's claims, on balance most agreed that it was not appropriate to take these public, rather than adjudicating them internally. The image of the league was perceived to be at stake. As Tyrone argued, "Some of her tweets are so outlandish, it gets her in trouble. And people are like, 'Well, she can say what she wants. It's a free country.' Until it becomes detrimental to the team or the league, she's crossed the line. And an already fragile league, because at no point should any single player, single owner, single executive put themselves bigger than the league." Anne also felt that Solo's "Twitter battles" were inappropriate and brought negative attention to the league. "I'm just like, why even put it out there?" she said.

Thirty-five-year-old Brittany argued that players who had entered professional soccer before social media encountered a culture of silence, but that social media gave players greater opportunities to break this silence. Hope Solo was one example of a player who had done this. To Brittany, this behavior was "irresponsible" and presented a "problem" for the league:

We were sort of old school, you don't say anything, you just keep your mouth shut. And then you fast forward to these Twitter and Facebook and players like Hope are firing off all these tweets. It's just sort of culturally mind-blowing, like, "Why are you even saying anything at all?" You've got your PR person saying, "Yes we want you commenting on social media." Well no wonder you guys are having problems, then, because you're encouraging players to say stuff! You expect a twenty-two-year-old who's fired up after a game and pissed off about a bad call not to say anything about it? So I think the responsibility of social media is a challenge.

While players did have greater control over their image on social media compared to mainstream media, if their preferred image was particularly sexualized, highly opinionated, or even merely silly, they had to assert this control against the WPS players, team owners, and managers who sought a wholesome, "family-friendly," and uncontroversial image for women's soccer.[49]

Conclusion

To be a female athlete is to feel as if she is the sum total of her physical assets—
or invisible.

—Karen Crouse, "Why Female Athletes Remain on Sport's Periphery"

WPS, like all women's sports leagues and some men's sports leagues, faced the challenge of breaking into mass media news cycles already organized around men's football, basketball, baseball, and ice hockey. Mainstream media invisibility made it hard for WPS to engage with existing fans, make news ones, or gain corporate sponsors. The most obvious way in was through sex appeal, the possibility for media coverage seemingly predicated on players' willingness to pose for hypersexualized photos. While some players took these opportunities and were understood to be pragmatic in their decision making, the downside was again a delegitimizing of women's sports. Cultural ideologies of the inferiority of women's sports lurked on both sides of a damning either-or. When women athletes weren't in the media, this was because their sports drew less interest, presumably because they just weren't as exciting as men's sports. And when they were in the media, the nature of their presentation suggested that their sports still must be inferior to men's, requiring a little something extra to draw interest above and beyond athleticism.

Faced with an impossible trade-off between no coverage and perceived harmful coverage, the Momentum found a middle ground. They separated "glamour" from "sexualization" and accepted the first while rejecting the second. Sexualization was how women were presented in men's magazines, their bodies exposed to titillate a male audience. Beauty, in contrast, was something far more "classy," involving signifiers of heterosexual femininity. In contrast to sexualized imagery, "glamming up" players' image would not put off the family audience the Momentum desired. Instead, it would appeal to them. And this invocation of sexuality as gender-normative heterosexuality was not perceived to detract from the players' athleticism. Rather, femininity and soccer talent could coexist, if in distinct on- and off-field places. Separating "sexy" from "beautiful" was a strategy to protect the "family-friendly" heterosexuality of women's soccer without threatening its status as a "real" sports league.

The investment I witnessed in defining "sexy" from "glamorous" and accepting one while denigrating the other was a function of beauty's ability to normalize both women athletes and women working in sports. Simultaneously, however, the promotion of physical attractiveness established the normalcy of white, class-privileged definitions of femininity.

Conclusion

Kicking Forward?

In the first week of June 2015, I packed a small suitcase with soccer-themed apparel and boarded a plane for Winnipeg, the capital city of the Canadian province Manitoba. I was headed to see the United States' opening games of the 2015 Women's World Cup. Winnipeg was warm and buzzed with excitement, the streets filled with fans and all restaurant and bar televisions tuned in to broadcasts of the tournament. I met fans from Minnesota, Vancouver, and Australia and was elated to run into American midfielder Megan Rapinoe at a local diner. Just as in 2011, nearly all mainstream media outlets turned to women's soccer. And once again, the dominant media narrative was the link between past and present. The United States had not won a World Cup since that golden moment in 1999. Would this team at last build on the legacy of the "Girls of Summer"?[1] Nowhere was the expectation of continuity more clear than in Fox Sports' "Score to Settle" advertising campaign, complete with Twitter hashtag. In the ads, team stars Alex Morgan, Sydney Leroux, and Abby Wambach were "getting ready" to defend the team's reputation for excellence first established in 1999.[2]

Winnipeg Stadium thrilled the crowd of more than thirty thousand fans for first-round games against Australia and Sweden. I arrived home after a week but continued to watch the tournament on television. On July 5, with an astounding three goals from midfielder Carli Lloyd, the United States defeated Japan five to two to win the Women's World Cup. Watching the cup raised high amid a shower of brightly colored confetti, I cried from my couch at home, caught up in the emotion of the event. On July 10, just five days after the tournament's finale, New York City held a ticker tape parade

FIGURE 5 Women's National Team members attend a ticker tape parade in honor of their victory in the 2015 Women's World Cup, July 10, 2015. Mayoral Photography Office/Alamy Stock Photo.

to celebrate the team's victory, the first such parade for a women's sports team in history.

In many ways, the 2015 tournament paralleled the 1999 event. The U.S. women were victorious not only on the field but also off the field in attendance figures, television viewership statistics, and social media attention. More people watched this tournament than had in 2011. In fact, the Women's World Cup garnered more views on TV than many men's professional events. American studies scholar Cheryl Cooky summarized this media success: "The 2015 Women's World Cup final was the most watched soccer game—men's or women's—in the U.S., with almost 25 million viewers at home and 750 million internationally. Indeed, the 2015 World Cup garnered higher ratings in the U.S. than the NBA finals, the Stanley Cup finals, and baseball's World Series."[3]

Like 1999, the 2015 Women's World Cup was a marquee sporting event widely believed to represent improvement in the status of women's sports and to catalyze continued change. The players were heralded for their inspiration of the next generation of youth. The team's victory was again incorporated into a narrative of progressive gender transformation in sport, presented as the next step in the march toward equality. Mainstream media focused on the historic nature of the New York City parade, calling it a breakthrough for women athletes that signaled widespread cultural acceptance and recognition. As scholars of gender and sport have argued, however, such stories of progress tend to obscure many of the systematic, structural inequalities that women in sport continue to face.[4] Yet at the same time as the U.S. women's soccer team was celebrated within liberal feminist framings of incremental and continued positive change, team members themselves fractured these narratives.

The 2015 event departed from its 1999 counterpart in several important ways. For one, celebration coexisted with an unprecedented attention to inequality.[5] Several U.S. players, in addition to others from around the world, sued Fédération Internationale de Football Association (FIFA) and the Canadian Soccer Association over the so-called grass ceiling, noting that the women's tournament was scheduled on turf fields and not the safer, more preferred grass fields that all men's World Cup games were held on. Although the lawsuit was dropped before the Women's World Cup, well-known players like Hope Solo and Abby Wambach publicly lambasted field conditions over social media during the World Cup and the immediate post-tournament victory tour. The day after midfielder Megan Rapinoe suffered a knee injury training on a field of suspect quality, a game in Hawaii was cancelled at the last minute due to poor field conditions. In an article on Fox Sports, forward Alex Morgan argued, "The training grounds that we were given and the playing surface of the stadium were horrible. I think it's hard because no one's really going to protect us but ourselves. So we're put in a very hard position because obviously we want to play in front of these fans and we want to train before the game but injuries happen when you don't protect yourself and when you're not protected from those higher up from you."[6]

During and after the tournament, players also pushed against gender disparities in pay and prize money. For instance, the U.S. team was awarded a two-million-dollar total bonus for winning the Women's World Cup, compared to the thirty-five million allotted the men's World Cup victor. Five women's players appeared on NBC's *Today* in early 2016 to argue forcefully against pay inequality. Their campaign, "Equal Play, Equal Pay," accompanied a claim of wage discrimination filed with the Equal Employment Opportunity Commission. A year later, the U.S. Women's National Team signed a five-year collective bargaining agreement with the U.S. Soccer Federation that gained them higher pay, greater per diems on par with those their male counterparts received, improved travel and playing conditions, and a portion of licensing rights. Importantly, the deal also ensured U.S. Soccer's continued financial investment in the national women's professional league.

Women's soccer players leveraged the attention of their 2015 win to build support for their cause, rejecting not only resource inequalities but also the ideological justifications that had made these seem natural and acceptable. In a 2016 op-ed in the *New York Times*, goal-scoring phenomenon Carli Lloyd argued against an essentialist reading of the issue, holding that men's and women's National Team members did the same job and thus should be compensated equally. Lloyd wrote of the wage discrimination complaint, "It had everything to do with what's right and what's fair, and with upholding a fundamental American concept: equal pay for equal play. Even if you are female. Simply put, we're sick of being treated like second-class citizens. It wears on you after a while. And we are done with it."[7]

The 2015 Women's World Cup was also different for its open embrace of lesbian sexuality. When marriage equality became federal law following the U.S. Supreme Court's late June 2015 decision in *Obergefell v. Hodges*, the U.S. Soccer Federation joined many U.S. players in celebrating this as a positive change toward greater inclusivity and fairness via social media.[8] And Abby Wambach, who had publicly "come out" as lesbian since the Women's Professional Soccer (WPS) years, was captured kissing her wife immediately after the final game against Japan ended. Video and photos of the two women were circulated widely in mainstream and social media to welcome reaction. A CNN article posttournament pointed to the novelty of this public embrace, concluding, "If the lasting image of the 1999 World Cup win is that of Brandi Chastain taking off her shirt and lifting her arms in triumph, the iconic moment of the 2015 may be this: forward Abby Wambach rushing to the stands after the game and kissing her wife, Sarah Huffman, as the crowd of 53,341 awwed. This is soccer for the new century."[9]

Comparing the 1999 and 2015 Women's World Cups highlights both continuity and change in the ever-shifting landscape of professional women's sports. The trajectory of professional women's soccer also evidences these dynamics. The league that I studied, Women's Professional Soccer, folded in 2012, a seeming replication of the failure of the Women's United Soccer Association (WUSA) nearly a decade earlier. Yet the project of professional women's soccer continued, driven by a core of dedicated investors and managers. A new league formed almost immediately and launched in 2013 as the National Women's Soccer League (NWSL). As of this writing, the NWSL is well into its fifth season, the first women's soccer league to last beyond three seasons. But this longevity has been accompanied by intermittent struggles to garner mainstream media coverage, sponsorship deals, and, in many cases, fans. So what, if anything, has changed about women's professional soccer since 2012? And what can the case of women's soccer reveal about the contemporary environment for elite women's sports?

Women's Soccer and Dilemmas of Difference

U.S. women's professional soccer was founded to capitalize on two related trends: the increased popularity of soccer in the United States and the feminization of sports participation. And by capitalize, I mean to make money. Early organizers and investors believed that women's professional soccer could generate financial gains within the commercialized, corporatized world of U.S. professional sport. It would do this by appealing to an emergent and untapped market of sports playing girls and women. Like its male counterpart leagues, women's professional soccer sought television deals, corporate partners, and sellout crowds. In the eyes of league creators, being a *women's* sports league was not a barrier but an advantage to gaining this capital considering the opportunities created by the changing demographics of sports participation in the United States.

From its inception, then, women's professional soccer was seeking the same resources as men's professional sports, but emphasized a unique source of value that lay firmly within the gender of the players. Women's sports, simply put, were different than men's sports and women soccer players could appeal to girls and women in a way that men could not. This was not only because the quality of the soccer was excellent, which it was, but also because women athletes were assumed to be uniquely inspirational for other women. Women connected to others, were positive role models for youth, and were playing in service of the larger goal of women's advancement in sport.[10] Women's soccer would sell, then, as much for its social appeal as for the excitement of its on-field product. In creating professional women's soccer, the changing status of women in American society was packaged and sold to make money for individual and corporate investors. Unspoken and assumed was the wholesale adoption of the model of success presented by men's professional sports. A new professional league in women's soccer would be just like any big-time men's league—only women!

Academics have vigorously debated the consequences of uncritical adoption of the so-called male model of aggressive, hypercompetitive, and commercialized sport. On the one hand, seeking inclusion without the simultaneous transformation of dominant values in sport has meant that problems endemic to men's sports like cheating, doping, and injury are increasingly true for women's sports as well. High and rising rates of injury in youth soccer, for example, reflect the increased professionalization and competitiveness of the sport among girls.[11] And buying in gives corporations enormous influence over women's sports. One consequence of commercial forces has been the selective promotion of women athletes. Corporate and media power drive a star system whereby a few white and heterosexually attractive women derive rewards from media exposure and corporate sponsorship at the expense of the vast majority of players who struggle with the lack of resources comparative obscurity denies.[12] On the other hand, however, women's inclusion among the ranks of men's professional sports leagues challenges the assumed maleness of professional sports and breaks down stereotypes of women's weakness and inferiority to men.[13] Inclusion is one route toward social change, though a limited and imperfect one.

The questions that inform *Kicking Center* lie somewhat outside of this debate. Rather than investigating the wisdom of seeking entrance to men's sports culture, I ask what it looks like in practice to pursue it. And how successful is it possible to be in doing so? As women's professional soccer emerged after the 1999 Women's World Cup, it stressed the difference of women from men to seek footing among the ranks of existing pro sports leagues. The downside to this approach illustrates what legal scholar Deborah Brake calls the "dilemma of difference," where invoking gender difference reinforces ideologies of women's inferiority to men.[14] That is because difference is always and inevitably a basis for hierarchy. Selling women's sports as a different product than men's sports makes it seem as if women just aren't as physically capable as men. If they were, they wouldn't be different! Perhaps women's sports have to be sold as different, then, because similarity (as physical ability) is impossible. This dilemma was clearly articulated by opponents of what I have called the "cause" approach to selling women's professional soccer, who feared that appeals to gender and social change would undermine the players' athletic talents in public perception, making the league appear undeserving of investment.

Selling women's soccer as different from men's sports also sets up a challenging tangle of expectations for professional players. Women in soccer needed to excel on the field and connect with their young fans off it. These connections were clearly rooted in gender stereotypes, with women assumed to "naturally" inspire others. And these expectations extended beyond behavior to the very presentation of self, with players expected to present a welcoming and "professional" (meaning white, class-privileged, and [hetero]feminine) face to the public. While players were happy to role model their soccer skills, not all wanted or were able to meet expectations of availability, nurturance, and femininity. These expectations were particularly difficult to meet for rank-and-file professional players who needed to hold second jobs. And certainly gendered expectations for "professionalism" were more difficult, if not impossible, to meet for women of color and for players whose own self-presentations were more masculine than feminine. Thus the marketing value of women's supposedly natural "difference" from men relied on and reasserted the whiteness and heterosexuality of women's soccer. It also hid the time and financial resources required to meet gendered expectations, presenting what was demanding work as somehow the "natural" result of women's inner values and personalities. Presumably, a passion for seeing the sport grow and the league thrive overrode more superficial concerns about time and money. But is this the future that we want for girls, the dream that we sell them on when we say that professional players are role models—jobs as professional athletes that don't pay enough to live?

The 2016 Olympic Games were disappointing for the U.S. Women's National Team, who lost to Sweden in the quarterfinals. Following the loss, goalkeeper Hope Solo publicly insulted her Swedish opponents, calling them "cowards" for their defensive tactics. Similar to Solo's strongly worded public remarks in 2007, this comment generated swift and harsh blowback. She was suspended from the National Team for six months and her contract was terminated. Solo had broken the unspoken but powerful norms that dictated secrecy and conformity. Of course, her comments in Rio were just the latest in a series of incidents that many believed brought negative attention to women's soccer. It was the cumulative weight of her words and actions that drew such a harsh sentence. Fundamentally, though, she was punished for failing to meet gender expectations. A role model she was not.

The Women's National Team's fight for equal pay could also be viewed as a departure from long-standing expectations that conflict be kept internal for the sake of presenting a unified public image. However, players' arguments for greater pay equality tied the fight to the same media-friendly, forward-looking narrative of progress that accompanied the 2015 Women's World Cup win. According to this framing, the battle was not just for equality now but also for future generations of women players to come. And as in the "Equal Play, Equal Pay" slogan, women's soccer players were argued to be similar to men and not different from them, performing the exact same work and expecting the same reward. The presence of both future orientation and meritocratic rhetoric in this dispute points to an important counterpoint to constructions of gender difference in the selling of women's soccer.

The paradigm of difference evident at the founding of women's professional soccer has always competed with an alternative, liberal feminist conception of equality as women's sameness to men. This "gender-blind" approach is purportedly meritocratic in assessing value without direct reference to gender.[15] Yet it ends up punishing women for failing to meet what appear to be gender-neutral but are really male norms. Men's leagues like the National Football League (NFL) and Major League Baseball (MLB) form the undisputed cultural and economic epicenter of sport, the model against which new leagues inevitably define themselves. The existing model of professional sport is explicitly masculine and male dominated. Its core values, like aggression and winning at all costs, reflect culturally dominant definitions of masculinity. The practices of sport that reflect these values are most possible for highly gifted, trained male bodies. Women will always be at a disadvantage in meeting these standards. And their inability to do so equally to men is easily interpreted as evidence of their physical inferiority when the standards themselves are understood to be genderless.

Consider those "business" adherents in women's soccer who felt that return on investment, or ROI, was a gender-neutral measuring stick. When women's soccer failed to provide the same ROI as men's sports, and thus garnered less investment, this was believed to be a fair result. By promoting a level playing field without recognizing how the field was tilted by history and ideology, differential investment was understood to stem from lower levels of interest in what must be an inferior product. It was a slippery slope from sameness to essentialism, from gender neutrality to gender hierarchy.

Both similarity and difference provide avenues toward value and subsequent material reward for women's soccer, but both contain unavoidable trade-offs. The sex segregation of sports foregrounds difference, preventing women's sports from being perceived as fully equal to men's sports. But to claim and assert this difference, even as a unique, marketable source of value for women's sports, also reinforces perceptions of inferiority. Men's sports are the automatic point of reference for women's sports, and there is no getting around it. It is a frustrating and unforgiving paradox, with advocates for gender equality in sport "damned if they ignore gender and damned if they don't."[16]

More than mistaken business models or misplaced feminist ideals, persistent essentialist ideology is at the heart of the challenges that women's professional soccer has faced since 2001. The mass entrance of girls and women into sport since the 1970s has only slightly eroded hard essentialist beliefs in women's categorical physical inferiority to men. Men, in particular, maintain investment in sport as an institutional site where their privilege and power remain intact, especially given more successful challenges to essentialist beliefs and practices in other arenas.[17] Essentialism in sport has not disappeared, but has taken on newer, more publicly acceptable forms. Overtly sexist assertions that women uniformly lack athletic talent or that women's sports are boring and unexciting are far less acceptable than they were in the past. When these messages do crop up, they are roundly refuted. For instance, when *Sports Illustrated*'s Andy Benoit tweeted "Women's sports in general not worth watching" in 2015, the pushback was widespread and immediate. Former *Saturday Night Live* comedians Amy Poehler and Seth Meyers produced a comedy segment for *Late Night with Seth Meyers* that poked holes in this argument. In the video, Poehler argued sarcastically, "Really?! Really, Andy Benoit? There's *nothing* in women's sports worth watching? I think a lot of people would love to watch you say that to Serena Williams. Really." To date, the video has garnered more than two million views on YouTube.

Faced with declining legitimacy, essentialism has gone underground, persisting largely in the guise of market ideology.[18] Gender-neutral market principles, and not cultural beliefs and organizational practices, are now argued to account for gender disparities in investment and resources between elite men and women's sports. In professional sports today, essentialism operates as an "ideology of interest" that moves responsibility for inequality from sports, media, and corporate organizations and their constituent decision makers onto sports fans. Fan interests are the demand, and investment is merely the supply that responds to this demand. Interest drives investment. Of course, what this "interest ideology" fails to consider is the two-way street that is opportunity and interest. Interest itself is a function of existing cultural and social ideas and material opportunity structures. But by couching essentialism in economic terms, low levels of investment in women's sports are justified as a matter of universal principle and not gender; rejections of women's sports on the part of corporations and media entities reflect merely "business decisions" and not sexist attitudes.

Lingering essentialism also helps explain why the promise of women's professional team sports has not materialized in the ways expected by sports apparel companies in the 1990s. Corporations eagerly anticipated that the swelling number of girls and women who played sports would also follow and watch women's sports. But this hasn't happened, at least not in great numbers. Instead, women have become fans of men's sports.[19] Relationships with men are central in many women's lives, and fandom of men's sports is one way women can connect to and spend time with sons, brothers, fathers, and husbands. Men's sports are simply more readily available to fans. And women, no less than men, have been sold on the "legitimacy gap," where "we have learned to think that the female-centered variations of organized sports are less valuable than corresponding male-centered variations."[20]

Arguably, women's soccer, of any women's team sport in the United States, has come closest to closing this gap. Yet the reasons for this comparative success invoke a second and perhaps more damning "dilemma of difference." Both sameness and difference as selling strategies presume that all women share a single set of experiences, interests, and desires. Similarly, liberal feminist narratives of continual progress also flatten the diverse experiences of girls and women. As a result, the roles of race, class, and sexuality in the development and marketing of women's professional soccer have been systematically ignored. Differences among women have taken a backseat to presumptions of similarity.

The increased youth sports participation that drove the creation of elite women's leagues did not take place equally across all groups but occurred largely among white, class-privileged, and suburban youth. The ideology of women's physical weakness and inferiority to men that women's professional leagues purportedly challenge has historically applied largely to white, middle- and upper-class women. And the universal female subject within women's soccer has been white, heterosexual, and solidly middle class. The undeniable truth is that professional women's soccer was created for a privileged audience. In many ways, its operations have reflected these social locations.

Women's professional soccer has relied on whiteness, class privilege, and heterosexuality to push for inclusion in male-dominated sport. It has struck something of a devil's bargain, making the inclusion of women more palatable through racial, sexual, and class normativity. It is as if women's soccer has said, "Maybe they will let us in if our image isn't too threatening." This bargain is what underpinned the deep concern for and policing of image within the league I studied. The prospects for success seemed to hinge on the cultivation of an image of good (white) girl players next door who were beautiful and sexually appealing without crossing the line into sexual promiscuity.

Limited inclusion has been bought at the expense of inclusivity and diversity. Women's professional soccer has created and solidified associations of their sport with racial, class, and sexual privilege. The symbolic exclusion of people of color, the poor and working classes, and sexual minorities from women's soccer as players, fans, and employees limits the sport's future growth and potential to meaningfully transform professional sport. It also makes those within excluded categories invisible, their contributions to the league's development a footnote when it often ought to be a chapter. The irony is that as women's soccer itself is fighting for recognition, it has denied recognition to others.

Kicking Forward: The National Women's Soccer League

The National Women's Soccer League (NWSL) has achieved the longevity and stability that previous iterations of women's professional soccer could not. The league is into its fifth season, with little suggestion of impending failure. The number of teams has grown from eight to ten, with future expansion likely. One team, the Portland Thorns, has attracted a massive fan following and has already turned a profit.[21] The Thorns are also notable for the gender and sexual diversity of their fan base. As a whole, the league has shown greater acceptance of lesbian and bisexual players than its predecessors, and the number of publicly "out" players and staff members has increased. There are also hints of growing racial diversity in women's professional soccer. Half of the top ten first-round draft picks for the 2017 season were women of color. The growing representation of racial minority players is a function of the increasing diversity of collegiate women's soccer. For instance, from 1999–2000 to 2016–2017, the percentage of white NCAA Division I women's soccer players dropped from 84 to 71 percent.[22] In early 2017, NWSL announced that A&E Networks had purchased a stake in the league, with the jointly formed NWSL Media taking over broadcasting, streaming, and digital media platforms, with weekly games to be televised on sponsor network Lifetime.

Yet the league faces a bevy of challenges both familiar and new. Increasing racial and sexual orientation diversity has not dislodged the role of class privilege in facilitating players' careers and fans' attachments. While NWSL teams sometimes market to childless adult fans, including LGB fans, they also continue to prioritize partnerships with youth soccer organizations. As in WPS, men disproportionately occupy ownership, management, and coaching positions in this league.[23] And like with the WUSA, the failure of WPS was understood to be the partial result of an errant business model. In comparison, the NWSL has been even more pared down. Although players' pay has increased each season since 2013, it started at a lower point to begin with. Many players are still not paid a livable wage and must take on side jobs to pursue the "dream" of professionalism. Early retirement is not unusual.

The NWSL's stability has been attributed to greater financial investment on the part of the U.S. Soccer Federation and MLS. U.S. Soccer has paid for the salaries of Women's National Team players and contributed funding for the league's main office. MLS franchises own several NWSL teams. While these new partnerships are advantageous in bringing resources and experience, they simultaneously bring women's soccer under the increased control of men and men's sports. It remains to be seen whether affiliation with men's soccer will compromise the NWSL's ability to be taken "seriously" by presenting teams as secondary or "little sister" accompaniments to the "real thing."

Also, the NWSL has been slow to sign many corporate partners or attract large numbers of fans. With the exception of the NWSL partnership with Lifetime, marketing remains minor, with social media a key form of advertising. While game attendance is higher for this league than for WPS, many prospective fans across the country are still in the dark when it comes to women's professional soccer. In an April 2016 article in the *New York Times*, forward Natasha Kai argued that "a lot of people don't even know this league exists. So something's got to change. We just want to play."[24] And essentialism persists in inevitable comparisons with men's sports leagues. In a 2015 interview with soccer journalist Meg Linehan, NWSL midfielder Keelin Winters concluded, "Women's sports in general are different from men's sports. And because they're different, people want to say they're better or worse. And there was this sense that no one wants to go out to women's sports, because men's sports are better."[25]

What is clear is that the NWSL is already the longest-lasting women's professional soccer league in history. It is poised to become a fixture of the U.S. professional sports scene. As this league continues to seek inroads into professional sports culture, the culture itself will adapt and respond. As this book has shown, it has often pushed back, repelling women's soccer through the (re)assertion of ideologies of difference and inferiority. Yet the history of women's professional soccer is nothing if not a story of persistence. The NWSL has and will continue to push (or kick) forward. As it does, it should keep in mind the lessons of the past.

Rather than castigate sameness or difference as strategies for gaining investment, it should call out essentialist ideology in its contemporary manifestations and challenge the ways it complicates equality via either route. Similarly, it should take on one-sided views of the relationship between resource investment and audience interest, emphasizing that interest grows with increased awareness and opportunity. And it should continue to expand and recognize representational diversity and build inclusivity in how women's soccer is marketed and to whom. To do this requires the NWSL to forgo the long-standing politics of image that traded the selective mainstream inclusion of the few for the construction of exclusionary symbolic boundaries around race, class, and sexuality. Although rejecting the construction of a singular image for the NWSL may seem risky in the short term, the long-term benefits are clear. A vibrant, diverse women's soccer community is best positioned to fight the battles to come.

Appendix A

Participant Demographic
Information

Table A.1
Interview Participants

Pseudonym	Gender	Age	Affiliation
Alice	F	35	Player
Alicia	F	18	Media
Amy	F	40	Manager
Anne	F	45	Staff
April	F	42	Fan
Ashley	F	33	Player
Barbara	F	32	Media
Brad	M	36	Media
Brittany	F	35	Player
Brooke	F	37	Player
Cara	F	29	Player
Carl	M	38	Fan
Carol	F	31	Fan
Catherine	F	42	Fan
Cherish	F	54	Fan
Chris	M	36	Manager
Christine	F	50	Manager
Corrine	F	32	Player
Courtney	F	44	Manager
Cristina	F	20	Fan
Crystal	F	24	Player

(continued)

Table A.1
Interview Participant

Pseudonym	Gender	Age	Affiliation
Curtis	M	45	Sponsor
Daniel	M	41	Staff
David	M	35	Staff
Davis	M	55	Manager
Dean	M	37	Fan
Derrick	M	30	Media
Diane	F	29	Player
Dillon	M	20	Staff
Donna	F	38	Fan
Elizabeth	F	26	Player
Erin	F	32	Fan
Grace	F	24	Manager
Hannah	F	25	Media
Helen	F	30	Player
James	M	43	Staff
Janine	F	25	Media
Jared	M	30	Fan
Jason	M	25	Staff
Jeanette	F	22	Player
Jerome	M	52	Sponsor
Jerry	M	49	Staff
Jessie	F	27	Media
Jim	M	44	Fan
Jordan	F	23	Manager
Joseph	M	42	Staff
Joshua	M	26	Media
Joyce	F	29	Player
Justine	F	32	Player
Keegan	F	26	Player
Keith	M	38	Media
Kendall	F	30	Manager
Kristy	F	24	Fan
Kyle	M	24	Media
Leslie	F	31	Manager
Liz	F	35	Fan
Marcus	M	50	Coach
Marcy	F	39	Player
Margaret	F	60	Fan
Marie	F	28	Player
Mary Anne	F	34	Fan
Michael	M	36	Staff
Nathan	M	46	Sponsor
Nina	F	37	Player
Paul	M	53	Fan
Raina	F	29	Player
Raymond	M	30	Media

Pseudonym	Gender	Age	Affiliation
Renee	F	38	Staff
Robin	F	27	Player
Rochelle	F	31	Staff
Ronald	M	56	Staff
Sarah	F	35	Player
Stan	M	62	Sponsor
Stephen	M	41	Staff
Susannah	F	34	Fan
Tanya	F	29	Manager
Thomas	M	28	Staff
Tyrone	M	48	Staff
Vincent	M	36	Manager
Virginia	F	32	Player

N = 80

Table A.2
Survey Participants

	Percent	
Gender		
Women	53.0	
Men	47.0	
Age		
18–19	19.6	
20–29	17.1	
30–39	15.3	
40–49	31.1	
50–59	12.0	
60+	4.9	
Children under 18?		
Yes	48.2	
No	51.8	

N= 450

Appendix B

Methods

When I tell people that I study women's professional soccer, the first question they often ask is, "Have you met [famous Women's National Team member]?" That I get this question so frequently reveals a limited familiarity with women's soccer outside the few celebrity players featured during televised Women's World Cup and Olympic tournaments. This question also contains several assumptions—namely, that I have had easy, perhaps even unlimited access to players and that I find it exciting to meet them. On one count, these assumptions hold. I have found it exciting to meet and talk with professional players.

Like many scholars of sport, I am also a sports fan.[1] In designing, carrying out, and writing up this project, I have thought deeply about how my demographic background and history playing and watching soccer have shaped the expectations I brought to the research and my interactions in the field. Reflexivity, or "recognition of the researcher's particular social positioning and its impact on research," enhances the credibility of qualitative research by enabling readers to assess the data and their interpretation.[2] To maintain reflexivity, I kept a field journal while collecting data that documented not only what I observed but also my own thoughts, feelings, and interpretations.

From the perspective of a former player and fan, I wanted the league I studied to stick around. I wanted WPS to reach its goals for growth, vitality, and longevity. I was acutely aware of persistent gender inequality in sport and felt a commitment to both understanding and alleviating it. From the beginning, then, I conceptualized my study as a feminist ethnography that merged analytic and political aims as "complementary sides of a feminist coin."[3] Yet while feminist ethnography was easy to claim, it was challenging to do.

As a white, middle-class woman in her twenties at the time of this study, I had grown up with liberal feminist and postfeminist understandings of inequality and social change. Messages of "Girl Power" and empowerment through sports were often aimed directly at young women like me, and I was not immune to them. I recognize that my question concerning how inclusion in professional sport is pursued and not whether it should be reflects this orientation. Yet at the same time, my academic training had sensitized me to the downsides of seeking inclusion among the ranks of men's sports leagues as the hallmark of "success." My education had altered my "feminist habitus" to incorporate alternative and critical perspectives.[4] Some scholars have questioned the need for or utility of professional leagues for women at all, pointing to problems with violence, injury, and hypercommercialism endemic to professional sports. And scholars writing from intersectional perspectives have pointed to systematic exclusions based on race, ethnicity, social class, and sexuality that are often created and subsequently made invisible within liberal feminist and postfeminist narratives and projects. So while I understood and shared the desire for a professional women's league that could rival men's leagues in stature and resources, I also wondered, what form of gender equality is truly advanced by such a league, and who stands to benefit from it? From the onset, I struggled to square my hope for the league's success with a critical, feminist orientation to research. I was challenged to balance the voices of my participants with a contextualization of these perspectives within existing cultural and institutional contexts of power.

This balancing act generated frequent tensions as I did the research. As a white, middle-class, and college-educated woman who had played and followed soccer, I was demographically and socially similar to most of my participants. In several ways, my "insider" status was a methodological advantage.[5] It facilitated my access to the Momentum, helped me form positive relationships with others quickly, and built the trust that allowed for disclosure of sensitive information. As I have written about previously, this was truer for women than for men.[6] I shared the "cultural knowledge" typical of my racial and social class locations, and this smoothed my integration into the Momentum.[7] Before my first day of fieldwork at the Momentum's office, for instance, I nervously agonized over my choice of clothing, not sure what the office dress code was. I opted for formality, choosing a tan pencil skirt, purple silk blouse, and heels. I carefully applied makeup and curled my long hair. I was complimented on my appearance by almost everyone in the office that day. As I realized later, I had successfully performed heterofeminine "professionalism" without being told to do so or seeing it done firsthand.

At the same time, others often assumed that I shared their perspectives when I did not. At times, I faced the "feminist ethnographer's dilemma," referring to the "clash" of feminist orientation with empirical evidence.[8] For me, this "clash" emerged in the espousal of hard essentialism and market rhetoric among those otherwise invested in women's professional soccer. I understood belief in women's universal physical inferiority to men, as well as subsequent belief in lower levels of public interest in women's sports on these grounds, to undermine efforts to build and sell women's professional soccer. While I hadn't expected all or even many I met to identify as feminist, I did anticipate widespread condemnation of essentialism. Yet I found a not-so-small group of people who embraced essentialist beliefs and yet were highly committed to, even passionate about this league.

The "clash" also emerged in the adoption of terms like *empowerment*, yet simultaneous repudiation of feminism. I found that feminist goals and language had become separated from their origins and entangled with corporations, these commercial links largely invisible and unquestioned. On one occasion, I was asked to write a letter thanking a family for hosting a dinner for the Momentum and a local girls' club team. When I asked about the letter's tone, I was instructed in writing, "Girls rule, anything-you-can-do-I-can-do-better." This saying referenced the song accompanying a 1990s Gatorade commercial featuring soccer star Mia Hamm facing off in multiple sports against basketball's Michael Jordan. In the ad, Mia bests Michael, the duo spurred to athletic greatness by the power of Gatorade. This commercial had become so familiar a message of commercialized empowerment in sports that it was referenced as shorthand without acknowledgment of its source. I knew exactly the tone I was being asked to convey and I wrote the letter, but was concerned about repeating (and thus solidifying) postfeminist ideas of equality achieved and change through consumption. Was I telling girls they can have and do it all with the right attitudes and consumer purchases?

I struggled to know whether I should express an opinion in the field and, if so, when and how to do so. Speaking up may compromise access to field sites, the honesty of participants, or even the safety of the researcher. Yet remaining silent makes us complicit with the social inequalities that we seek to change as feminist scholars.[9] I confess that I rarely spoke up. I nodded when interview participants argued that women soccer players were less physically capable than men and wrote letters encouraging girls to "reach for the stars." In part, this was a function of my position at the Momentum. I was defined as a student and intern who possessed little expertise and no decision-making authority. I was not often asked for my opinion by those who did. Of course, this is not to say that I had no impact on the social relations I observed. I recognize that I was an active participant in these relations as they unfolded. But by position and by choice, I had a nearly nonexistent influence on the outcomes of these relations for this team and league. Even now, however, I reflect on my "feminist failures" and wonder whether I could or should have made my own perspectives more explicit.[10]

Although emotions are a rarely discussed, "hidden" component of qualitative research, ethnography is emotional labor.[11] Doing this research was an emotional roller-coaster ride, from the tedium of stuffing hundreds of gift bags to the exhilaration of game days to the exhaustion of late nights writing field notes. But strong emotions were not just a by-product of entering this world. I also carefully managed and deployed emotions to build and maintain relationships with others.[12] This emotion management sometimes felt disingenuous but was necessary as I navigated conflicts between participants. Foremost among these was a conflict between Momentum players and team staff. Despite the popular assumption that I regularly socialized with the Women's National Team, I had only partial access to Momentum players due to time and space issues. Players spent much of their time training and only rarely came to the team's office. These groups also had different perspectives on unpaid marketing initiatives and community events. Many players found this work exploitative and unfair and preferred to prioritize other paid work. In contrast, staff members saw these events as obligations that they too participated in, often going above and beyond the bounds of their job descriptions. As I joined the Momentum, I quickly had to choose where to locate myself. That I spent most of my time in the office made players skeptical of me, despite efforts to present myself as friendly and supportive. As a result, I spent less time observing and talking with players than I wanted to.

As the 2011 Women's Professional Soccer season got under way, I compiled names, job titles, and publicly available contact information of the league's owners, managers, and other staff members. This spreadsheet came in handy when the league folded unexpectedly, allowing me to contact those employed by WPS with requests for interviews. I also contacted those who had owned or worked for failed WPS teams. While I was neither seeking nor expecting a generalizable sample of interview participants, I was attuned to diversity by team, job, and gender, among other axes. And although I cannot know how the experiences and perspectives of those who did not respond to my interview requests differ from those who did, those who agreed were managers and staff members and not team owners. I also received a response from only one player. Several years after the league folded I had much better luck, with about half of the players I contacted over email agreeing to interviews. When I asked these players about the rejection I had previously faced, they explained that team staff members typically dealt with requests for interviews. In addition, they acknowledged that many had been hesitant to air the "dirty laundry" of this league, fearing their disclosures would risk the wrath of others, compromise the health of a tenuous league, and/or jeopardize the already uncertain longevity of their playing careers. I conducted interviews until I reached the point of saturation, where I did not learn anything new from additional data.

By necessity, a subset of my interviews was conducted over the phone. As research has found, phone interviews tend to be somewhat shorter than face-to-face interviews, with participants giving truncated responses to questions. At the same time, phone interviews can foster perceptions of distance that enable the disclosure of sensitive or personal information.[13] And participants are more easily able to fit phone interviews into their existing schedules than to meet researchers in person. Analysis of my notes following interviews showed that the level of detail and the depth of disclosure did not vary between modes of interviewing and in some cases was greater in phone interviews.[14] However, given that I was interviewing a group used to phone interviews with media, I had to explain carefully (and often several times) who I was, what I was doing, and how interview data would be used.

Prompted by questions regarding identity protections on my Institutional Review Board (IRB) application, I assumed that removal of identifying information was a requirement for institutional permission to do this research. Assurances of confidentiality also helped me to secure participation in interviews. Yet truly masking our field sites and our participants' identities can be next to impossible, especially given the extent of information online. In addition, masking risks the erasure of information that is sociologically significant.[15] As I wrote this book, I concluded (and the IRB agreed) that it was simply not possible to obscure the name of the only professional soccer league for women operating at the time of my research. I do retain a pseudonym for the team I studied, although some of the information I present may enable identification for those highly knowledgeable about this league or committed to finding out. In choosing to present possible identifiers, such as the racial composition of the Momentum's metropolitan area, I balanced the sociological importance of this information against the risks of unmasking the team, deciding that these risks were minimal for a now defunct team and league. I did take care to mask the identities of individuals, using pseudonyms, slightly altering or scrambling identifiers such as age or position, and omitting other identifying information. I made an exception when referring to public interviews with journalists or bloggers or when using excerpts from autobiographies, opting in these cases to use real names.

Acknowledgments

While I was writing this book, the brother of a colleague came to visit. The week after his trip, my colleague referred to me in a phone conversation. As she told me later, her brother had struggled to place me. "Who, the soccer nut?" he had finally asked.

Without a doubt, the best thing about writing a book on women's soccer has been connecting with my fellow "nuts" across the country. I am thankful for the players, owners, staff members, sponsors, journalists, and fans who graciously shared their perspectives with me. Thank you especially to all at the Momentum, who allowed me an inside glimpse into the exciting and challenging world of women's professional sports.

I also extend my gratitude to those who provided assistance and support while I conducted my research and wrote this book: Pallavi Banerjee, Bruce Berglund, Bill Bielby, Amy Brainer, Courtney Carter, Andrew Colver, George Cunningham, Georgiann Davis, Ilana Demantas, Jesse Grady, Margaret Hagerman, Stacy Haynes, Joseph Hodnette, Leslie Hossfeld, Kecia Johnson, Ryland Johnson, Shelley Keith, Kimberly Kelly, Adam Love, Paul-Brian McInerney, Ann Pegoraro, Lindsey Peterson, Pamela Popielarz, Nicole Rader, Margaret Ralston, Barbara Risman, Kelsey Risman, Sofia Skraba, and Linda Treiber. I am deeply grateful for the insights of series editors Douglas Hartmann and Michael Messner, several peer reviewers, and Rutgers University Press editor Peter Mickulas.

The arguments in this book previously appeared in *Journal of Sport & Social Issues* and *Social Currents*. Chapter 2 was previously published as Rachel Allison, "Business or Cause? Gendered Institutional Logics in Women's Professional Soccer," Journal of Sport & Social Issues 40, no. 3 (2016): 237–262. Reprinted by permission of SAGE Publications, http://journals.sagepub .com/doi/full/10.1177/0193723515615349. Chapter 3 was previously published as Rachel Allison, "From Oversight to Autonomy: Gendered Organizational Change in Women's Soccer," *Social Currents* 4, no. 1 (2017): 71–86. Reprinted by permission of SAGE Publications, http://journals.sagepub.com/doi/full/10.1177/2329496516651637.

I have presented this work at meetings of the North American Society for the Sociology of Sport, the Society for the Study of Social Problems, and the Southern Sociological Society. This research was supported by grants from the Center for Research on Women and Gender at the University of Illinois at Chicago, the Laboratory for Diversity in Sport at Texas A&M University, and the Midwest Sociological Society.

Finally, thank you to my family. This book would not be possible without the unwavering support of my parents, Grant and Lynne Allison. My sisters, Grace and Jordan, suffered through the endless youth soccer tournaments that sparked my love of the game. I do not apologize for this.

Notes

Introduction

1 Jay Coakley, "Youth Sports: What Counts as 'Positive Development?,'" *Journal of Sport & Social Issues* 35, no. 3 (2011): 306–324.

2 Natalie Adams and Pamela Bettis, "Commanding the Room in Short Skirts: Cheering as the Embodiment of Ideal Girlhood," *Gender & Society* 17, no. 1 (2003): 73–91; Laura Azzarito, "Future Girls, Transcendent Femininities, and New Pedagogies: Toward Girls' Hybrid Bodies?," *Sport, Education, and Society* 15, no. 3 (2010): 261–275; Ruth Jeanes, "'I'm into High Heels and Makeup but I Still Love Football': Exploring Gender Identity and Football Participation with Preadolescent Girls," *Soccer & Society* 12, no. 3 (2011): 402–420; Michael A. Messner and Michela Musto, eds., *Child's Play: Sport in Kids' Worlds* (New Brunswick, N.J.: Rutgers University Press, 2016).

3 Dolores P. Martinez, "Soccer in the USA: 'Holding Out for a Hero?,'" *Soccer & Society* 9, no. 2 (2008): 231–243; Michael A. Messner, *It's All for the Kids: Gender, Families, and Youth Sports* (Berkeley: University of California Press, 2009); Welch Suggs, *A Place on the Team: The Triumph and Tragedy of Title IX* (Princeton: Princeton University Press, 2006).

4 National Federation of State High School Associations, "2013–14 Annual Report," http://www.nfhs.org/media/1014511/2013-14-annual-report_website.pdf.

5 Jaime Schultz, *Qualifying Times: Points of Change in U.S. Women's Sport* (Champaign: University of Illinois Press, 2014).

6 Cheryl Cooky, "Do Girls Rule? Understanding Popular Culture Images of 'Girl Power!' and Sport," in *Learning Culture through Sports: Perspectives on Society and Organized Sports*, ed. Sandra Spickard Prettyman and Brian Lampman (Lanham, Md.: Rowman & Littlefield, 2011), 210.

7 "Women's World Cup: And Strong TV Ratings, Too," *New York Times*, July 12, 1999, http://www.nytimes.com/1999/07/12/sports/women-s-world-cup-and-strong-tv-ratings-too.html.

8 C. L. Cole, "The Year That Girls Ruled," *Journal of Sport & Social Issues* 24, no. 1 (2000): 3–7; Leslie Heywood and Shari L. Dworkin, *Built to Win: The Female Athlete as Cultural Icon* (Minneapolis: University of Minnesota Press, 2003).

9 Adams and Bettis, "Commanding the Room"; Timothy F. Grainey, *Beyond* Bend It like Beckham*: The Global Phenomenon of Women's Soccer* (Lincoln: University of Nebraska Press, 2012).

10 Neal Christopherson, Michelle Janning, and Eileen Diaz McConnell, "Two Kicks Forward, One Kick Back: A Content Analysis of Media Discourses on the 1999 Women's World Cup Soccer Championship," *Sociology of Sport Journal* 19, no. 2 (2012): 170–188; Cole, "Year That Girls Ruled."

11 Eileen Narcotta-Welp, "A Black Fly in White Milk: The 1999 Women's World Cup, Briana Scurry, and the Politics of Inclusion," *Journal of Sport History* 42, no. 3 (2016): 382–393; Helene Shugart, "She Shoots, She Scores: Mediated Constructions of Contemporary Female Athletes in Coverage of the 1999 US Women's Soccer Team," *Western Journal of Communication* 67, no. 1 (2003): 1–31.

12 Jeré Longman, *The Girls of Summer: The U.S. Women's Soccer Team and How It Changed the World* (New York: Harper Perennial, 2001).

13 Christopherson, Janning, and McConnell, "Two Kicks Forward," 182–183.

14 Michael A. Messner, *Taking the Field: Women, Men & Sports* (Minneapolis: University of Minnesota Press, 2002).

15 Cole, "Year That Girls Ruled."

16 Jayne Caudwell, "Gender, Feminism, and Football Studies," *Soccer & Society* 12, no. 3 (2011): 330–344; Schultz, *Qualifying Times*.

17 Briana Scurry, "Women's World Cup Champ: Today Women's Players Are Appreciated for Their Achievements—Not for How They Look," *Time*, July 6, 2015, http://time.com/3947113/world-cup-women-players-today/.

18 Michael D. Giardina and Jennifer L. Metz, "All-American Girls? Corporatizing National Identity and Cultural Citizenship with/in the WUSA," in *Sport and Corporate Nationalisms*, ed. Michael L. Silk, David L. Andrews, and C. L. Cole (Oxford: Berg, 2004), 109–126.

19 Cole, "Year That Girls Ruled," 6.

20 Heywood and Dworkin, *Built to Win*.

21 Giardina and Metz, "All-American Girls?"; Mary G. McDonald, "The Marketing of the Women's National Basketball Association and the Making of Postfeminism," *International Review for the Sociology of Sport* 35, no. 1 (2000): 35–47.

22 Christopherson, Janning, and McConnell, "Two Kicks Forward," 171.

23 Cooky, "Do Girls Rule?," 211.

24 Sean Brown, "Critical Events or Critical Conditions: The 1999 Women's World Cup and the Women's United Soccer Association," *Soccer & Society* 7, nos. 2–3 (2006): 385–400; Beau Dure, *Long-Range Goals: The Success Story of Major League Soccer* (Washington, D.C.: Potomac Books, 2010).

25 Messner, *Taking the Field*.

26 Messner, 66.

27 Michael Kimmel, "Baseball and the Reconstitution of American Masculinity, 1880–1920," in *Sport, Men, and the Gender Order: Critical Feminist Perspectives*, ed. Don Sabo and Michael Messner (Champaign, Ill.: Human Kinetics Press, 2005), 55–66; Andrei Markovits and Emily Albertson, *Sportista! Female Fandom in the United States* (Philadelphia: Temple University Press, 2012); Michael A. Messner, *Out of Play: Critical Essays on Gender & Sport* (New York: State University of New York Press, 2007).

28 Kimmel, "Baseball and the Reconstitution," 50.

29 Markovits and Albertson, *Sportista!*; Messner, *Taking the Field*; Messner, *Out of Play*; Jeffrey Montez de Oca, *Discipline and Indulgence: College Football, Media,*

and the American Way of Life During the Cold War (New Brunswick, N.J.: Rutgers University Press, 2013); Mariah Burton Nelson, *The Stronger Women Get, the More Men Love Football* (New York: Harcourt, Brace, 1994).

30 Sara L. Crawley, "Visible Bodies, Vicarious Masculinity, and the 'Gender Revolution': A Comment on England," *Gender & Society* 25, no. 1 (2011): 111; Sara L. Crawley, Lara J. Foley, and Constance L. Shehan, *Gendering Bodies* (Lanham, Md.: Rowman & Littlefield, 2008).

31 Messner, *Out of Play*, 4; Faye Linda Wachs, "Leveling the Playing Field: Negotiating Gendered Rules in Coed Softball," *Journal of Sport & Social Issues* 26, no. 3 (2002): 300–316.

32 Adam Love and Kimberly Kelly, "Equity or Essentialism? U.S. Courts and the Legitimation of Girls' Teams in High School Sport," *Gender & Society* 25, no. 2 (2011): 227–249; Michael A. Messner, "Gender Ideologies, Youth Sports, and the Production of Soft Essentialism," *Sociology of Sport Journal* 28, no. 2 (2011): 151–170.

33 Georgiann Davis, *Contesting Intersex: The Dubious Diagnosis* (New York: New York University Press, 2015), 2.

34 Georgiann Davis and Erin L. Murphy, "Intersex Bodies as States of Exception: An Empirical Explanation for Unnecessary Surgical Modification," *Feminist Formations* 25, no. 2 (2013): 129–152.

35 Crawley, Foley, and Shehan, *Gendering Bodies*; Mary Jo Kane, "Resistance/Transformation of the Oppositional Binary: Exposing Sport as a Continuum," *Journal of Sport & Social Issues* 19, no. 2 (1995): 191–218.

36 Messner, "Gender Ideologies."

37 Markovits and Albertson, *Sportista!*, 3; Janet Fink, "Hiding in Plain Sight: The Embedded Nature of Sexism in Sport," *Journal of Sport Management* 30, no. 1 (2016): 1–7.

38 Kane, "Resistance/Transformation"; Michael A. Messner, "Sports and Male Domination: The Female Athlete as Contested Ideological Terrain," *Sociology of Sport Journal* 5, no. 3 (1988): 197–211; Sohaila Shakib and Michele D. Dunbar, "The Social Construction of Female and Male High School Basketball Participation: Reproducing the Gender Order through a Two-Tiered Sporting Institution," *Sociological Perspectives* 45, no. 4 (2002): 353–378; Belinda Wheaton and Alan Tomlinson, "The Changing Gender Order in Sport? The Case of Windsurfing Subcultures," *Journal of Sport & Social Issues* 22, no. 3 (1998): 252–274.

39 Faye Linda Wachs, "The Boundaries of Difference: Negotiating Gender in Recreational Sport," *Sociological Inquiry* 75, no. 4 (2005): 527–547.

40 Corentin Clement-Guillotin, Aina Chalabaev, and Paul Fontayne, "Is Sport Still a Masculine Domain? A Psychological Glance," *International Journal of Sport Psychology* 43, no. 1 (2012): 1–12.

41 Marie Hardin and Jennifer D. Greer, "The Influence of Gender-Role Socialization, Media Use and Sports Participation on Perceptions of Gender-Appropriate Sports," *Journal of Sport Behavior* 32, no. 2 (2009): 207–226; Mary Jo Kane and E. E. Snyder, "Sport Typing: The Social 'Containment' of Women in Sport," *Arena Review* 13, no. 2 (1989): 77–96.

42 Crawley, Foley, and Shehan, *Gendering Bodies*; Nathalie Koivula, "Perceived Characteristics of Sports Categorized as Gender-Neutral, Feminine, and Masculine," *Journal of Sport Behavior* 24, no. 4 (2001): 377–393.

43 Barbara J. Risman and Elizabeth Seale, "Betwixt and Between: Gender Contradictions among Middle Schoolers," in *Families as They Really Are*, ed. Barbara J. Risman (New York: Norton, 2010), 340–361.

44 Adams Mary Louise, *Artistic Impressions: Figure Skating, Masculinity, and the Limits of Sport* (Toronto: University of Toronto Press, 2011).

45 Susan K. Cahn, "From the 'Muscle Moll' to the 'Butch' Ballplayer: Mannishness, Lesbianism, and Homophobia in U.S. Women's Sport," *Feminist Studies* 19, no. 2 (1993): 343–368; Susan K. Cahn, *Coming on Strong: Gender and Sexuality in Women's Sport*, 2nd ed. (Urbana: University of Illinois Press, 2015); Pat Griffin, *Strong Women, Deep Closets: Lesbians and Homophobia in Sport* (Champaign, Ill.: Human Kinetics, 1998); Helen Jefferson Lenskyj, *Out on the Field: Gender, Sport and Sexualities* (Toronto: Women's Press, 2003).

46 M. Ann Hall, "The Discourse of Gender and Sport: From Femininity to Feminism," *Sociology of Sport Journal* 5, no. 4 (1988): 333.

47 Melanie L. Sartore and George B. Cunningham, "The Lesbian Stigma in the Sport Context: Implications for Women of Every Sexual Orientation," *Quest* 61, no. 3 (2009): 289–305.

48 Laurel R. Davis-Delano, April Pollock, and Jennifer Ellsworth Vose, "Apologetic Behavior among Female Athletes: A New Questionnaire and Initial Results," *International Review for the Sociology of Sport* 44, nos. 2–3 (2009): 131–150; Shari L. Dworkin and Michael A. Messner, "Just Do . . . What? Sport, Bodies, Gender," in *Gender and Sport: A Reader*, ed. Sheila Scraton and Anne Flintoff (New York: Routledge, 2002), 17–29; Jan Felshin, "The Triple Option . . . for Women in Sport," *Quest* 21, no. 1 (1974): 36–40; Vikki Krane, "We Can Be Athletic and Feminine, but Do We Want To? Challenging Hegemonic Femininity in Women's Sport," *Quest* 53, no. 1 (2001): 115–133; J. B. Rohrbaugh, "Femininity on the Line," *Psychology Today* 13, no. 3 (1979): 31–33.

49 Anima Adjepong, "'We're like a Cute Rugby Team': How Whiteness and Heterosexuality Shape Women's Sense of Belonging in Rugby," *International Review for the Sociology of Sport* 52, no. 2 (2017): 209–222; Kane and. Snyder, "Sport Typing."

50 Maddie Breeze, "Analysing 'Seriousness' in Roller Derby: Speaking Critically with the Serious Leisure Perspective," *Sociological Research Online* 18, no. 4 (2013): 1–13.

51 Adams and Bettis, "Commanding the Room"; Laura Grindstaff and Emily West, "Cheerleading and the Gendered Politics of Sport," *Social Problems* 53, no. 4 (2006): 500–518.

52 Sartore and Cunningham, "Lesbian Stigma," 294.

53 Jennifer Hargreaves, *Sporting Females: Critical Issues in the History and Sociology of Women's Sports* (New York: Routledge, 2002).

54 Gerald R. Gems and Gertrud Pfister, *Understanding American Sports* (New York: Routledge, 2009).

55 Mary G. McDonald, "Queering Whiteness: The Particular Case of the Women's National Basketball Association," *Sociological Perspectives* 45, no. 4 (2002): 379–396; Patricia Vertinsky and Gwendolyn Captain, "More Myth than History: American Culture and Representations of the Black Female's Athletic Ability," *Journal of Sport History* 25, no. 3 (1998): 532–561.

56 Markovits and Albertson, *Sportista!*

57 Sylvain Ferez, "From Women's Exclusion to Gender Institution: A Brief History of the Sexual Categorisation Process in Sport," *International Journal of the History of Sport* 29, no. 2 (2012): 272–285; Jennifer Ring, *Stolen Bases: Why American Girls Don't Play Baseball* (Champaign: University of Illinois Press, 2013).

58 Eric D. Anderson, "'I Used to Think Women Were Weak': Orthodox Masculinity, Gender Segregation, and Sport," *Sociological Forum* 23, no. 2 (2008): 257–280;

Deborah L. Brake, *Getting in the Game: Title IX and the Women's Sports Revolution* (New York: New York University Press, 2010); Eileen McDonagh and Laura Pappano, *Playing with the Boys: Why Separate Is Not Equal in Sports* (New York: Oxford University Press, 2008); Adrienne Milner and Jomills Henry Braddock III, *Sex Segregation in Sports: Why Separate Is Not Equal* (Santa Barbara, Calif.: Praeger, 2016); Ann Travers, "The Sport Nexus and Gender Injustice," *Studies in Social Justice* 2, no. 1 (2008): 79–101.

59 Kathryn E. Henne, *Testing for Athlete Citizenship: Regulating Doping and Sex in Sport* (New Brunswick, N.J.: Rutgers University Press, 2015).

60 Sylvia Camporesi, "Ethics of Regulating Competition for Women with Hyperandrogenism," *Clinics in Sports Medicine* 35, no. 2 (2016): 293–301.

61 Katrina Karkazis, Rebecca Jordan-Young, Georgiann Davis, and Sylvia Camporesi, "Out of Bounds? A Critique of the New Policies on Hyperandrogenism in Elite Female Athletes," *American Journal of Bioethics* 12, no. 7 (2012): 3–16.

62 Carrie Dunn, *Football and the Women's World Cup: Organisation, Media, and Fandom* (New York: Palgrave Pivot, 2016).

63 Cheryl Cooky, Michael A. Messner, and Michaela Musto, "'It's Dude Time!' A Quarter Century of Excluding Women's Sports in Televised News and Highlights Shows," *Communication & Sport* 3, no. 3 (2015): 261–287; Cheryl Cooky, Michael A. Messner, and Robin Hextrum, "Women Play Sports, but Not on TV: A Longitudinal Study of Televised News Media," *Communication & Sport* 1, no. 3 (2013): 203–230.

64 Toni Bruce, "Assessing the Sociology of Sport: On Media and Representations of Sportswomen," *International Review for the Sociology of Sport* 50, nos. 4–5 (2015): 380–384; Marie Hardin and Stacie Shain, "Female Sports Journalists: Are We There Yet? No," *Newspaper Research Journal* 26, no. 4 (2005): 22–35; Marie Hardin and Stacie Shain, "Strength in Numbers? The Experiences and Attitudes of Women in Sports Media Careers," *Journalism & Mass Communication Quarterly* 82, no. 4 (2005): 804–819; Annelies Knoppers and Agnes Elling, "'We Do Not Engage in Promotional Journalism': Discursive Strategies Used by Sport Journalists to Describe the Selection Process," *International Review for the Sociology of Sport* 39, no. 1 (2004): 57–73.

65 Toni Bruce, "Reflections on Communication and Sport: On Women and Femininities," *Communication & Sport* 1, nos. 1–2 (2013): 131; Cheryl Cooky and Nicole M. LaVoi, "Playing but Losing: Women's Sports after Title IX," *Contexts* 11, no. 1 (2012): 42–46; Cooky, Messner, and Musto, "'It's Dude Time!'"

66 Schultz, *Qualifying Times*.

67 Gertrud Pfister, "Assessing the Sociology of Sport: On Women and Football," *International Review for the Sociology of Sport* 50, nos. 4–5 (2015): 563–569.

68 K. L. Broad, "The Gendered Unapologetic: Queer Resistance in Women's Sport," *Sociology of Sport Journal* 18, no. 2 (2001): 181–204.

69 Schultz, *Qualifying Times*, 196.

70 Susan Birrell, "Feminist Theories for Sport," in *Handbook of Sports Studies*, ed. Jay Coakley and Eric Dunning (London: SAGE, 2000), 61–76; Varda Burstyn, *The Rites of Men: Manhood, Politics, and the Culture of Sport* (Toronto: University of Toronto Press, 1999); Jennifer Hargreaves, "Querying Sport Feminism: Personal or Political?," in *Sport and Modern Social Theorists*, ed. Richard Giulianotti (New York: Palgrave Macmillan, 2004), 187–206.

71 Caudwell, "Gender, Feminism."

72 Barbara Barnett and Marie C. Hardin, "Advocacy from the Liberal Feminist Playbook: The Framing of Title IX and Women's Sports in News Releases from the Women's Sports Foundation," *International Journal of Sport Communication* 4, no. 2 (2011): 178–197.

73 Hargreaves, *Sporting Females*, 29.

74 Barnett and Hardin, "Advocacy."

75 Messner, "Gender Ideologies," 161; Caudwell, "Gender, Feminism."

76 Lauren Rauscher and Cheryl Cooky, "Ready for Anything the World Gives Her? A Critical Look at Sports-Based Positive Youth Development for Girls," *Sex Roles* 74, no. 7 (2015): 288–298.

77 Adjepong, "'We're like a Cute Rugby Team,'" 219; Bruce, "Assessing the Sociology of Sport"; David J. Leonard, *Playing While White: Privilege and Power On and Off the Field* (Seattle: University of Washington Press, 2017).

78 C. L. Cole and Amy Hribar, "Celebrity Feminism: Nike Style, Post-Fordism, Transcendence, and Consumer Power," *Sociology of Sport Journal* 12, no. 4 (1995): 347–369.

79 Rosalind Gill, "Postfeminist Media Culture: Elements of a Sensibility," *European Journal of Cultural Studies* 10, no. 2 (2007): 147–166.

80 Barbara Cox and Shona Thompson, "Multiple Bodies: Sportswomen, Soccer, and Sexuality," *International Review for the Sociology of Sport* 35, no. 1 (2000): 5–20; Shari L. Dworkin, "'Holding Back': Negotiating a Glass Ceiling on Women's Muscular Strength," *Sociological Perspectives* 44, no. 3 (2001): 333–350.

81 Heywood and Dworkin, *Built to Win*.

82 Matthew R. Hodler and Cathryn Lucas-Carr, "'The Mother of All Comebacks': A Critical Analysis of the Fitspirational Comeback Narrative of Dara Torres," *Communication & Sport* 4, no. 4 (2016): 442–459.

83 Shari L. Dworkin and Faye Linda Wachs, *Body Panic: Gender, Health, and the Selling of Fitness* (New York: New York University Press, 2009); Pirkko Markula, "Beyond the Perfect Body: Women's Body Image Distortion in Fitness Magazine Discourse," *Journal of Sport & Social Issues* 25, no. 2 (2001): 158–179.

84 Myra S. Washington and Megan Economides, "Strong Is the New Sexy: Women, Crossfit, and the Postfeminist Ideal," *Journal of Sport & Social Issues* 40, no. 2 (2016): 150.

85 Gregory A. Cranmer, Maria Brann, and Nicholas D. Bowman, "Male Athletes, Female Aesthetics: The Continued Ambivalence toward Female Athletes in ESPN's *The Body Issue*," *International Journal of Sport Communication* 7, no. 2 (2014): 145–165; Rachael R. Smallwood, Natalie A. Brown, and Andrew C. Billings, "Female Bodies on Display: Attitudes regarding Female Athlete Photos in *Sports Illustrated*'s Swimsuit Issue and *ESPN: The Magazine*'s Body Issue," *Journal of Sports Media* 9, no. 1 (2014): 1–22.

86 Shugart, "She Shoots, She Scores," 3.

87 Heywood and Dworkin, *Built to Win*.

88 Dworkin and Messner, "Just Do . . . What?"

89 Samantha King, "Marketing Generosity: The Avon Worldwide Fund for Women's Health and the Reinvention of Global Corporate Citizenship," in Silk, Andrews, and Cole, *Sport and Corporate Nationalisms*, 98; Shelley Lucas, "Nike's Commercial Solution: Girls, Sneakers, and Salvation," *International Review for the Sociology of Sport* 35, no. 2 (2000): 149–164.

90 Schultz, *Qualifying Times*, 135.

91 Cheryl Cooky, "'Girls Just Aren't Interested': The Social Construction of Interest in Girls' Sport," *Sociological Perspectives* 52, no. 2 (2009): 259–284.

92 Sarah Banet-Weiser, "Hoop Dreams: Professional Basketball and the Politics of Race and Gender," *Journal of Sport & Social Issues* 23, no. 4 (1999): 403–420; Cheryl Cooky and Mary G. McDonald, "'If You Let Me Play': Young Girls' Insider-Other Narratives of Sport," *Sociology of Sport Journal* 22, no. 2 (2005): 158–177; Jason Laurendeau and Nancy Shahara, "'Women Could Be Every Bit as Good as Guys': Reproductive and Resistant Agency in Two 'Action' Sports," *Journal of Sport & Social Issues* 32, no. 1 (2008): 24–47.

93 Cole and Hribar, "Celebrity Feminism," 351–352.

94 Gill, "Postfeminist Media Culture"; Angela McRobbie, *The Aftermath of Feminism: Gender, Culture, and Social Change* (Thousand Oaks, Calif.: SAGE, 2009); Jo Reger, *Everywhere and Nowhere: Contemporary Feminism in the United States* (Oxford: Oxford University Press, 2012).

95 Stephanie Genz, "Third Way/ve: The Politics of Postfeminism," *Feminist Theory* 7, no. 3 (2006): 337–338.

96 Travers, "Sport Nexus."

97 Bruce, "Assessing the Sociology of Sport."

98 Hargreaves, *Sporting Females*.

99 Heywood and Dworkin, *Built to Win*.

100 Toni Bruce, "New Rules for New Times: Sportswomen and Media Representation in the Third Wave," *Sex Roles* 74, no. 7 (2016): 361–376.

101 Michael A. Messner and Nancy M. Solomon, "Social Justice and Men's Interests: The Case of Title IX," *Journal of Sport & Social Issues* 31, no. 2 (2007): 163.

102 Banet-Weiser, "Hoop Dreams"; Todd W. Crosset, *Outsiders in the Clubhouse: The World of Women's Professional Golf* (Albany: State University of New York Press, 1995); Jennifer L. Hanis-Martin, "Embodying Contradictions: The Case of Professional Women's Basketball," *Journal of Sport & Social Issues* 30, no. 3 (2006): 265–288; Nancy Theberge, *Higher Goals: Women's Ice Hockey and the Politics of Gender* (Albany: State University of New York Press, 2000).

103 Michael Atkinson, *Key Concepts in Sport and Exercise Research Methods* (London: SAGE, 2011), 32.

Chapter 1 Women's Soccer in the United States

1 Kevin Tallec Marston, "Rethinking 'Ethnic' Soccer: The National Junior Challenge Cup and the Transformation of American Soccer's Identity (1935–1976)," *Soccer & Society* 18, nos. 2–3 (2017): 330–347.

2 Laura Grindstaff and Emily West, "Cheerleading and the Gendered Politics of Sport," *Social Problems* 53, no. 4 (2006): 500–518.

3 Ann Coulter, "America's Favorite National Past Time: Hating Soccer," Anncoulter.com, June 25, 2014, http://www.anncoulter.com/columns/2014-06-25.html.

4 Cheryl Cooky, Faye Linda Wachs, and Michael A. Messner, "It's Not about the Game: Don Imus, Race, Class, Gender and Sexuality in Contemporary Media," *Sociology of Sport Journal* 27, no. 2 (2010): 139–159; Ramon Spaaij, Karen Farquharson, and Timothy Marjoribanks, "Sport and Social Inequalities," *Sociology Compass* 9, no. 5 (2015): 400–411.

5 Adams Mary Louise, *Artistic Impressions: Figure Skating, Masculinity, and the Limits of Sport* (Toronto: University of Toronto Press, 2011); Inge Claringbould

and Johanna Adriaanse, "'Silver Cups Versus Ice Creams': Parental Involvement in the Construction of Gender in the Field of their Sons' Soccer," *Sociology of Sport Journal* 32, no. 2 (2015): 201–219.

6 Andrew M. Lindner and Daniel N. Hawkins, "Globalization, Culture Wars, and Attitudes toward Soccer in America: An Empirical Assessment of How Soccer Explains the World," *Sociological Quarterly* 53, no. 1 (2012): 68–91.

7 Dennis J. Seese, "New Traditionalists: The Emergence of Modern America and the Birth of the MLS Coalition," in *Soccer Culture in America: Essays on the World's Sport in Red, White, and Blue*, ed. Yuya Kiuchi (Jefferson, N.C.: McFarland, 2013), 45.

8 Daniel Taylor Buffington, "Us and Them: U.S. Ambivalence toward the World Cup and American Nationalism," *Journal of Sport & Social Issues* 26, no. 2 (2012): 144.

9 Buffington, 144; Gary Armstrong and James Rosbrook-Thompson, "Coming to America: Historical Ontologies and United States Soccer," *Identities: Global Studies in Culture and Power* 17, no. 4 (2010): 348–371; John Sugden, "USA and the World Cup: American Nativism and Rejection of the People's Game," in *Hosts and Champions: Soccer Cultures, National Identities, and the USA World Cup*, ed. John Sugden and Alan Tomlinson (Aldershot, U.K.: Ashgate, 1994), 215–252; John Sugden and Alan Tomlinson, "What's Left When the Circus Leaves Town? An Evaluation of World Cup USA 1994," *Sociology of Sport Journal* 13, no. 3 (1996): 238–258.

10 Andrei Markovits and Emily Albertson, *Sportista! Female Fandom in the United States* (Philadelphia: Temple University Press, 2012), 4.

11 Andrei S. Markovits and Steven L. Hellerman, *Offside: Soccer and American Exceptionalism* (Princeton: Princeton University Press, 2001).

12 David Keyes, "The Domestication of American Soccer," in *Soccer Culture in America: Essays on the World's Sport in Red, White, and Blue*, ed. Yuya Kiuchi (Jefferson, N.C.: McFarland, 2013), 9–24.

13 Nathan D. Abrams, "Inhibited but Not 'Crowded Out': The Strange Fate of Soccer in the United States," *International Journal of the History of Sport* 12, no. 3 (1995): 1–17; Benjamin James Dettmar, "'Fast-Kicking, Low-Scoring, and Ties': How Popular Culture Can Help the Global Game Become America's Game," in Kiuchi, *Soccer Culture in America*, 95–119; David Kilpatrick, "Amnesia and Animosity: An Assessment of Soccer in the States," *Sport in Society* 20, nos. 5–6 (2017): 627–640; Thom Satterlee, "Making Soccer a 'Kick in the Grass': The Media's Role in Promoting a Marginal Sport, 1975–1977," *International Review for the Sociology of Sport* 36, no. 3 (2001): 305–317.

14 Seese, "New Traditionalists," 49; Dwight Branch, "A Resounding Soccer Success . . . in the U.S.?," in Kiuchi, *Soccer Culture in America*, 84–94.

15 Mike Humes, "2014 World Cup Final on ABC: Most-Watched Men's World Cup Championship," *ESPN*, July 14, 2014, http://espnmediazone.com/us/press-releases/2014/07/2014-world-cup-final-on-abc-most-watched-mens-world-cup-championship-ever/.

16 Danielle Sarver Coombs, "Pitch Perfect: How the U.S. Women's National Soccer Team Brought the Game Home," in Kiuchi, *Soccer Culture in America*, 170.

17 Seese, "New Traditionalists."

18 Gregory G. Reck and Bruce Allen Dick, *American Soccer: History, Culture, Class* (Jefferson, N.C.: McFarland, 2015).

19 Andrei S. Markovits and Adam Isaiah Green, "FIFA, the Video Game: A Major Vehicle for Soccer's Popularization in the United States," *Sport in Society* 20, nos. 5–6 (2016): 716–734.

20 Glen M. E. Duerr, "Becoming Apple Pie: Soccer as the Fifth Major Team Sport in the United States?," in Kiuchi, *Soccer Culture in America*, 144.

21 Jean Williams, *A Beautiful Game: International Perspectives on Women's Football* (New York: Berg, 2007).

22 Sugden, "USA and the World Cup."

23 Andrei S. Markovits and Stephen L. Hellerman, "Women's Soccer in the United States: Yet Another American Exceptionalism," *Soccer & Society* 4, nos. 2–3 (2003): 14–29.

24 Markovits and Albertson, *Sportista!*, 94.

25 Williams, *Beautiful Game*, 36.

26 Williams, 39.

27 Williams, 66.

28 Williams.

29 Markovits and Green, "FIFA, the Video Game."

30 Keyes, "Domestication of American Soccer."

31 David L. Andrews, Robert Pitter, Detlev Zwick, and Darren Ambrose, "Soccer's Racial Frontier: Sport and the Suburbanization of Contemporary America," in *Entering the Field: New Perspectives on World Football*, ed. Gary Armstrong and Richard Giulianotti (Oxford: Berg, 1997), 261–282.

32 David L. Andrews, *Sport-Commerce-Culture: Essays on Sport in Late Capitalist America* (New York: Peter Lang, 2006), 85.

33 Andrews, 268–269.

34 Becky Nicolaides, "How Hell Moved from the City to the Suburbs: Urban Scholars and Changing Perceptions of Authentic Community," in *The New Suburban History*, ed. Kevin M. Kruse and Thomas J. Sugrue (Chicago: University of Chicago Press, 2006), 95.

35 Andrews et al., "Soccer's Racial Frontier," 270.

36 Andrews et al.

37 Annette Lareau, *Unequal Childhoods: Race, Class, and Family Life*, 2nd ed. (Berkeley: University of California Press, 2011).

38 Jay Coakley, "The Good Father: Parental Expectations and Youth Sports," *Leisure Studies* 25, no. 2 (2006): 153–163; Dawn E. Trussell and Susan M. Shaw, "Organized Youth Sport and Parenting in Public and Private Spaces," *Leisure Sciences* 34, no. 5 (2012): 377–394.

39 Hilary Levey Friedman, *Playing to Win: Raising Children in a Competitive Culture* (Berkeley: University of California Press, 2013).

40 Andrews et al., "Soccer's Racial Frontier," 274.

41 Timothy F. Grainey, *Beyond Bend It like Beckham: The Global Phenomenon of Women's Soccer* (Lincoln: University of Nebraska Press, 2012).

42 Kenneth T. Jackson, *Crabgrass Frontier: The Suburbanization of the United States* (New York: Oxford University Press, 1985), 289.

43 Reck and Dick, *American Soccer*.

44 Seese, "New Traditionalists."

45 Jay Coakley, "The 'Logic' of Specialization," *Journal of Physical Education, Recreation, & Dance* 81, no. 8 (2010): 16–25.

46 Friedman, *Playing to Win*, 40.

47 Lisa Swanson, "Soccer Fields of Cultural (Re)production: Creating 'Good Boys' in Suburban America," *Sociology of Sport Journal* 26, no. 3 (2009): 404–424.

48 Keyes, "Domestication of American Soccer."

49 Marston, "Rethinking 'Ethnic' Soccer," 337.

50 David Wangerin, *Soccer in a Football World: The Story of America's Forgotten Game* (Philadelphia: Temple University Press, 2006).

51 Annelies Knoppers and Anthony Anthonissen, "Women's Soccer in the United States and the Netherlands: Differences and Similarities in Regimes of Inequalities," *Sociology of Sport Journal* 20, no. 4 (2003): 351–370; Helene A. Shugart, "She Shoots, She Scores: Mediated Constructions of Contemporary Female Athletes in Coverage of the 1999 US Women's Soccer Team," *Western Journal of Communication* 67, no. 1 (2003): 1–31.

52 Reck and Dick, *American Soccer*, 18.

53 Eric D. Anderson, "The Maintenance of Masculinity among the Stakeholders of Sport," *Sport Management Review* 12, no. 1 (2009): 3–14.

54 Sandra Collins, "National Sports and Other Myths: The Failure of U.S. Soccer," *Soccer & Society* 7, nos. 2–3 (2006): 353–363.

55 Coombs, "Pitch Perfect," 162.

56 Sarah K. Fields, *Female Gladiators: Gender, Law, and Contact Sport in America* (Chicago: University of Illinois Press, 2005).

57 Fields, *Female Gladiators*.

58 Michael A. Messner, *It's All for the Kids: Gender, Families, and Youth Sports* (Berkeley: University of California Press, 2009).

59 Lucas Gottzén and Tamar Kremer-Sadlick, "Fatherhood and Youth Sports: A Balancing Act between Care and Expectations," *Gender & Society* 26, no. 4 (2012): 639–664.

60 Andrews et al., "Soccer's Racial Frontier."

61 Michael A. Messner, "Gender Ideologies, Youth Sports, and the Production of Soft Essentialism," *Sociology of Sport Journal* 28, no. 2 (2011): 151–170.

62 Messner, "Gender Ideologies," 155.

63 Deborah L. Brake, *Getting in the Game: Title IX and the Women's Sports Revolution* (New York: New York University Press, 2010).

64 Vivian R. Acosta and Linda Jean Carpenter, "Women in Intercollegiate Sport: A Longitudinal, National Study, Thirty Seven Year Update, 1977–2014" (unpublished manuscript), PDF file, http://www.acostacarpenter.org.

65 Rick Eckstein, *How College Athletics Are Hurting Girls' Sports: The Pay-to-Play Pipeline* (New York: Rowman & Littlefield, 2017).

66 Alan Tomlinson, Andrei S. Markovits, and Christopher Young, "Introduction: Mapping Sports Space," *American Behavioral Scientist* 46, no. 11 (2003): 1470.

67 Knoppers and Anthonissen, "Women's Soccer."

68 Eckstein, *How College Athletics*.

69 Messner, "Gender Ideologies."

70 Sean Brown, "Critical Events or Critical Conditions: The 1999 Women's World Cup and the Women's United Soccer Association," *Soccer & Society* 7, nos. 2–3 (2006): 385–400.

71 Derek Van Rheenen, "The Promise of Soccer in America: The Open Play of Ethnic Subcultures," *Soccer & Society* 10, no. 6 (2009): 784.

72 Hope Solo and Ann Killion, *Solo: A Memoir of Hope* (New York: HarperCollins, 2012), 105.

73 Carly Adams and Stacey Leavitt, "'It's Just Girls' Hockey': Troubling Progress Narratives in Girls' and Women's Sport," *International Review for the Sociology of Sport* 53, no. 2 (2018): 152–172.

74 Lindsey J. Meân, "The 99ers: Celebrating the Mythological," *Journal of Sports Media* 10, no. 2 (2015): 31–43.

75 Markovits and Hellerman, *Offside*, 21.

Chapter 2 Business or Cause? Contested Goals

1 David L. Andrews, *Sport-Commerce-Culture: Essays on Sport in Late Capitalist America* (New York: Peter Lang, 2006).

2 Laura Cousens and Trevor Slack, "Field-Level Change: The Case of North American Major League Professional Sports," *Journal of Sport Management* 19, no. 1 (2005): 13–42.

3 Jon Dart, "New Media, Professional Sport, and Political Economy," *Journal of Sport & Social Issues* 38, no. 6 (2014): 528–547.

4 Bente Ovèdie Skogvang, "Players' and Coaches' Experiences with the Gendered Sport/Media Complex in Elite Football," in *Gender and Sport: Changes and Challenges*, ed. Gertrud Pfister and Mari Kristin Sisjord (New York: Waxmann, 2013), 103–122.

5 Andrews, *Sport-Commerce-Culture*, 6.

6 Sean Brown, "Critical Events or Critical Conditions: The 1999 Women's World Cup and the Women's United Soccer Association," *Soccer & Society* 7, nos. 2–3 (2006): 395.

7 Rachel Allison, "Business or Cause? Gendered Institutional Logics in Women's Professional Soccer," *Journal of Sport & Social Issues* 40, no. 3 (2016): 237–262.

8 Michael D. Giardina and Jennifer L. Metz, "All-American Girls? Corporatizing National Identity and Cultural Citizenship With/in the WUSA," in *Sport and Corporate Nationalisms*, ed. Michael L. Silk, David L. Andrews, and C. L. Cole (Oxford: Berg, 2004), 109–126.

9 Timothy F. Grainey, *Beyond Bend It like Beckham: The Global Phenomenon of Women's Soccer* (Lincoln: University of Nebraska Press, 2012).

10 Han Arar and George Foster, "Women's Professional Soccer: Building a New League after WUSA Shutdown" (Stanford Graduate School of Business Case E-411A, 2012), 7.

11 Andrews, *Sport-Commerce-Culture*.

12 Clare Burton, "Merit and Gender: Organisations and the Mobilisation of Masculine Bias," *Australian Journal of Social Issues* 27, no. 2 (1987): 425.

13 Mary Jo Kane, "Resistance/Transformation of the Oppositional Binary: Exposing Sport as a Continuum," *Journal of Sport & Social Issues* 19, no. 2 (1995): 191–218.

14 Jean Williams, *A Beautiful Game: International Perspectives on Women's Football* (New York: Berg, 2007), 43.

15 Carrie Dunn, "Elite Footballers as Role Models: Promoting Young Women's Football Participation," *Soccer & Society* 17, no. 6 (2016): 843–855.

16 Andrew M. Guest and Stephanie Cox, "Using Athletes as Role Models? Conceptual and Empirical Perspectives from a Sample of Elite Women Soccer Players," *International Journal of Sport Science and Coaching* 4, no. 4 (2009): 567–581; Elsa Kristiansen, Trygve B. Broch, and Paul M. Pedersen, "Negotiating Gender in Professional Soccer: An Analysis of Female Footballers in the United States," *Choregia* 10, no. 1 (2014): 5–27.

17 Tim Nash, *It's Not the Glory: The Remarkable First Thirty Years of U.S. Women's Soccer* (Lulu, 2016), 88.

18 Jeré Longman, "After World Cup Thrills, Players Return to Unstable Women's League," *New York Times*, August 8, 2011, http://www.nytimes.com/2011/08/09/sports/soccer/unsteady-financial-footing-for-womens-soccer-league.html.

19 Michelle T. Helstein, "Rethinking Community: Introducing the 'Whatever' Female Athlete," *Sociology of Sport Journal* 21, no. 1 (2005): 1–18.

20 Andrews, *Sport-Commerce-Culture*, 6.

21 Andrews, 394.

Chapter 3 We're Taking Over! Constructing the Fan Base

1 Timothy Grainey, *Beyond* Bend It like Beckham: *The Global Phenomenon of Women's Soccer* (Lincoln: University of Nebraska Press, 2012), 60.

2 Richard M. Southall and Mark S. Nagel, "Marketing Professional Soccer in the United States: Lessons in Exchange Theory and Cause-Related Marketing," *Smart Journal* 3, no. 2 (2007): 54–69.

3 Grainey, *Beyond*, 75.

4 Sarah Banet-Weiser, "Hoop Dreams: Professional Basketball and the Politics of Race and Gender," *Journal of Sport & Social Issues* 23, no. 4 (1999): 403–420.

5 Tiffany Muller Myrdahl, "Producing Gender-Normative Spaces in U.S. Women's Professional Soccer," in *Stadium Worlds: Football, Space, and the Built Environment*, ed. Sybille Frank and Silke Steets (New York: Routledge, 2010), 201; Mary G. McDonald, "Queering Whiteness: The Particular Case of the Women's National Basketball Association," *Sociological Perspectives* 45, no. 4 (2002): 379–396.

6 McDonald, "Queering Whiteness."

7 Muller Myrdahl, "Producing Gender-Normative Spaces."

8 Anthony Kwame Harrison, "Black Skiing, Everyday Racism, and the Racial Spatiality of Whiteness," *Journal of Sport & Social Issues* 37, no. 4 (2013): 317.

9 Matthew Walker, Aubrey Kent, and John Vincent, "Communicating Socially Responsible Initiatives: An Analysis of U.S. Professional Teams," *Sport Marketing Quarterly* 19, no. 4 (2010): 187–195.

10 Grainey, *Beyond*.

11 Rachel Allison, "From Oversight to Autonomy: Gendered Organizational Change in Women's Soccer," *Social Currents* 4, no. 1 (2017): 71–86.

12 Muller Myrdahl, "Producing Gender-Normative Spaces," 197.

13 Muller Myrdahl, 203.

14 Carrie Dunn, *Football and the Women's World Cup: Organisation, Media, and Fandom* (New York: Palgrave Pivot, 2016); Tiffany Muller Myrdahl, "'Family-Friendly' without the Double Entendre: A Spatial Analysis of Normative Game Spaces and Lesbian Fans," *Journal of Lesbian Studies* 13, no. 1 (2009): 292.

15 "How Many Gays Must God Create before We Accept That He Wants Them Around?," YouTube, May 2, 2011, https://www.youtube.com/watch?v=hXpOA3jPC04.

16 Cathy van Ingen, "Geographies of Gender, Sexuality, and Race: Reframing the Focus on Space in Sport Sociology," *International Review for the Sociology of Sport* 32, no. 2 (2003): 201–216; Christopher Henderson, "Two Balls Is Too Many: Stadium Performance and Queerness among Portland's Rose City Riveters Supporters Club," *Sport in Society* (forthcoming).

17 Tiffany Muller, "'Lesbian Community' in Women's National Basketball Association (WNBA) Spaces," *Social & Cultural Geography* 8, no. 1 (2007): 9–28.

18 Andrei Markovits and Emily Albertson, *Sportista! Female Fandom in the United States* (Philadelphia: Temple University Press, 2012).

19 Katelyn Esmonde, Cheryl Cooky, and David L. Andrews, "'It's Supposed to Be about the Love of the Game, Not the Love of Aaron Rodgers' Eyes': Challenging the Exclusions of Women Sports Fans," *Sociology of Sport Journal* 32, no. 1 (2015): 22–48.

20 Annette Lareau, *Unequal Childhoods: Race, Class, and Family Life*, 2nd ed. (Berkeley: University of California Press, 2011).

21 Southall and Nagel, "Marketing Professional Soccer," 61.

22 Allison, "From Oversight to Autonomy."

23 Muller Myrdahl, "Producing Gender-Normative Spaces."

24 Esmonde, Cooky, and Andrews, "'It's Supposed to Be about the Love.'"

Chapter 4   Image Politics and Media (In)visibility

1 Tiffany Muller Myrdahl, "Producing Gender-Normative Spaces in U.S. Women's Professional Soccer," in *Stadium Worlds: Football, Space, and the Built Environment*, ed. Sybille Frank and Silke Steets (New York: Routledge, 2010), 196.

2 Jennifer Hargreaves, *Sporting Females: Critical Issues in the History and Sociology of Women's Sports* (New York: Routledge, 2002), 164.

3 Janet S. Fink, "Homophobia and the Marketing of Female Athletes and Women's Sport," in *Sexual Orientation and Gender Identity in Sport: Essays from Activists, Coaches, and Scholars*, ed. George B. Cunningham (College Station, Tex.: Center for Sport Management Research and Education, 2012), 49–60.

4 Maddie Breeze, *Seriousness and Women's Roller Derby: Gender, Organization, and Ambivalence* (New York: Palgrave Macmillan, 2015); Nancy Theberge, *Higher Goals: Women's Ice Hockey and the Politics of Gender* (Albany: State University of New York Press, 2000).

5 Janet S. Fink, "Female Athletes, Women's Sport and the Sport-Media-Commercial Complex: Have We Really 'Come a Long Way, Baby'?," *Sport Management Review* 18, no. 3 (2015): 331–342.

6 David Rowe, "Assessing the Sociology of Sport: On Media and Power," *International Review for the Sociology of Sport* 50, nos. 4–5 (2015): 577; Lawrence A. Wenner, "Assessing the Sociology of Sport: On the Mediasport Interpellation and Commodity Narratives," *International Review for the Sociology of Sport* 50, nos. 4–5 (2015): 628–633.

7 Fink, "Female Athletes."

8 Andrew C. Billings and Brittany D. Young, "Comparing Flagship News Programs: Women's Sports Coverage in ESPN's SportsCenter and FOX Sports 1's Sports Live," *Electronic News* 9, no. 1 (2015): 3–16; Cheryl Cooky, Michael A. Messner, and Robin Hextrum, "Women Play Sports, but Not on TV: A Longitudinal Study of Televised News Media," *Communication & Sport* 1, no. 3 (2013): 203–230.

9 Terry Adams and C. A. Tuggle, "ESPN's Sports Center and Coverage of Women's Athletics: 'It's a Boys' Club,'" *Mass Communication and Society* 7, no. 2 (2004): 237–248.

10 Cheryl Cooky, Michael A. Messner, and Michaela Musto, "'It's Dude Time!' A Quarter Century of Excluding Women's Sports in Televised News and Highlights Shows," *Communication & Sport* 3, no. 3 (2015): 261–287.

11 Mary Jo Kane, "The Better Sportswomen Get, the More the Media Ignore Them," *Communication & Sport* 1, no. 3 (2013): 231–236.

12 Nancy Theberge and Alan Cronk, "Work Routines in Newspaper Sports Departments and the Coverage of Women's Sports," *Sociology of Sport Journal* 3, no. 3 (1986): 197.

13 Marie Hardin, "Stopped at the Gate: Women's Sports, 'Reader Interest,' and Decision Making by Editors," *Journalism & Mass Communication Quarterly* 82, no. 1 (2005): 62–77.

14 Annelies Knoppers and Agnes Elling, "'We Do Not Engage in Promotional Journalism': Discursive Strategies Used by Sport Journalists to Describe the Selection Process," *International Review for the Sociology of Sport* 39, no. 1 (2004): 57–73.

15 Toni Bruce, "Reflections on Communication and Sport: On Women and Femininities," *Communication & Sport* 1, nos. 1–2 (2013): 130–131.

16 Fink, "Female Athletes"; Michael A. Messner, Margaret Carlisle Duncan, and Faye Linda Wachs, "The Gender of Audience Building: Televised Coverage of Women's and Men's NCAA Basketball," *Sociological Inquiry* 66, no. 4 (1996): 422–439.

17 Michael A. Messner, *Taking the Field: Women, Men & Sports* (Minneapolis: University of Minnesota Press, 2002).

18 Cooky, Messner, and Musto, "'It's Dude Time!'"

19 Fink, "Female Athletes."

20 Michela Musto, Cheryl Cooky, and Michael A. Messner, "'From Fizzle to Sizzle': Televised Sports News and the Production of Gender-Bland Sexism," *Gender & Society* 31, no. 5 (2017): 590.

21 Musto, Cooky, and Messner, 590.

22 Paul Davis, "Sexualization and Sexuality in Sport," in *Philosophical Perspectives on Gender in Sport and Physical Activity*, ed. Paul Davis and Charlene Weaving (New York: Routledge, 2010), 57–63.

23 Allen Guttman, *The Erotic in Sports* (New York: Columbia University Press, 1996).

24 Cooky, Messner, and Musto, "'It's Dude Time!'"; Helene A. Shugart, "She Shoots, She Scores: Mediated Constructions of Contemporary Female Athletes in Coverage of the 1999 US Women's Soccer Team," *Western Journal of Communication* 67, no. 1 (2003): 7; Emma Sherry, Angela Osborne, and Matthew Nicholson, "Images of Sports Women: A Review," *Sex Roles* 74, no. 7 (2016): 299–309.

25 Cooky, Messner, and Musto, "'It's Dude Time!'," 277.

26 Shugart, "She Shoots, She Scores."

27 Jaime Schultz, *Qualifying Times: Points of Change in U.S. Women's Sport* (Champaign: University of Illinois Press, 2014).

28 Hargreaves, *Sporting Females*, 163.

29 Timothy F. Grainey, *Beyond Bend It like Beckham: The Global Phenomenon of Women's Soccer* (Lincoln: University of Nebraska Press, 2012), 76.

30 Elsa Kristiansen, Trygve B. Broch, and Paul M. Pedersen, "Negotiating Gender in Professional Soccer: An Analysis of Female Footballers in the United States," *Choregia* 10, no. 1 (2014): 5–27.

31 Elizabeth Daniels and Heidi Wartena, "Athlete or Sex Symbol: What Boys Think of Media Representations of Female Athletes," *Sex Roles* 65, nos. 7–8 (2011): 566–579; Mary Jo Kane, Nicole M. LaVoi, and Janet S. Fink, "Exploring Elite Female Athletes' Interpretations of Sport Media Images: A Window into the Construction of Social Identity and 'Selling Sex' in Women's Sports," *Communication & Sport* 1, no. 3 (2013): 269–298.

32 George B. Cunningham, Janet S. Fink, and Linda Jean Kenix, "Choosing an Endorser for a Women's Sporting Event: The Interaction of Attractiveness and Expertise," *Sex*

Roles 58, nos. 5–6 (2008): 371–378; Janet S. Fink, George B. Cunningham, and Linda Jean Kensicki, "Using Athletes as Endorsers to Sell Women's Sport: Attractiveness vs. Expertise," *Journal of Sport Management* 18, no. 4 (2004): 350–367; Mary Jo Kane and Heather D. Maxwell, "Expanding the Boundaries of Sport Media Research: Using Critical Theory to Explore Consumer Reponses to Representations of Women's Sports," *Journal of Sport Management* 25, no. 3 (2011): 202–216.

33 Jayne Caudwell, "Gender, Feminism, and Football Studies," *Soccer & Society* 12, no. 3 (2011): 338; Rachael R. Smallwood, Natalie A. Brown, and Andrew C. Billings. "Female Bodies on Display: Attitudes regarding Female Athlete Photos in *Sports Illustrated*'s Swimsuit Issue and *ESPN: The Magazine*'s Body Issue," *Journal of Sports Media* 9, no. 1 (2014): 1–22.

34 Michael D. Giardina and Jennifer L. Metz, "All-American Girls? Corporatizing National Identity and Cultural Citizenship With/in the WUSA," in *Sport and Corporate Nationalisms*, ed. Michael L. Silk, David L. Andrews, and C. L. Cole (Oxford: Berg, 2004), 109–126.

35 Annelies Knoppers and Anthony Anthonissen, "Women's Soccer in the United States and the Netherlands: Differences and Similarities in Regimes of Inequalities," *Sociology of Sport Journal* 20, no. 4 (2003): 351–370.

36 Cheryl Cooky, Faye Linda Wachs, and Michael A. Messner, "It's Not about the Game: Don Imus, Race, Class, Gender and Sexuality in Contemporary Media," *Sociology of Sport Journal* 27, no. 2 (2010): 139–159.

37 Barbara Cox and Shona Thompson, "Multiple Bodies: Sportswomen, Soccer, and Sexuality," *International Review for the Sociology of Sport* 35, no. 1 (2000): 5–20; Schultz, *Qualifying Times*; Shugart, "She Shoots, She Scores."

38 Michela Musto and P. J. McGann, "Strike a Pose! The Femininity Effect in Collegiate Women's Sport," *Sociology of Sport Journal* 33, no. 2 (2016): 109.

39 Theberge, *Higher Goals*.

40 Jamie Skerski, "From Sideline to Centerfold: The Sexual Commodification of Female Sportscasters," in *Sex in Consumer Culture: The Erotic Content of Media and Marketing*, ed. Tom Reichert and Jacqueline Lambiase (New York: Routledge, 2006), 88; Barbara Thomas Coventry, "On the Sidelines: Sex and Racial Segregation in Television Sports Broadcasting," *Sociology of Sport Journal* 21, no. 3 (2004): 322–341.

41 Candace West and Don H. Zimmerman, "Doing Gender," *Gender & Society* 1, no. 2 (1987): 125–151.

42 Rachel Allison, "From Oversight to Autonomy: Gendered Organizational Change in Women's Soccer," *Social Currents* 4, no. 1 (2017): 71–86.

43 Elizabeth A. Armstrong et al., "'Good Girls': Gender, Social Class, and Slut Discourse on Campus," *Social Psychology Quarterly* 77, no. 2 (2014): 100–122; Matthew B. Ezzell, "'Barbie Dolls' on the Pitch: Identity Work, Defensive Othering, and Inequality in Women's Rugby," *Social Problems* 56, no. 1 (2009): 111–131.

44 Ann Pegoraro, "Look Who's Talking—Athletes on Twitter: A Case Study," *International Journal of Sport Communication* 3, no. 4 (2010): 501–514.

45 Toni Bruce and Marie Hardin, "Reclaiming Our Voices: Sportswomen and Social Media," in *Routledge Handbook of Sport and New Media*, ed. Andrew C. Billings and Marie Hardin (New York: Routledge, 2014), 311–319.

46 Grainey, *Beyond*, 80.

47 Evan Frederick et al., "Choosing between the One-Way or Two-Way Street: An Exploration of Relationship Promotion by Professional Athletes on Twitter," *Communication & Sport* 2, no. 1 (2014): 80–99.

48 Eileen Narcotta-Welp, "Going Solo: The Specter of the 1999ers, Hope Solo, and the 'Conscious Pariah,'" *Sport in Society* (forthcoming).

49 Brandi Watkins and Regina Lewis, "I Am Woman, but Not Roaring: An Examination of Similarities and Differences in How Male and Female Professional Athletes are Using Twitter," *Journal of Social Media in Society* 5, no. 3 (2016): 5–36.

Conclusion

1 Jeré Longman, *The Girls of Summer: The U.S. Women's Soccer Team and How It Changed the World* (New York: Harper Perennial, 2001).

2 Rachel Allison, "One Nation Under (Women's) Soccer?" *Gender & Society* (blog), April 6, 2015, https://gendersociety.wordpress.com/2015/04/06/one-nation-under -womens-soccer/.

3 Cheryl Cooky, "Striking Goals for Pay and Prize Parity in Sport," *Society Pages*, June 17, 2016, https://thesocietypages.org/papers/pay-and-prize-parity-in -soccer/.

4 Erin Whiteside and Amber Roessner, "Forgotten and Left Behind: Political Apathy and Privilege at Title IX's 40th Anniversary," *Communication & Sport* 6, no. 1 (2018): 3–24.

5 Cheryl Cooky, "'We Cannot Stand Idly By': A Necessary Call for a Public Sociology of Sport," *Sociology of Sport Journal* 34, no. 1 (2017): 1–11.

6 Lauren Vecsey, "Rapinoe Injury Reignites Turf, Player Safety Debate for USWNT," Fox Sports, December 5, 2015, http://www.foxsports.com/soccer/story/megan -rapinoe-uswnt-proclaim-outrage-field-conditions-stadium-training-grounds -hawaii-120515.

7 Carli Lloyd, "Why I'm Fighting for Equal Pay," *New York Times*, April 10, 2016, https://www.nytimes.com/2016/04/11/sports/soccer/carli-lloyd-why-im-fighting -for-equal-pay.html.

8 Elizabeth Cavalier and Kristine Newhall, "'Stick to Soccer': Fan Reaction and Inclusion Rhetoric on Social Media," *Sport in Society* (forthcoming).

9 Saeed Ahmed and Steve Almasy, "Women's World Cup: Carli Lloyd's Hat Trick Leads U.S. to Third Title," *CNN*, July 6, 2015, http://edition.cnn.com/2015/07/06/ football/womens-world-cup-final/.

10 Michelle T. Helstein, "Rethinking Community: Introducing the 'Whatever' Female Athlete," *Sociology of Sport Journal* 21, no. 1 (2005): 1–18.

11 Nicholas A. Smith, Thiphalak Chounthirath, and Huiyan Xiang, "Soccer-Related Injuries Treated in Emergency Departments: 1990–2014," *Pediatrics* 138, no. 4 (2016): e20160346.

12 Michael A. Messner, *Taking the Field: Women, Men & Sports* (Minneapolis: University of Minnesota Press, 2002).

13 Leslie Heywood and Shari L. Dworkin, *Built to Win: The Female Athlete as Cultural Icon* (Minneapolis: University of Minnesota Press, 2003).

14 Deborah L. Brake, *Getting in the Game: Title IX and the Women's Sports Revolution* (New York: New York University Press, 2010).

15 Brake.

16 Brake, 17.

17 Sara L. Crawley, Lara J. Foley, and Constance L. Shehan, *Gendering Bodies* (Lanham, Md.: Rowman & Littlefield, 2008).

18 Musto, Cooky, and Messner, "'From Fizzle to Sizzle.'"

19 Rebecca Joyce Kissane and Sarah Winslow, "Bonding and Abandoning: Gender, Social Interaction, and Relationships in Fantasy Sports," *Social Currents* 3, no. 3 (2016): 256–272; Erin Whiteside and Marie Hardin, "Women (Not) Watching Women: Leisure Time, Television, and Implications for Televised Coverage of Women's Sports," *Communication, Culture & Critique* 4, no. 2 (2011): 122–143.

20 Rick Eckstein, *How College Athletics Are Hurting Girls' Sports: The Pay-to-Play Pipeline* (New York: Rowman & Littlefield, 2017), 22.

21 Andrew M. Guest and Anne Luijten, "Fan Culture and Motivation in the Context of Successful Women's Professional Team Sports: A Mixed Methods Case Study of Portland Thorns Fandom," *Sport in Society* (forthcoming); Christopher Henderson, "Two Balls Is Too Many: Stadium Performance and Queerness among Portland's Rose City Riveters Supporters Club," *Sport in Society* (forthcoming).

22 Graham Hays, "United State of Soccer Represented in USC-West Virginia College Cup Final," espnW, December 3, 2016, http://www.espn.com/espnw/sports/article/18196581/ncaa-women-soccer-west-virginia-mountaineers-usc-trojans-represent-diversity-women-college-cup-final.

23 Rachel Allison, "From Oversight to Autonomy: Gendered Organizational Change in Women's Soccer," *Social Currents* 4, no. 1 (2017): 71–86.

24 Juliet Macur, "For Most in Women's Soccer, Hashtags Don't Pay the Bills," *New York Times*, April 25, 2016, https://www.nytimes.com/2016/04/26/sports/women-soccer-equal-pay.html?smid=tw-share.

25 Meg Linehan, "A Long Road to NWSL 2.0, but Hopeful First Steps," *Meg Linehan* (blog), July 8, 2015, http://www.meglinehan.com/blog/repost-a-long-road-to-nwsl-20-but-hopeful-first-steps-originally-from-bright-select-42214.

Appendix B

1 Shannon Kerwin and Larena Hoeber, "Collaborative Self-Ethnography: Navigating Self-Reflexivity in a Sport Management Context," *Journal of Sport Management* 29, no. 5 (2015): 498–509.

2 Orit Avishai, Lynne Gerber, and Jennifer Randles, "The Feminist Ethnographer's Dilemma: Reconciling Progressive Research Agendas with Fieldwork Realities," *Journal of Contemporary Ethnography* 42, no. 4 (2013): 397.

3 Matthew Ezzell, "Getting the Story Right: A Response to 'The Feminist Ethnographer's Dilemma,'" *Journal of Contemporary Ethnography* 42, no. 4 (2013): 449.

4 Rebecca Olive and Holly Thorpe, "Negotiating the 'F-Word' in the Field: Doing Feminist Ethnography in Action Sport Cultures," *Sociology of Sport Journal* 28, no. 4 (2011): 425.

5 Roni Berger, "Now I See It, Now I Don't: Researcher's Position and Reflexivity in Qualitative Research," *Qualitative Research* 15, no. 2 (2015): 220.

6 Rachel Allison, "From Oversight to Autonomy: Gendered Organizational Change in Women's Soccer," *Social Currents* 4, no. 1 (2017): 71–86.

7 Annette Lareau, "Cultural Knowledge and Social Inequality," *American Sociological Review* 80, no. 1 (2015): 1–27.

8 Avishai, Gerber, and Randles, "Feminist Ethnographer's Dilemma."

9 Olive and Thorpe, "Negotiating the 'F-Word.'"

10 Olive and Thorpe, 427.

11 Shane J. Blackman, "'Hidden Ethnography': Crossing Emotional Borders in Qualitative Accounts of Young People's Lives," *Sociology* 41, no. 4 (2007): 699–716.

12 Stina Bergman Blix and Asa Wettergren, "The Emotional Labor of Gaining and Maintaining Access to the Field," *Qualitative Research* 15, no. 6 (2015): 688–704.

13 Annie Irvine, Paul Drew, and Roy Sainsbury, "'Am I Not Answering Your Questions Properly?' Clarification, Adequacy and Responsiveness in Semi-structured Telephone and Face-to-Face Interviews," *Qualitative Research* 13, no. 1 (2013): 87–106.

14 Judith E. Sturges and Kathleen J. Hanrahan, "Comparing Telephone and Face-to-Face Qualitative Interviewing: a Research Note," *Qualitative Research* 4, no. 1 (2004): 107–118.

15 Colin Jerolmack and Alexandra K. Murphy, "The Ethical Dilemmas and Social Scientific Tradeoffs of Masking in Ethnography," *Sociological Methods & Research* (2017): doi:10.1177/0049124117701483.

Bibliography

Abrams, Nathan D. "Inhibited but Not 'Crowded Out': The Strange Fate of Soccer in the United States." *International Journal of the History of Sport* 12, no. 3 (1995): 1–17.

Acosta, R. Vivian, and Linda Jean Carpenter. "Women in Intercollegiate Sport: A Longitudinal, National Study. Thirty-Seven Year Update, 1977–2014." Unpublished manuscript. http://www.acostacarpenter.org. PDF file.

Adams, Carly, and Stacey Leavitt. "'It's Just Girls' Hockey': Troubling Progress Narratives in Girls' and Women's Sport." *International Review for the Sociology of Sport* 53, no. 2 (2018): 152–172.

Adams, Mary Louise. *Artistic Impressions: Figure Skating, Masculinity, and the Limits of Sport*. Toronto: University of Toronto Press, 2011.

Adams, Natalie, and Pamela Bettis. "Commanding the Room in Short Skirts: Cheering as the Embodiment of Ideal Girlhood." *Gender & Society* 17, no. 1 (2003): 73–91.

Adams, Terry, and C. A. Tuggle. "ESPN's Sports Center and Coverage of Women's Athletics: 'It's a Boys' Club.'" *Mass Communication and Society* 7, no. 2 (2004): 237–248.

Adjepong, Anima. "'We're like a Cute Rugby Team': How Whiteness and Heterosexuality Shape Women's Sense of Belonging in Rugby." *International Review for the Sociology of Sport* 52, no. 2 (2017): 209–222.

Ahmed, Saeed, and Steve Almasy. "Women's World Cup: Carli Lloyd's Hat Trick Leads U.S. to Third Title." *CNN*, July 6, 2015. http://edition.cnn.com/2015/07/06/football/womens-world-cup-final/.

Allison, Rachel. "Business or Cause? Gendered Institutional Logics in Women's Professional Soccer." *Journal of Sport & Social Issues* 40, no. 3 (2016): 237–262.

———. "From Oversight to Autonomy: Gendered Organizational Change in Women's Soccer." *Social Currents* 4, no. 1 (2017): 71–86.

———. "One Nation under (Women's) Soccer?" *Gender & Society* (blog), April 6, 2015. https://gendersociety.wordpress.com/2015/04/06/one-nation-under-womens-soccer/.

Anderson, Eric D. "'I Used to Think Women Were Weak': Orthodox Masculinity, Gender Segregation, and Sport." *Sociological Forum* 23, no. 2 (2008): 257–280.

———. "The Maintenance of Masculinity among the Stakeholders of Sport." *Sport Management Review* 12, no. 1 (2009): 3–14.

Andrews, David L. "Contextualizing Suburban Soccer: Consumer Culture, Lifestyle Differentiation and Suburban America." *Culture, Sport, and Society* 2, no. 3 (1999): 31–53.

———. *Sport-Commerce-Culture: Essays on Sport in Late Capitalist America.* New York: Peter Lang, 2006.

Andrews, David L., Robert Pitter, Detlev Zwick, and Darren Ambrose. "Soccer's Racial Frontier: Sport and the Suburbanization of Contemporary America." In *Entering the Field: New Perspectives on World Football*, edited by Gary Armstrong and Richard Giulianotti, 261–282. Oxford: Berg, 1997.

Arar, Han, and George Foster. "Women's Professional Soccer: Building a New League after WUSA Shutdown." Stanford Graduate School of Business Case E-411A, 2012.

Armstrong, Elizabeth A., Laura T. Hamilton, Elizabeth M. Armstrong, and J. Lotus Seeley. "'Good Girls': Gender, Social Class, and Slut Discourse on Campus." *Social Psychology Quarterly* 77, no. 2 (2014): 100–122.

Armstrong, Gary, and James Rosbrook-Thompson. "Coming to America: Historical Ontologies and United States Soccer." *Identities: Global Studies in Culture and Power* 17, no. 4 (2010): 348–371.

Atkinson, Michael. *Key Concepts in Sport and Exercise Research Methods.* London: SAGE, 2011.

Avishai, Orit, Lynne Gerber, and Jennifer Randles. "The Feminist Ethnographer's Dilemma: Reconciling Progressive Research Agendas with Fieldwork Realities." *Journal of Contemporary Ethnography* 42, no. 4 (2013): 394–426.

Azzarito, Laura. "Future Girls, Transcendent Femininities, and New Pedagogies: Toward Girls' Hybrid Bodies?" *Sport, Education, and Society* 15, no. 3 (2010): 261–275.

Banet-Weiser, Sarah. "Hoop Dreams: Professional Basketball and the Politics of Race and Gender." *Journal of Sport & Social Issues* 23, no. 4 (1999): 403–420.

Barnett, Barbara, and Marie C. Hardin. "Advocacy from the Liberal Feminist Playbook: The Framing of Title IX and Women's Sports in News Releases from the Women's Sports Foundation." *International Journal of Sport Communication* 4, no. 2 (2011): 178–197.

Berger, Roni. "Now I See It, Now I Don't: Researcher's Position and Reflexivity in Qualitative Research." *Qualitative Research* 15, no. 2 (2015): 219–234.

Billings, Andrew C., and Brittany D. Young. "Comparing Flagship News Programs: Women's Sports Coverage in ESPN's SportsCenter and FOX Sports 1's Sports Live." *Electronic News* 9, no. 1 (2015): 3–16.

Birrell, Susan. "Feminist Theories for Sport." In *Handbook of Sports Studies*, edited by Jay Coakley and Eric Dunning, 61–76. London: SAGE, 2000.

Blackman, Shane J. "'Hidden Ethnography': Crossing Emotional Borders in Qualitative Accounts of Young People's Lives." *Sociology* 41, no. 4 (2007): 699–716.

Blix, Stina Bergman, and Asa Wettergren. "The Emotional Labor of Gaining and Maintaining Access to the Field." *Qualitative Research* 15, no. 6 (2015): 688–704.

Brake, Deborah L. *Getting in the Game: Title IX and the Women's Sports Revolution.* New York: New York University Press, 2010.

Branch, Dwight. "A Resounding Soccer Success . . . in the U.S.?" In *Soccer Culture in America: Essays on the World's Sport in Red, White, and Blue*, edited by Yuya Kiuchi, 84–94. Jefferson, N.C.: McFarland, 2013.

Breeze, Maddie. "Analysing 'Seriousness' in Roller Derby: Speaking Critically with the Serious Leisure Perspective." *Sociological Research Online* 18, no. 4 (2013): 1–13.

———. *Seriousness and Women's Roller Derby: Gender, Organization, and Ambivalence.* New York: Palgrave Macmillan, 2015.

Broad, K. L. "The Gendered Unapologetic: Queer Resistance in Women's Sport." *Sociology of Sport Journal* 18, no. 2 (2001): 181–204.

Brown, Sean. "Critical Events or Critical Conditions: The 1999 Women's World Cup and the Women's United Soccer Association." *Soccer & Society* 7, nos. 2–3 (2006): 385–400.

Bruce, Toni. "Assessing the Sociology of Sport: On Media and Representations of Sports-women." *International Review for the Sociology of Sport* 50, nos. 4–5 (2015): 380–384.

———. "New Rules for New Times: Sportswomen and Media Representation in the Third Wave." *Sex Roles* 74, no. 7 (2016): 361–376.

———. "Reflections on Communication and Sport: On Women and Femininities." *Communication & Sport* 1, nos. 1–2 (2013): 125–137.

Bruce, Toni, and Marie Hardin. "Reclaiming Our Voices: Sportswomen and Social Media." In *Routledge Handbook of Sport and New Media*, edited by Andrew C. Billings and Marie Hardin, 311–319. New York: Routledge, 2014.

Buffington, Daniel Taylor. "Us and Them: U.S. Ambivalence toward the World Cup and American Nationalism." *Journal of Sport & Social Issues* 26, no. 2 (2012): 135–154.

Burstyn, Varda. *The Rites of Men: Manhood, Politics, and the Culture of Sport*. Toronto: University of Toronto Press, 1999.

Burton, Clare. "Merit and Gender: Organisations and the Mobilisation of Masculine Bias." *Australian Journal of Social Issues* 27, no. 2 (1987): 424–435.

Cahn, Susan K. *Coming on Strong: Gender and Sexuality in Women's Sport*. 2nd ed. Urbana: University of Illinois Press, 2015.

———. "From the 'Muscle Moll' to the 'Butch' Ballplayer: Mannishness, Lesbianism, and Homophobia in U.S. Women's Sport." *Feminist Studies* 19, no. 2 (1993): 343–368.

Camporesi, Sylvia. "Ethics of Regulating Competition for Women with Hyperandrogenism." *Clinics in Sports Medicine* 35, no. 2 (2016): 293–301.

Caudwell, Jayne. "Gender, Feminism, and Football Studies." *Soccer & Society* 12, no. 3 (2011): 330–344.

Cavalier, Elizabeth, and Kristine Newhall. "'Stick to Soccer': Fan Reaction and Inclusion Rhetoric on Social Media." *Sport in Society* (forthcoming).

Christopherson, Neal, Michelle Janning, and Eileen Diaz McConnell. "Two Kicks Forward, One Kick Back: A Content Analysis of Media Discourses on the 1999 Women's World Cup Soccer Championship." *Sociology of Sport Journal* 19, no. 2 (2012): 170–188.

Claringbould, Inge, and Johanna Adriaanse. "'Silver Cups versus Ice Creams': Parental Involvement in the Construction of Gender in the Field of Their Sons' Soccer." *Sociology of Sport Journal* 32, no. 2 (2015): 201–219.

Clement-Guillotin, Corentin, Aina Chalabaev, and Paul Fontayne. "Is Sport Still a Masculine Domain? A Psychological Glance." *International Journal of Sport Psychology* 43, no. 1 (2012): 1–12.

Coakley, Jay. "The Good Father: Parental Expectations and Youth Sports." *Leisure Studies* 25, no. 2 (2006): 153–163.

———. "The 'Logic' of Specialization." *Journal of Physical Education, Recreation, & Dance* 81, no. 8 (2010): 16–25.

———. "Youth Sports: What Counts as 'Positive Development?'" *Journal of Sport & Social Issues* 35, no. 3 (2011): 306–324.

Cole, C. L. "The Year That Girls Ruled." *Journal of Sport & Social Issues* 24, no. 1 (2000): 3–7.

Cole, C. L., and Amy Hribar. "Celebrity Feminism: Nike Style, Post-Fordism, Transcendence, and Consumer Power." *Sociology of Sport Journal* 12, no. 4 (1995): 347–369.

Collins, Sandra. "National Sports and Other Myths: The Failure of U.S. Soccer." *Soccer & Society* 7, nos. 2–3 (2006): 353–363.

Cooky, Cheryl. "Do Girls Rule? Understanding Popular Culture Images of 'Girl Power!' and Sport." In *Learning Culture through Sports: Perspectives on Society and Organized Sports*, edited by Sandra Spickard Prettyman and Brian Lampman, 210–226. Lanham, Md.: Rowman & Littlefield, 2011.

———. "'Girls Just Aren't Interested': The Social Construction of Interest in Girls' Sport." *Sociological Perspectives* 52, no. 2 (2009): 259–284.

———. "Striking Goals for Pay and Prize Parity in Sport." *Society Pages*, June 17, 2016. https://thesocietypages.org/papers/pay-and-prize-parity-in-soccer/.

———. "'We Cannot Stand Idly By': A Necessary Call for a Public Sociology of Sport." *Sociology of Sport Journal* 34, no. 1 (2017): 1–11.

Cooky, Cheryl, and Nicole M. LaVoi. "Playing but Losing: Women's Sports after Title IX." *Contexts* 11, no. 1 (2012): 42–46.

Cooky, Cheryl, and Mary G. McDonald. "'If You Let Me Play': Young Girls' Insider-Other Narratives of Sport." *Sociology of Sport Journal* 22, no. 2 (2005): 158–177.

Cooky, Cheryl, Michael A. Messner, and Robin Hextrum. "Women Play Sports, but Not on TV: A Longitudinal Study of Televised News Media." *Communication & Sport* 1, no. 3 (2013): 203–230.

Cooky, Cheryl, Michael A. Messner, and Michaela Musto. "'It's Dude Time!' A Quarter Century of Excluding Women's Sports in Televised News and Highlights Shows." *Communication & Sport* 3, no. 3 (2015): 261–287.

Cooky, Cheryl, and Lauren Rauscher. "Girls and the Racialization of Female Bodies in Sport Contexts." In *Child's Play: Sport in Kids' Worlds*, edited by Michael Messner and Michela Musto, 61–81. New Brunswick, N.J.: Rutgers University Press, 2016.

Cooky, Cheryl, Faye Linda Wachs, and Michael A. Messner. "It's Not about the Game: Don Imus, Race, Class, Gender and Sexuality in Contemporary Media." *Sociology of Sport Journal* 27, no. 2 (2010): 139–159.

Coombs, Danielle Sarver. "Pitch Perfect: How the U.S. Women's National Soccer Team Brought the Game Home." In Soccer Culture in America: Essays on the World's Sport in Red, White, and Blue, edited by Yuya Kiuchi, 160–178. Jefferson, N.C.: McFarland, 2013.

Cousens, Laura, and Trevor Slack. "Field-Level Change: The Case of North American Major League Professional Sports." *Journal of Sport Management* 19, no. 1 (2005): 13–42.

Coventry, Barbara Thomas. "On the Sidelines: Sex and Racial Segregation in Television Sports Broadcasting." *Sociology of Sport Journal* 21, no. 3 (2004): 322–341.

Cox, Barbara, and Shona Thompson. "Multiple Bodies: Sportswomen, Soccer, and Sexuality." *International Review for the Sociology of Sport* 35, no. 1 (2000): 5–20.

Cranmer, Gregory A., Maria Brann, and Nicholas D. Bowman. "Male Athletes, Female Aesthetics: The Continued Ambivalence toward Female Athletes in ESPN's *The Body Issue*." *International Journal of Sport Communication* 7, no. 2 (2014): 145–165.

Crawley, Sara L. "Visible Bodies, Vicarious Masculinity, and the 'Gender Revolution': A Comment on England." *Gender & Society* 25, no. 1 (2011): 108–112.

Crawley, Sara L., Lara J. Foley, and Constance L. Shehan. *Gendering Bodies*. Lanham, Md.: Rowman & Littlefield, 2008.

Crosset, Todd W. *Outsiders in the Clubhouse: The World of Women's Professional Golf*. Albany: State University of New York Press, 1995.

Crouse, Karen. "Why Female Athletes Remain on Sport's Periphery." *Communication & Sport* 1, no. 3 (2013): 237–240.

Cunningham, George, Janet S. Fink, and Linda Jean Kenix. "Choosing an Endorser for a Women's Sporting Event: The Interaction of Attractiveness and Expertise." *Sex Roles* 58, nos. 5–6 (2008): 371–378.

Daniels, Elizabeth, and Heidi Wartena. "Athlete or Sex Symbol: What Boys Think of Media Representations of Female Athletes." *Sex Roles* 65, nos. 7–8 (2011): 566–579.

Dart, Jon. "New Media, Professional Sport, and Political Economy." *Journal of Sport & Social Issues* 38, no. 6 (2014): 528–547.

Davis, Georgiann. *Contesting Intersex: The Dubious Diagnosis*. New York: New York University Press, 2015.

Davis, Georgiann, and Erin L. Murphy. "Intersex Bodies as States of Exception: An Empirical Explanation for Unnecessary Surgical Modification." *Feminist Formations* 25, no. 2 (2013): 129–152.

Davis, Paul. "Sexualization and Sexuality in Sport." In *Philosophical Perspectives on Gender in Sport and Physical Activity*, edited by Paul Davis and Charlene Weaving, 57–63. New York: Routledge, 2010.

Davis-Delano, Laurel R., April Pollock, and Jennifer Ellsworth Vose. "Apologetic Behavior among Female Athletes: A New Questionnaire and Initial Results." *International Review for the Sociology of Sport* 44, nos. 2–3 (2009): 131–150.

Dettmar, Benjamin James. "'Fast-Kicking, Low-Scoring, and Ties': How Popular Culture Can Help the Global Game Become America's Game." In *Soccer Culture in America: Essays on the World's Sport in Red, White, and Blue*, edited by Yuya Kiuchi, 95–119. Jefferson, N.C.: McFarland, 2013.

Duerr, Glen M. E. "Becoming Apple Pie: Soccer as the Fifth Major Team Sport in the United States?" In *Soccer Culture in America: Essays on the World's Sport in Red, White, and Blue*, edited by Yuya Kiuchi, 143–159. Jefferson, N.C.: McFarland, 2013.

Dunn, Carrie. "Elite Footballers as Role Models: Promoting Young Women's Football Participation." *Soccer & Society* 17, no. 6 (2016): 843–855.

———. *Football and the Women's World Cup: Organisation, Media, and Fandom*. New York: Palgrave Pivot, 2016.

Dure, Beau. *Long-Range Goals: The Success Story of Major League Soccer*. Washington, D.C.: Potomac Books, 2010.

Dworkin, Shari L. "'Holding Back': Negotiating a Glass Ceiling on Women's Muscular Strength." *Sociological Perspectives* 44, no. 3 (2001): 333–350.

Dworkin, Shari L., and Michael A. Messner. "Just Do . . . What? Sport, Bodies, Gender." In *Gender and Sport: A Reader*, edited by Sheila Scraton and Anne Flintoff, 17–29. New York: Routledge, 2002.

Dworkin, Shari L., and Faye Linda Wachs. *Body Panic: Gender, Health, and the Selling of Fitness*. New York: New York University Press, 2009.

Eckstein, Rick. *How College Athletics Are Hurting Girls' Sports: The Pay-to-Play Pipeline*. New York: Rowman & Littlefield, 2017.

Esmonde, Katelyn, Cheryl Cooky, and David L. Andrews. "'It's Supposed to Be about the Love of the Game, Not the Love of Aaron Rodgers' Eyes': Challenging the Exclusions of Women Sports Fans." *Sociology of Sport Journal* 32, no. 1 (2015): 22–48.

Ezzell, Matthew B. "'Barbie Dolls' on the Pitch: Identity Work, Defensive Othering, and Inequality in Women's Rugby." *Social Problems* 56, no. 1 (2009): 111–131.

———. "Getting the Story Right: A Response to 'The Feminist Ethnographer's Dilemma.'" *Journal of Contemporary Ethnography* 42, no. 4 (2013): 439–450.

Felshin, Jan. "The Triple Option . . . for Women in Sport." *Quest* 21, no. 1 (1974): 36–40.

Ferez, Sylvain. "From Women's Exclusion to Gender Institution: A Brief History of the Sexual Categorisation Process in Sport." *International Journal of the History of Sport* 29, no. 2 (2012): 272–285.

Fields, Sarah K. *Female Gladiators: Gender, Law, and Contact Sport in America*. Chicago: University of Illinois Press, 2005.

Fink, Janet S. "Female Athletes, Women's Sport and the Sport-Media-Commercial Complex: Have We Really 'Come a Long Way, Baby'?" *Sport Management Review* 18, no. 3 (2015): 331–342.

———. "Hiding in Plain Sight: The Embedded Nature of Sexism in Sport." *Journal of Sport Management* 30, no. 1 (2016): 1–7.

———. "Homophobia and the Marketing of Female Athletes and Women's Sport." In *Sexual Orientation and Gender Identity in Sport: Essays from Activists, Coaches, and Scholars*, edited by George B. Cunningham, 49–60. College Station, Tex.: Center for Sport Management Research and Education, 2012.

Fink, Janet S., George B. Cunningham, and Linda Jean Kensicki. "Using Athletes as Endorsers to Sell Women's Sport: Attractiveness vs. Expertise." *Journal of Sport Management* 18, no. 4 (2004): 350–367.

Fink, Janet S., Mary Jo Kane, and Nicole M. LaVoi. "Freedom to Choose: Elite Female Athletes' Preferred Representations within Endorsement Opportunities." *Journal of Sport Management* 28, no. 2 (2014): 207–219.

Frederick, Evan, Choong Hoon Lim, Galen Clavio, Paul M. Pederson, and Lauren Burch. "Choosing between the One-Way or Two-Way Street: An Exploration of Relationship Promotion by Professional Athletes on Twitter." *Communication & Sport* 2, no. 1 (2014): 80–99.

Friedman, Hilary Levey. *Playing to Win: Raising Children in a Competitive Culture*. Berkeley: University of California Press, 2013.

Gems, Gerald R., and Gertrud Pfister. *Understanding American Sports*. New York: Routledge, 2009.

Genz, Stephanie. "Third Way/ve: The Politics of Postfeminism." *Feminist Theory* 7, no. 3 (2006): 333–353.

Giardina, Michael D., and Jennifer L. Metz. "All-American Girls? Corporatizing National Identity and Cultural Citizenship with/in the WUSA." In *Sport and Corporate Nationalisms*, edited by Michael L. Silk, David L. Andrews, and C. L. Cole, 109–126. Oxford: Berg, 2004.

Gill, Rosalind. "Postfeminist Media Culture: Elements of a Sensibility." *European Journal of Cultural Studies* 10, no. 2 (2007): 147–166.

Gottzén, Lucas, and Tamar Kremer-Sadlick. "Fatherhood and Youth Sports: A Balancing Act between Care and Expectations." *Gender & Society* 26, no. 4 (2012): 639–664.

Grainey, Timothy F. *Beyond Bend It like Beckham: The Global Phenomenon of Women's Soccer*. Lincoln: University of Nebraska Press, 2012.

Griffin, Pat. *Strong Women, Deep Closets: Lesbians and Homophobia in Sport*. Champaign, Ill.: Human Kinetics Press, 1998.

Grindstaff, Laura, and Emily West. "Cheerleading and the Gendered Politics of Sport." *Social Problems* 53, no. 4 (2006): 500–518.

Guest, Andrew M., and Stephanie Cox. "Using Athletes as Role Models? Conceptual and Empirical Perspectives from a Sample of Elite Women Soccer Players." *International Journal of Sport Science and Coaching* 4, no. 4 (2009): 567–581.

Guest, Andrew M., and Anne Luijten. "Fan Culture and Motivation in the Context of Successful Women's Professional Team Sports: A Mixed Methods Case Study of Portland Thorns Fandom." *Sport in Society* (forthcoming).

Guttman, Allen. *The Erotic in Sports*. New York: Columbia University Press, 1996.

Hall, M. Ann. "The Discourse of Gender and Sport: From Femininity to Feminism." *Sociology of Sport Journal* 5, no. 4 (1988): 330–340.

Han, Arar, and George Foster. "Women's Professional Soccer: Building a New League after WUSA Shutdown." Stanford Graduate School of Business Case E-411A, 2012.

Hanis-Martin, Jennifer L. "Embodying Contradictions: The Case of Professional Women's Basketball." *Journal of Sport & Social Issues* 30, no. 3 (2006): 265–288.

Hardin, Marie. "Stopped at the Gate: Women's Sports, 'Reader Interest,' and Decision Making by Editors." *Journalism & Mass Communication Quarterly* 82, no. 1 (2005): 62–77.

Hardin, Marie, and Jennifer D. Greer. "The Influence of Gender-Role Socialization, Media Use and Sports Participation on Perceptions of Gender-Appropriate Sports." *Journal of Sport Behavior* 32, no. 2 (2009): 207–226.

Hardin, Marie, and Stacie Shain. "Female Sports Journalists: Are We There Yet? No." *Newspaper Research Journal* 26, no. 4 (2005): 22–35.

———. "Strength in Numbers? The Experiences and Attitudes of Women in Sports Media Careers." *Journalism & Mass Communication Quarterly* 82, no. 4 (2005): 804–819.

Hargreaves, Jennifer. "Querying Sport Feminism: Personal or Political?" In *Sport and Modern Social Theorists*, edited by Richard Giulianotti, 187–206. New York: Palgrave Macmillan, 2004.

———. *Sporting Females: Critical Issues in the History and Sociology of Women's Sports.* New York: Routledge, 2002.

Harrison, Anthony Kwame. "Black Skiing, Everyday Racism, and the Racial Spatiality of Whiteness." *Journal of Sport & Social Issues* 37, no. 4 (2013): 315–339.

Hays, Graham. "United State of Soccer Represented in USC-West Virginia College Cup Final." espnW, December 3, 2016. http://www.espn.com/espnw/sports/article/18196581/ncaa-women-soccer-west-virginia-mountaineers-usc-trojans-represent-diversity-women-college-cup-final.

Helstein, Michelle T. "Rethinking Community: Introducing the 'Whatever' Female Athlete." *Sociology of Sport Journal* 21, no. 1 (2005): 1–18.

Henderson, Christopher. "Two Balls Is Too Many: Stadium Performance and Queerness among Portland's Rose City Riveters Supporters Club." *Sport in Society* (forthcoming).

Henne, Kathryn E. *Testing for Athlete Citizenship: Regulating Doping and Sex in Sport.* New Brunswick, N.J.: Rutgers University Press, 2015.

Heywood, Leslie, and Shari L. Dworkin. *Built to Win: The Female Athlete as Cultural Icon.* Minneapolis: University of Minnesota Press, 2003.

Hodler, Matthew R., and Cathryn Lucas-Carr. "'The Mother of All Comebacks': A Critical Analysis of the Fitspirational Comeback Narrative of Dara Torres." *Communication & Sport* 4, no. 4 (2016): 442–459.

Hull, Kevin, Lauren R. Smith, and Annelie Schmittel. "Form or Function? An Examination of ESPN Magazine's 'Body Issue.'" *Visual Communication Quarterly* 22, no. 2 (2015): 106–117.

Humes, Mike. "2014 World Cup Final on ABC: Most-Watched Men's World Cup Championship." *ESPN*, July 14, 2014. http://espnmediazone.com/us/press-releases/2014/07/2014-world-cup-final-on-abc-most-watched-mens-world-cup-championship-ever/.

Irvine, Annie, Paul Drew, and Roy Sainsbury. "'Am I Not Answering Your Questions Properly?' Clarification, Adequacy and Responsiveness in Semi-structured Telephone and Face-to-Face Interviews." *Qualitative Research* 13, no. 1 (2013): 87–106.

Jackson, Kenneth T. *Crabgrass Frontier: The Suburbanization of the United States.* New York: Oxford University Press, 1985.

Jeanes, Ruth. "'I'm into High Heels and Makeup but I Still Love Football': Exploring Gender Identity and Football Participation with Preadolescent Girls." *Soccer & Society* 12, no. 3 (2011): 402–420.

Jerolmack, Colin, and Alexandra K. Murphy. "The Ethical Dilemmas and Social Scientific Tradeoffs of Masking in Ethnography." *Sociological Methods & Research* (2017): doi:10.1177/0049124117701483.

Kane, Mary Jo. "The Better Sportswomen Get, the More the Media Ignore Them." *Communication & Sport* 1, no. 3 (2013): 231–236.

———. "Resistance/Transformation of the Oppositional Binary: Exposing Sport as a Continuum." *Journal of Sport & Social Issues* 19, no. 2 (1995): 191–218.

———. "Sex Sells Sex, Not Women's Sports." *Nation*, August 2011.

Kane, Mary Jo, Nicole M. LaVoi, and Janet S. Fink. "Exploring Elite Female Athletes' Interpretations of Sport Media Images: A Window into the Construction of Social Identity and 'Selling Sex' in Women's Sports." *Communication & Sport* 1, no. 3 (2013): 269–298.

Kane, Mary Jo, and Heather D. Maxwell. "Expanding the Boundaries of Sport Media Research: Using Critical Theory to Explore Consumer Reponses to Representations of Women's Sports." *Journal of Sport Management* 25, no. 3 (2011): 202–216.

Kane, Mary Jo, and E. E. Snyder. "Sport Typing: The Social 'Containment' of Women in Sport." *Arena Review* 13, no. 2 (1989): 77–96.

Karkazis, Katrina, Rebecca Jordan-Young, Georgiann Davis, and Sylvia Camporesi. "Out of Bounds? A Critique of the New Policies on Hyperandrogenism in Elite Female Athletes." *American Journal of Bioethics* 12, no. 7 (2012): 3–16.

Kerwin, Shannon, and Larena Hoeber. "Collaborative Self-Ethnography: Navigating Self-Reflexivity in a Sport Management Context." *Journal of Sport Management* 29, no. 5 (2015): 498–509.

Keyes, David. "The Domestication of American Soccer." In *Soccer Culture in America: Essays on the World's Sport in Red, White, and Blue*, edited by Yuya Kiuchi, 9–24. Jefferson, N.C.: McFarland, 2013.

Kilpatrick, David. "Amnesia and Animosity: An Assessment of Soccer in the States." *Sport in Society* 20, nos. 5–6 (2017): 627–640.

Kimmel, Michael. "Baseball and the Reconstitution of American Masculinity, 1880–1920." In *Sport, Men, and the Gender Order: Critical Feminist Perspectives*, edited by Don Sabo and Michael Messner, 55–66. Champaign, Ill.: Human Kinetics Press, 2005.

King, Samantha. "Marketing Generosity: The Avon Worldwide Fund for Women's Health and the Reinvention of Global Corporate Citizenship." In *Sport and Corporate Nationalisms*, edited by Michael L. Silk, David L. Andrews, and C. L. Cole, 83–108. Oxford: Berg, 2004.

Kissane, Rebecca Joyce, and Sarah Winslow. "Bonding and Abandoning: Gender, Social Interaction, and Relationships in Fantasy Sports." *Social Currents* 3, no. 3 (2016): 256–272.

Kiuchi, Yuya, ed. *Soccer Culture in America: Essays on the World's Sport in Red, White, and Blue*. Jefferson, N.C.: McFarland, 2013.

Knoppers, Annelies, and Anthony Anthonissen. "Women's Soccer in the United States and the Netherlands: Differences and Similarities in Regimes of Inequalities." *Sociology of Sport Journal* 20, no. 4 (2003): 351–370.

Knoppers, Annelies, and Agnes Elling. "'We Do Not Engage in Promotional Journalism': Discursive Strategies Used by Sport Journalists to Describe the Selection Process." *International Review for the Sociology of Sport* 39, no. 1 (2004): 57–73.

Koivula, Nathalie. "Perceived Characteristics of Sports Categorized as Gender-Neutral, Feminine, and Masculine." *Journal of Sport Behavior* 24, no. 4 (2001): 377–393.

Krane, Vikki. "We Can Be Athletic and Feminine, but Do We Want To? Challenging Hegemonic Femininity in Women's Sport." *Quest* 53, no. 1 (2001): 115–133.

Kristiansen, Elsa, Trygve B. Broch, and Paul M. Pedersen. "Negotiating Gender in Professional Soccer: An Analysis of Female Footballers in the United States." *Choregia* 10, no. 1 (2014): 5–27.

Lareau, Annette. "Cultural Knowledge and Social Inequality." *American Sociological Review* 80, no. 1 (2015): 1–27.

———. *Unequal Childhoods: Class, Race, and Family Life.* 2nd ed. Berkeley: University of California Press, 2011.

Laurendeau, Jason, and Nancy Shahara. "'Women Could Be Every Bit as Good as Guys': Reproductive and Resistant Agency in Two 'Action' Sports." *Journal of Sport & Social Issues* 32, no. 1 (2008): 24–47.

Lenskyj, Helen Jefferson. *Out on the Field: Gender, Sport and Sexualities.* Toronto: Women's Press, 2003.

Leonard, David J. *Playing While White: Privilege and Power On and Off the Field.* Seattle: University of Washington Press, 2017.

Lindner, Andrew M., and Daniel N. Hawkins. "Globalization, Culture Wars, and Attitudes toward Soccer in America: An Empirical Assessment of How Soccer Explains the World." *Sociological Quarterly* 53, no. 1 (2012): 68–91.

Linehan, Meg. "A Long Road to NWSL 2.0, but Hopeful First Steps." *Meg Linehan* (blog), July 8, 2015. http://www.meglinehan.com/blog/repost-a-long-road-to-nwsl-20-but-hopeful-first-steps-originally-from-bright-select-42214.

Lloyd, Carli. "Why I'm Fighting for Equal Pay." *New York Times*, April 10, 2016. https://www.nytimes.com/2016/04/11/sports/soccer/carli-lloyd-why-im-fighting-for-equal-pay.html.

Longman, Jeré. "After World Cup Thrills, Players Return to Unstable Women's League." *New York Times*, August 8, 2011. http://www.nytimes.com/2011/08/09/sports/soccer/unsteady-financial-footing-for-womens-soccer-league.html.

———. *The Girls of Summer: The U.S. Women's Soccer Team and How It Changed the World.* New York: Harper Perennial, 2001.

Love, Adam, and Kimberly Kelly. "Equity or Essentialism? U.S. Courts and the Legitimation of Girls' Teams in High School Sport." *Gender & Society* 25, no. 2 (2011): 227–249.

Lucas, Shelley. "Nike's Commercial Solution: Girls, Sneakers, and Salvation." *International Review for the Sociology of Sport* 35, no. 2 (2000): 149–164.

Macur, Juliet. "For Most in Women's Soccer, Hashtags Don't Pay the Bills." *New York Times*, April 25, 2016. https://www.nytimes.com/2016/04/26/sports/women-soccer-equal-pay.html?smid=tw-share.

Markovits, Andrei S., and Emily Albertson. *Sportista! Female Fandom in the United States.* Philadelphia: Temple University Press, 2012.

Markovits, Andrei S., and Adam I. Green. "FIFA, the Video Game: A Major Vehicle for Soccer's Popularization in the United States." *Sport in Society* 20, nos. 5–6 (2016): 716–734.

Markovits, Andrei S., and Steven L. Hellerman. *Offside: Soccer and American Exceptionalism.* Princeton: Princeton University Press, 2001.

———. "Women's Soccer in the United States: Yet Another American Exceptionalism." *Soccer & Society* 4, nos. 2–3 (2003): 14–29.

Markula, Pirkko. "Beyond the Perfect Body: Women's Body Image Distortion in Fitness Magazine Discourse." *Journal of Sport & Social Issues* 25, no. 2 (2001): 158–179.

Marston, Kevin Tallec. "Rethinking 'Ethnic' Soccer: The National Junior Challenge Cup and the Transformation of American Soccer's Identity (1935–1976)." *Soccer & Society* 18, nos. 2–3 (2017): 330–347.

Martinez, Dolores P. "Soccer in the USA: 'Holding Out for a Hero?'" *Soccer & Society* 9, no. 2 (2008): 231–243.

McDonagh, Eileen, and Laura Pappano. *Playing with the Boys: Why Separate Is Not Equal in Sports.* New York: Oxford University Press, 2008.

McDonald, Mary G. "The Marketing of the Women's National Basketball Association and the Making of Postfeminism." *International Review for the Sociology of Sport* 35, no. 1 (2000): 35–47.

———. "Queering Whiteness: The Particular Case of the Women's National Basketball Association." *Sociological Perspectives* 45, no. 4 (2002): 379–396.

McRobbie, Angela. *The Aftermath of Feminism: Gender, Culture, and Social Change.* Thousand Oaks, Calif.: SAGE, 2009.

Meân, Lindsey J. "The 99ers: Celebrating the Mythological." *Journal of Sports Media* 10, no. 2 (2015): 31–43.

Messner, Michael A. "Gender Ideologies, Youth Sports, and the Production of Soft Essentialism." *Sociology of Sport Journal* 28, no. 2 (2011): 151–170.

———. *It's All for the Kids: Gender, Families, and Youth Sports.* Berkeley: University of California Press, 2009.

———. *Out of Play: Critical Essays on Gender & Sport.* New York: State University of New York Press, 2007.

———. "Sports and Male Domination: The Female Athlete as Contested Ideological Terrain." *Sociology of Sport Journal* 5, no. 3 (1988): 197–211.

———. *Taking the Field: Women, Men, and Sports.* Minneapolis: University of Minnesota Press, 2002.

Messner, Michael A., Margaret Carlisle Duncan, and Faye Linda Wachs. "The Gender of Audience Building: Televised Coverage of Women's and Men's NCAA Basketball." *Sociological Inquiry* 66, no. 4 (1996): 422–439.

Messner, Michael A., and Michela Musto, eds. *Child's Play: Sport in Kids' Worlds.* New Brunswick, N.J.: Rutgers University Press, 2016.

Messner, Michael A., and Nancy M. Solomon. "Social Justice and Men's Interests: The Case of Title IX." *Journal of Sport & Social Issues* 31, no. 2 (2007): 162–178.

Milner, Adrienne, and Jomills Henry Braddock, III. *Sex Segregation in Sports: Why Separate Is Not Equal.* Santa Barbara, Calif.: Praeger, 2016.

Montez de Oca, Jeffrey. *Discipline and Indulgence: College Football, Media, and the American Way of Life during the Cold War.* New Brunswick, N.J.: Rutgers University Press, 2013.

Muller, Tiffany. "'Lesbian Community' in Women's National Basketball Association (WNBA) Spaces." *Social & Cultural Geography* 8, no. 1 (2007): 9–28.

Muller Myrdahl, Tiffany. "'Family-Friendly' without the Double Entendre: A Spatial Analysis of Normative Game Spaces and Lesbian Fans." *Journal of Lesbian Studies* 13, no. 1 (2009): 291–305.

———. "Producing Gender-Normative Spaces in U.S. Women's Professional Soccer." In *Stadium Worlds: Football, Space, and the Built Environment*, edited by Sybille Frank and Silke Steets, 195–212. New York: Routledge, 2010.

Musto, Michela, Cheryl Cooky, and Michael A. Messner. "'From Fizzle to Sizzle': Televised Sports News and the Production of Gender-Bland Sexism." *Gender & Society* 31, no. 5 (2017): 573–596.

Musto, Michela, and P. J. McGann. "Strike a Pose! The Femininity Effect in Collegiate Women's Sport." *Sociology of Sport Journal* 33, no. 2 (2016): 101–112.

Narcotta-Welp, Eileen. "A Black Fly in White Milk: The 1999 Women's World Cup, Briana Scurry, and the Politics of Inclusion." *Journal of Sport History* 42, no. 3 (2016): 382–393.

———. "Going Solo: The Specter of the 1999ers and Hope Solo as the 'Conscious Pariah.'" *Sport in Society* (forthcoming).

Nash, Tim. *It's Not the Glory: The Remarkable First Thirty Years of U.S. Women's Soccer.* Morrisville, N.C.: Lulu, 2016.

National Federation of State High School Associations. "2013–14 Annual Report." http://www.nfhs.org/media/1014511/2013-14-annual-report_website.pdf.

Nelson, Mariah Burton. *The Stronger Women Get, the More Men Love Football*. New York: Harcourt, Brace, 1994.

Nicolaides, Becky. "How Hell Moved from the City to the Suburbs: Urban Scholars and Changing Perceptions of Authentic Community." In *The New Suburban History*, edited by Kevin M. Kruse and Thomas J. Sugrue, 80–98. Chicago: University of Chicago Press, 2006.

Olive, Rebecca, and Holly Thorpe. "Negotiating the 'F-Word' in the Field: Doing Feminist Ethnography in Action Sport Cultures." *Sociology of Sport Journal* 28, no. 4 (2011): 421–440.

Pegoraro, Ann. "Look Who's Talking—Athletes on Twitter: A Case Study." *International Journal of Sport Communication* 3, no. 4 (2010): 501–514.

Pfister, Gertrud. "Assessing the Sociology of Sport: On Women and Football." *International Review for the Sociology of Sport* 50, nos. 4–5 (2015): 563–569.

Rauscher, Lauren, and Cheryl Cooky. "Ready for Anything the World Gives Her? A Critical Look at Sports-Based Positive Youth Development for Girls." *Sex Roles* 74, no. 7 (2015): 288–298.

Reck, Gregory G., and Bruce Allen Dick. *American Soccer: History, Culture, Class*. Jefferson, N.C.: McFarland, 2015.

Reger, Jo. *Everywhere and Nowhere: Contemporary Feminism in the United States*. Oxford: Oxford University Press, 2012.

Ring, Jennifer. *Stolen Bases: Why American Girls Don't Play Baseball*. Champaign: University of Illinois Press, 2013.

Risman, Barbara J., and Elizabeth Seale. "Betwixt and Between: Gender Contradictions among Middle Schoolers." In *Families as They Really Are*, edited by Barbara J. Risman, 340–361. New York: Norton, 2010.

Rohrbaugh, J. B. "Femininity on the Line." *Psychology Today* 13, no. 3 (1979): 31–33.

Rowe, David. "Assessing the Sociology of Sport: On Media and Power." *International Review for the Sociology of Sport* 50, nos. 4–5 (2015): 575–579.

Sartore, Melanie L., and George B. Cunningham. "The Lesbian Stigma in the Sport Context: Implications for Women of Every Sexual Orientation." *Quest* 61, no. 3 (2009): 289–305.

Satterlee, Thom. "Making Soccer a 'Kick in the Grass': The Media's Role in Promoting a Marginal Sport, 1975–1977." *International Review for the Sociology of Sport* 36, no. 3 (2001): 305–317.

Schultz, Jaime. *Qualifying Times: Points of Change in U.S. Women's Sport*. Champaign: University of Illinois Press, 2014.

Scurry, Briana. "Women's World Cup Champ: Today Women's Players Are Appreciated for Their Achievements—Not for How They Look." *Time*, July 6, 2015. http://time.com/3947113/world-cup-women-players-today/.

Seese, Dennis J. "New Traditionalists: The Emergence of Modern America and the Birth of the MLS Coalition." In *Soccer Culture in America: Essays on the World's Sport in Red, White, and Blue*, edited by Yuya Kiuchi, 43–70. Jefferson, N.C.: McFarland, 2013.

Shakib, Sohaila, and Michele D. Dunbar. "The Social Construction of Female and Male High School Basketball Participation: Reproducing the Gender Order through a Two-Tiered Sporting Institution." *Sociological Perspectives* 45, no. 4 (2002): 353–378.

Sherry, Emma, Angela Osborne, and Matthew Nicholson. "Images of Sports Women: A Review." *Sex Roles* 74, no. 7 (2016): 299–309.

Shugart, Helene A. "She Shoots, She Scores: Mediated Constructions of Contemporary Female Athletes in Coverage of the 1999 US Women's Soccer Team." *Western Journal of Communication* 67, no. 1 (2003): 1–31.

Silk, Michael L., David L. Andrews, and C. L. Cole, eds. *Sport and Corporate Nationalisms.* Oxford: Berg, 2004.

Skerski, Jamie. "From Sideline to Centerfold: The Sexual Commodification of Female Sportscasters." In *Sex in Consumer Culture: The Erotic Content of Media and Marketing,* edited by Tom Reichert and Jacqueline Lambiase, 87–106. New York: Routledge, 2006.

Skogvang, Bente Ovèdie. "Players' and Coaches' Experiences with the Gendered Sport/Media Complex in Elite Football." In *Gender and Sport: Changes and Challenges,* edited by Gertrud Pfister and Mari Kristin Sisjord, 103–122. New York: Waxmann, 2013.

Smallwood, Rachael R., Natalie A. Brown, and Andrew C. Billings. "Female Bodies on Display: Attitudes regarding Female Athlete Photos in *Sports Illustrated*'s Swimsuit Issue and *ESPN: The Magazine*'s Body Issue." *Journal of Sports Media* 9, no. 1 (2014): 1–22.

Smith, Nicholas A., Thiphalak Chounthirath, and Huiyan Xiang. "Soccer-Related Injuries Treated in Emergency Departments: 1990–2014." *Pediatrics* 138, no. 4 (2016): e20160346.

Solo, Hope, and Ann Killion. *Solo: A Memoir of Hope.* New York: HarperCollins, 2012.

Southall, Richard M., and Mark S. Nagel. "Marketing Professional Soccer in the United States: Lessons in Exchange Theory and Cause-Related Marketing." *Smart Journal* 3, no. 2 (2007): 54–69.

Spaaij, Ramon, Karen Farquharson, and Timothy Marjoribanks. "Sport and Social Inequalities." *Sociology Compass* 9, no. 5 (2015): 400–411.

Sturges, Judith E., and Kathleen J. Hanrahan. "Comparing Telephone and Face-to-Face Qualitative Interviewing: A Research Note." *Qualitative Research* 4, no. 1 (2004): 107–118.

Sugden, John. "USA and the World Cup: American Nativism and Rejection of the People's Game." In *Hosts and Champions: Soccer Cultures, National Identities, and the USA World Cup,* edited by John Sugden and Alan Tomlinson, 215–252. Aldershot, U.K.: Ashgate, 1994.

Sugden, John, and Alan Tomlinson. *FIFA and the Contest for World Football: Who Rules the People's Game?* Malden, Mass.: Polity, 1998.

———. "What's Left When the Circus Leaves Town? An Evaluation of World Cup USA 1994." *Sociology of Sport Journal* 13, no. 3 (1996): 238–258.

Suggs, Welch. *A Place on the Team: The Triumph and Tragedy of Title IX.* Princeton: Princeton University Press, 2006.

Swanson, Lisa. "Soccer Fields of Cultural (Re)production: Creating 'Good Boys' in Suburban America." *Sociology of Sport Journal* 26, no. 3 (2009): 404–424.

Theberge, Nancy. *Higher Goals: Women's Ice Hockey and the Politics of Gender.* Albany: State University of New York Press, 2000.

Theberge, Nancy, and Alan Cronk. "Work Routines in Newspaper Sports Departments and the Coverage of Women's Sports." *Sociology of Sport Journal* 3, no. 3 (1986): 195–203.

Tomlinson, Alan, Andrei S. Markovits, and Christopher Young. "Introduction: Mapping Sports Space." *American Behavioral Scientist* 46, no. 11 (2003): 1463–1475.

Travers, Ann. "The Sport Nexus and Gender Injustice." *Studies in Social Justice* 2, no. 1 (2008): 79–101.

Trussell, Dawn E., and Susan M. Shaw. "Organized Youth Sport and Parenting in Public and Private Spaces." *Leisure Sciences* 34, no. 5 (2012): 377–394.

van Ingen, Cathy. "Geographies of Gender, Sexuality, and Race: Reframing the Focus on Space in Sport Sociology." *International Review for the Sociology of Sport* 32, no. 2 (2003): 201–216.

Van Rheenen, Derek. "The Promise of Soccer in America: The Open Play of Ethnic Subcultures." *Soccer & Society* 10, no. 6 (2009): 781–794.

Vecsey, Lauren. "Rapinoe Injury Reignites Turf, Player Safety Debate for USWNT." Fox Sports, December 5, 2015. http://www.foxsports.com/soccer/story/megan-rapinoe-uswnt-proclaim-outrage-field-conditions-stadium-training-grounds-hawaii-120515.

Vertinsky, Patricia, and Gwendolyn Captain. "More Myth than History: American Culture and Representations of the Black Female's Athletic Ability." *Journal of Sport History* 25, no. 3 (1998): 532–561.

Wachs, Faye Linda. "The Boundaries of Difference: Negotiating Gender in Recreational Sport." *Sociological Inquiry* 75, no. 4 (2005): 527–547.

———. "Leveling the Playing Field: Negotiating Gendered Rules in Coed Softball." *Journal of Sport & Social Issues* 26, no. 3 (2002): 300–316.

Walker, Matthew, Aubrey Kent, and John Vincent. "Communicating Socially Responsible Initiatives: An Analysis of U.S. Professional Teams." *Sport Marketing Quarterly* 19, no. 4 (2010): 187–195.

Wangerin, David. *Soccer in a Football World: The Story of America's Forgotten Game*. Philadelphia: Temple University Press, 2006.

Washington, Myra S., and Megan Economides. "Strong Is the New Sexy: Women, Crossfit, and the Postfeminist Ideal." *Journal of Sport & Social Issues* 40, no. 2 (2016): 143–161.

Watkins, Brandi, and Regina Lewis. "I Am Woman, but Not Roaring: An Examination of Similarities and Differences in How Male and Female Professional Athletes Are Using Twitter." *Journal of Social Media in Society* 5, no. 3 (2016): 5–36.

Wenner, Lawrence A. "Assessing the Sociology of Sport: On the Mediasport Interpellation and Commodity Narratives." *International Review for the Sociology of Sport* 50, nos. 4–5 (2015): 628–633.

West, Candace, and Don H. Zimmerman. "Doing Gender." *Gender & Society* 1, no. 2 (1987): 125–151.

Wheaton, Belinda, and Alan Tomlinson. "The Changing Gender Order in Sport? The Case of Windsurfing Subcultures." *Journal of Sport & Social Issues* 22, no. 3 (1998): 252–274.

Whiteside, Erin, and Marie Hardin. "Women (Not) Watching Women: Leisure Time, Television, and Implications for Televised Coverage of Women's Sports." *Communication, Culture & Critique* 4, no. 2 (2011): 122–143.

Whiteside, Erin, and Amber Roessner. "Forgotten and Left Behind: Political Apathy and Privilege at Title IX's 40th Anniversary." *Communication & Sport* 6, no. 1 (2018): 3–24.

Williams, Jean. *A Beautiful Game: International Perspectives on Women's Football*. New York: Berg, 2007.

Index

Page numbers in *italics* refer to figures.

About the Author

RACHEL ALLISON is an assistant professor of sociology and faculty affiliate of gender studies at Mississippi State University in Starkville, Mississippi.